# AMERICAN WEST

History of the Wild West
and Westward Expansion
★ 1803–1890 ★

# AMERICAN WEST

### History of the Wild West and Westward Expansion
### ★ 1803–1890 ★

## FOX CHAPEL
PUBLISHING
www.FoxChapelPublishing.com

## VISUAL HISTORY CONTRIBUTORS
### Alice Barnes-Brown, Walter Borneman, Nell Darby

F U T U R E

Used under license. All rights reserved. This version published by
Fox Chapel Publishing Company, Inc., 903 Square Street, Mount Joy, PA 17552.

For more information about the Future plc group, go to *http://www.futureplc.com*.

ISBN 978-1-4971-0374-0

Library of Congress Cataloging-in-Publication Data

To learn more about the other great books from Fox Chapel Publishing, or to find a retailer near you,
call toll-free 800-457-9112 or visit us at *www.FoxChapelPublishing.com*.

We are always looking for talented authors. To submit an idea, please send a brief inquiry to
acquisitions@foxchapelpublishing.com.

Printed in China
First printing

# WELCOME

As the American Revolution drew to a close and the colonies claimed independence from Britain, the United States' gaze turned west to the vast expanse of land that was seemingly ripe for the taking. After all, according to their Manifest Destiny, it was their God-given right to expand.

In *American West*, uncover the resistance that these enterprising settlers faced, from the Native Americans to the unforgiving terrain. Discover the reality of what life was like on the frontier, and meet some of the key figures in creating the legend of the Wild West, including Billy the Kid and Wyatt Earp. Elsewhere, find out how the Native Americans suffered at the hands of the settlers, from wars and legislation that stripped them of their rights, to attempts at crushing existing cultures.

# CONTENTS

61

26

72

# LEGACY OF THE FRONTIER

# HOW WAS THE WILD WEST WON?

From Jefferson to Geronimo, discover the wars, people, and events that moved the American frontier west during the 19th century

**July 4, 1803**

## Louisiana Purchase
*Washington, D.C.*

On July 4, 1803, exactly 27 years after the American colonies declared their independence from Britain, President Thomas Jefferson signed an agreement to buy a vast tract of North America from France. By paying $15 million to Paris, Jefferson secured 827,000 square miles of territory stretching from the Gulf of Mexico to the Canadian border, nearly doubling the size of the United States in the largest single-land gain in American history. Jefferson initially only sought to buy New Orleans and its environs, but Napoleon was bogged down in war with Britain and the French colonies of the New World held little value to him. When the French emperor offered a much larger area for less than three cents an acre, the American negotiators were quick to agree. The land they bought eventually became part of 15 US states and 2 Canadian provinces, taking in New Orleans, Denver, St. Louis, and Calgary.

# Lewis and Clark
## St. Louis, Missouri Territory

Two years, four months, and ten days after setting out, 32 men (and a dog) returned to St. Louis having traveled from the Mississippi to the Pacific Ocean and back again. Captain Meriwether Lewis and his friend, Second Lieutenant William Clark, had been commissioned to map the newly acquired Louisiana Purchase and to find a safe route across the continent, allowing the USA to lay claim to the Pacific coast before any European powers did. The expedition largely traveled by boat, following the course of the Missouri and Columbia Rivers across the Great Plains and Rocky Mountains. They encountered at least 24 Native Americans tribes, without whose help the expedition would have starved during the winter months—only the Teton-Sioux treated the White explorers with a degree of suspicion. Along the way, Lewis and Clark discovered more than 200 new plant and animal species and drew 140 maps of their route. One member of the party died on the trip, probably caused by appendicitis.

**September 23, 1806**

---

**February 12, 1809**
### Abraham Lincoln is born in a simple one-room log cabin
*Hodgenville, Kentucky*

**August 24, 1812**
### The White House and Capitol are attacked by the British in the War of 1812
*Washington, D.C.*

**May 8, 1820**
### The Missouri Compromise allows slavery in western territories south of latitude 36°30
*Washington, D.C.*

**September 16, 1810**

**June 20, 1819**
### S.S. Savannah becomes the first steamship to cross the Atlantic
*Liverpool, UK*

**September 27, 1821**
### Mexico wins independence from Spain
*Mexico City, Mexico*

**1822**

# Cry of Dolores
## Dolores Hidalgo, Mexico

The small town of Dolores Hidalgo near Guanajuato stamped its name in Mexican history in September 1810 when Miguel Hidalgo y Costilla, a Catholic priest, rang his church bells in the early hours to gather his congregation. He spoke to the assembled crowds, giving what became known as the Grito de Dolores (Cry of Dolores), calling on the people of his parish to leave their homes and join him in a rebellion against the Spanish colonial government. Six hundred men joined his insurrection and, although he would be captured and executed within a year, his was the first step in the Mexican War of Independence. That conflict would end, 11 years later, with Mexico as an independent country.

# Rocky Mountain Fur Company
## St. Louis, Missouri

An ad in an 1822 edition of the Missouri Republican sought out 100 men who were prepared "to ascend the river Missouri to its source, there to be employed for one, two, or three years." The work they were going to carry out was fur trapping, a lucrative trade since beaver fur was highly fashionable at the time. The trappers were often the first White men to explore the treacherous terrain, and it was dangerous work. Among those employed by the Rocky Mountain Fur Company was Hugh Glass, who would be abandoned without supplies in the wilderness during an 1823 expedition and forced to travel 200 miles back to Fort Kiowa alone.

## Indian Removal Act
### Washington, D.C.

President Andrew Jackson was an ardent believer in manifest destiny, the idea that the USA should expand into the west, but the inconvenient truth was that Native American tribes already occupied much of the land he coveted. His solution was the Indian Removal Act, which allowed the president to negotiate with tribes to move west of the Mississippi in exchange for their ancestral lands in the east. The act was controversial and narrowly passed the House of Representatives; it was particularly opposed by Christian missionaries. However, Jackson was blunt—he saw the demise of the Native American tribes as inevitable, a judgement sadly proven true.

## Bonneville Expedition
### St. Louis, Missouri

Benjamin Bonneville left Missouri in May 1832 with 110 men and orders from John Jacob Astor to establish a new fur trapping operation to rival the Hudson's Bay Company. The expedition trekked across present-day Wyoming, Idaho, Nevada, and Oregon and a secondary party discovered a route along the Humboldt River and across the Sierra Nevada to California. Bonneville may have been laying the groundwork for a possible invasion of California, then part of Mexico, and the path he discovered was eventually used as the primary route to the gold fields during the California Gold Rush. However, the expedition failed in its primary aim to trap beaver fur—the Hudson's Bay Company refused to allow their traders to do business with Bonneville and many Native Americans also refused them.

March 4, 1831

**Davy Crockett loses his seat in the Congressional Election after opposing the Indian Removal Act**
*Tennessee*

May 28, 1830

November 1, 1831

May 1832

July 4, 1826

**Thomas Jefferson dies on Independence Day**
*Monticello, Virginia*

## Trail of Tears
### Mississippi

The first tribe displaced by the Indian Removal Act was the Choctaw nation, who agreed to give up 11 million acres of ancestral land in Mississippi in exchange for 15 million acres in Oklahoma. It was agreed that the Choctaw would gather in November 1831 at Memphis and Vicksburg to be relocated. However, conditions were harsh and the US government did little to relieve Choctaw suffering. Flash floods prevented any travel by wagon and rivers were clogged up with ice. Rations were limited to a handful of boiled corn, one turnip, and two cups of heated water per day, and incompetent guides got the Choctaw lost in the Lake Providence swamps. Of 17,000 Choctaws who left Mississippi, up to 6,000 died en route on a trek described by a tribal chief as a "trail of tears and death." However, few lessons were learned and the removals of the Chickasaw, Creek, Seminole, and Cherokee tribes would also turn into death marches.

## Battle of the Alamo
*San Antonio, Mexican Texas*

The Texan Revolution that began at Gonzalez soon pushed Mexican troops out of the province, but the Mexican government responded with a fierce counter-attack— and nowhere was it more vicious than the Alamo. The Catholic mission and fortress, garrisoned by around 200 revolutionaries, was surrounded by a Mexican army numbering around 1,800. A 13-day siege ended on March 6 when the Mexicans launched a frontal assault. Two attacks were repulsed, but a third broke the walls and nearly all the revolutionary combatants were killed, including politician-turned-soldier Davy Crockett. Although the Alamo was a defeat for the Texan revolutionaries, it was a turning point in the war. Buoyed by a desire for revenge against General Antonio Lopez de Santa Anna, many Texans flooded to the revolutionary armies and six weeks later the Mexicans were defeated at the Battle of San Jacinto. The Mexican government withdrew from the province and Texas became an independent republic.

**November 6-23, 1833**
**Mormons are forcibly evicted from Jackson County**
*Missouri*

**March 4, 1837**
**Andrew Jackson leaves the White House after two terms as president**
*Washington, D.C.*

October 2, 1835 · 1836 · March 6, 1836

## Texan Revolution
*Gonzalez, Mexican Texas*

When Mexico won independence from Spain, the province of Texas had a population of only 3,500. Hoping that an influx of settlers would stop Native American raids, the bankrupt Mexican government allowed immigrants from the United States into Texas. Soon Tejanos (Mexican-Spanish Texans) were outnumbered by Anglos (English-speaking Texans). Relations between the two groups were tense and, in October 1835, the Anglos rose in rebellion against the Mexican Army, earning a victory in a small skirmish at Gonzalez. The Texan journey to become the Lone Star State had begun.

AND TAKE IT.

## Oregon Trail
*Independence, Missouri*

Fur trappers may have been among the first to explore the west, but large-scale migration required an easier route than those which the trappers were able to take. By 1836, a trail had been cleared from Independence, Missouri to Fort Hall, Idaho. A missionary party led by Henry Spalding and Marcus Whitman became the first wagon train of migrants to set off to settle west via the trail. Each year, the trail was cleared a little further until it reached Oregon City, a stone's throw from the Pacific coast. Annual improvements also made the route better, with bridges, ferries, and resurfaced roads making the journey quicker and safer. Some 400,000 people traveled along the Oregon Trail to reach the coast and wagon trains continued to be the main form of migration until the Transcontinental Railroad.

## Donner Party Tragedy
*Nevada mountains*

When 87 settlers left Missouri for California in May 1846, they were full of hope for the future. Within months, their dream had turned into a nightmare. The pioneers were led by George Donner and James Reed, but the choice of route they made was not the best. They lost time by following an alterNative path that diverted from the Oregon Trail and Reed killed a fellow settler in an argument and was banished from the group. Wagons and cattle were lost on the Humboldt River before the party tried to cross the Sierra Nevada mountains in November. A heavy snowfall trapped them on a high pass and, as food supplies ran low, a group set out on foot to seek help. Rescue parties eventually arrived after four months, but not before several of the survivors had resorted to cannibalism. The Donner Party was not the only wagon train to suffer fatalities on the trek west, but tales of desperate settlers eating each other led to it becoming one of the most infamous.

### April 25, 1846
**Mexico declares war on the USA**
*Mexico City*

### June 27, 1844
**Mormon leader Joseph Smith is killed by a mob breaking into Carthage Jail**
*Carthage, Illinois*

## Battle of the Neches
*Tyler, Texas*

In order to avoid relocation under the Indian Removal Act, many members of the Cherokee nation moved to the new republic of Texas during the 1830s. Initially welcomed by President Sam Houston, attitudes began to change when Mirabeau Lamar was voted into power. He demanded that the Cherokee move out of Texas and into the territory provided for them by the USA. After only three days of negotiation, Texan troops moved against the Cherokee. Eighteen were killed as the Cherokee retreated into a ravine, the following day around 100 were killed near the source of the River Neches. Faced with annihilation, the Cherokee reluctantly moved out of Texas and into Indian Territory.

| August 6-November 1, 1838 | July 15-16, 1839 | December 29, 1845 | Winter 1846-47 |
|---|---|---|---|

### December 5, 1839
**George Custer is born**
*New Rumley, Ohio*

## Mormon War
*Missouri*

New Yorker Joseph Smith's religious visions led him to establish a new Christian church, the members of which were called Mormons. Smith and his followers moved west in 1831, settling around Independence, Missouri, a place which they thought would be the location for the City of Zion. However, tensions between the Mormons and the rest of the Missouri population quickly grew, particularly as non-Mormons suspected that the newcomers sold their votes to the highest bidder. During election day in Gallatin County in 1838, a crowd tried to prevent Mormons from voting and a brawl developed. Attempts to calm the situation failed and skirmishes broke out between Mormon and non-Mormon mobs, culminating in the Haun's Mill Massacre where 17 Mormons were killed. Despite the killings, Joseph Smith and the Mormon leaders were blamed for the violence and nearly all Mormons were forced to leave the state, retreating east to Illinois.

## Annexation of Texas
*Texas*

The life of the independent Texan republic was short. Most Texans favored joining the United States, although there was little enthusiasm for the cause in Washington, D.C.. Only when President John Tyler moved into the White House did things begin to change—Tyler was fiercely independent of party politics and a great believer in westward expansion. Over his four years in office, he gradually changed minds and, under his successor James Polk, Congress passed a resolution accepting Texas as the 28th state.

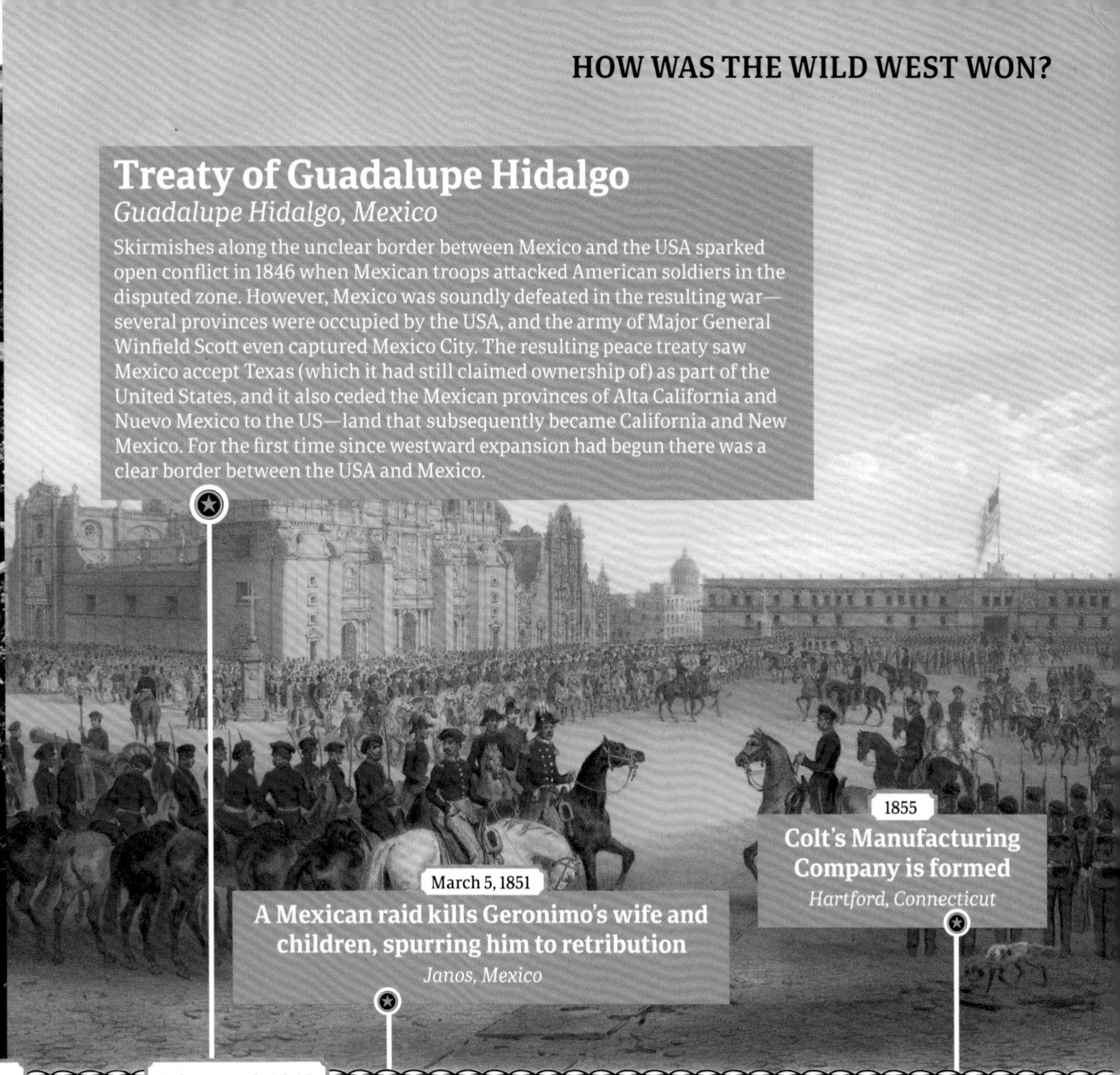

## Treaty of Guadalupe Hidalgo
*Guadalupe Hidalgo, Mexico*

Skirmishes along the unclear border between Mexico and the USA sparked open conflict in 1846 when Mexican troops attacked American soldiers in the disputed zone. However, Mexico was soundly defeated in the resulting war—several provinces were occupied by the USA, and the army of Major General Winfield Scott even captured Mexico City. The resulting peace treaty saw Mexico accept Texas (which it had still claimed ownership of) as part of the United States, and it also ceded the Mexican provinces of Alta California and Nuevo Mexico to the US—land that subsequently became California and New Mexico. For the first time since westward expansion had begun there was a clear border between the USA and Mexico.

**1855**
**Colt's Manufacturing Company is formed**
*Hartford, Connecticut*

**March 5, 1851**
**A Mexican raid kills Geronimo's wife and children, spurring him to retribution**
*Janos, Mexico*

**January 24, 1848**

**February 2, 1848**

**May-July 1857**
**Second Bonneville Expedition attacks Apache tribes**
*Arizona*

## California Gold Rush
*Sutter's Mill, California*

Early on a winter morning, James Marshall noticed some shiny flecks in the water channel feeding a sawmill. He had discovered gold. News quickly filtered out and, over the next seven years, 300,000 prospectors—nicknamed forty-niners after the peak year of the gold rush—flocked to California hoping to make their own valuable discovery. Many traveled overland, diverting from the Oregon Trail at Fort Hall in Idaho, others sailed from the east coast on steamships. The population of California boomed and the land was quickly adopted as a state after it was ceded from Mexico, but most who sought a quick buck were disappointed as nearly all prospectors failed. Those who did best were the merchants who supplied the miners, but undoubtedly those who did worst were the Native Americans who were driven off the land claimed by forty-niners—100,000 were killed through violence or starvation in what has subsequently been named the Californian Genocide.

A NEW AND MAGNIFICENT CLIPPER FOR SAN FRANCI
MERCHANTS' EXPRESS LINE OF C
Loading none but First-Class Vessels and Regularly
THE SPLENDID NEW OUT-AND-OUT

FORNI

HENRY BARBER, Commander, AT PIER 13 EAST RIVER.

This elegant Clipper Ship was built expressly for this trade by Samuel Hall, Esq., of East Boston, the builder of the celebrate "SURPRISE," "GAMECOCK," "JOHN GILPIN," and others. **She will fully equal them in speed!** Unusually promp and a very quick trip may be relied upon. Engagements should be completed at once.

Agents in San Francisco,

RANDOLPH M. COOLEY, 88 Wall Street, Tontine B

## PONY EXPRESS !

CHANGE OF      NEWS!!      REDUCED

TIME!      RATES!

### 10 Days to San Francisco!

## LETTERS

WILL BE RECEIVED AT THE

## OFFICE, 84 BROADWAY,

### NEW YORK,

Up t...

Which ...

Every ...

Sent to
meet with ...

LETT...
For ever...
In all cases to be enclosed in 10 cent Government Stamped Envelopes,
And all Express CHARGES Pre-paid.

☞ PONY EXPRESS ENVELOPES For Sale at our Office.

WELLS, FARGO & CO., Ag'ts.

*New York, July 1, 1861.*

## Pony Express
### St. Joseph, Missouri

The Pony Express may have had a short life, but during its 19 months of operation it helped to link the east and west coasts as never before. Messages and letters were carried by horse riders who set out from Missouri and raced from one station to the next, changing to a fresh horse at every stop, until they reached the final destination at Sacramento, California. It took about ten days to deliver a message from east to west, but even that was slow compared to the new technology that would soon render the Pony Express obsolete: the telegraph.

## Dakota War
### Dakota Territory

Fed up with settlers encroaching onto their territory and late annuity payments from the US government, in 1862 the Dakota tribes along the Minnesota River decided to act. When a Dakota brave killed five White settlers, his tribal chiefs decided to respond with further attacks aimed at pushing White settlers out of their reservation. Over the next few months, several pitched battles between the Dakota and the US Army gradually crushed the Natives, although not before 77 soldiers and up to 800 settlers were killed. Thirty-eight Dakotan prisoners were sentenced to death, some of whose trials lasted only five minutes, and the rest of the Dakotans were expelled and pushed further west. The United States had sent a signal that it was prepared to act ruthlessly against any Native Americans who defied its authority.

**April 12, 1861**
### Bombardment of Fort Sumter begins the Civil War
*Fort Sumter, South Carolina*

**July 1-3, 1863**
### Battle of Gettysburg
*Gettysburg, Pennsylvania*

**December 1861-January 1862**
### Great Flood causes widespread damage
*California, Oregon, and Nevada*

**July 26, 1863**
### Sam Houston, Founding Father of Texas, dies
*Huntsville, Texas*

| September 11, 1857 | April 3, 1860 | August 17-December 26, 1862 | August 21, 1863 |

**October 24, 1861**
### Transcontinental telegraph line is completed
*Sacramento, California*

## Mountain Meadows Massacre
### Mountain Meadows, Utah

The migrants who left Arkansas for California as part of the Baker-Fancher wagon train crossed Utah Territory in the middle of the Utah War, a year-long conflict between Mormons and non-Mormons. Suspicion of the settlers led the Mormons to attack the wagon train, disguising themselves as Native Americans to avoid reprisals. The settlers put up stern resistance until several members of the Mormon militia approached under a White flag. The settlers left the safety of their wagons and the Mormons turned on them, killing all over seven years of age. Around 130 men and women were murdered in the most infamous bout of paranoid hysteria that struck the west.

## Quantrill's Raid
### Lawrence, Kansas

The west was as fractured by the Civil War as the east—Texas and Louisiana were among the states that seceded from the USA to form the Confederacy, while Oregon and California remained loyal to the Union. Although few set-piece battles took place in the west, mainly due to a lack of Confederate manpower, there were extensive guerrilla raids carried out by roving bands of unofficial soldiers. Among them were William Quantrill's Confederate raiders, who targeted the pro-abolition town of Lawrence for retribution. Around 450 guerrillas attacked the settlement, looting and killing any men they came across; 164 died, most of whom were civilians, several of whom had surrendered. Quantrill had a list of men he specifically sought out, including Senator James Lane who had led his own raids against Confederate targets, but Lane escaped through a cornfield.

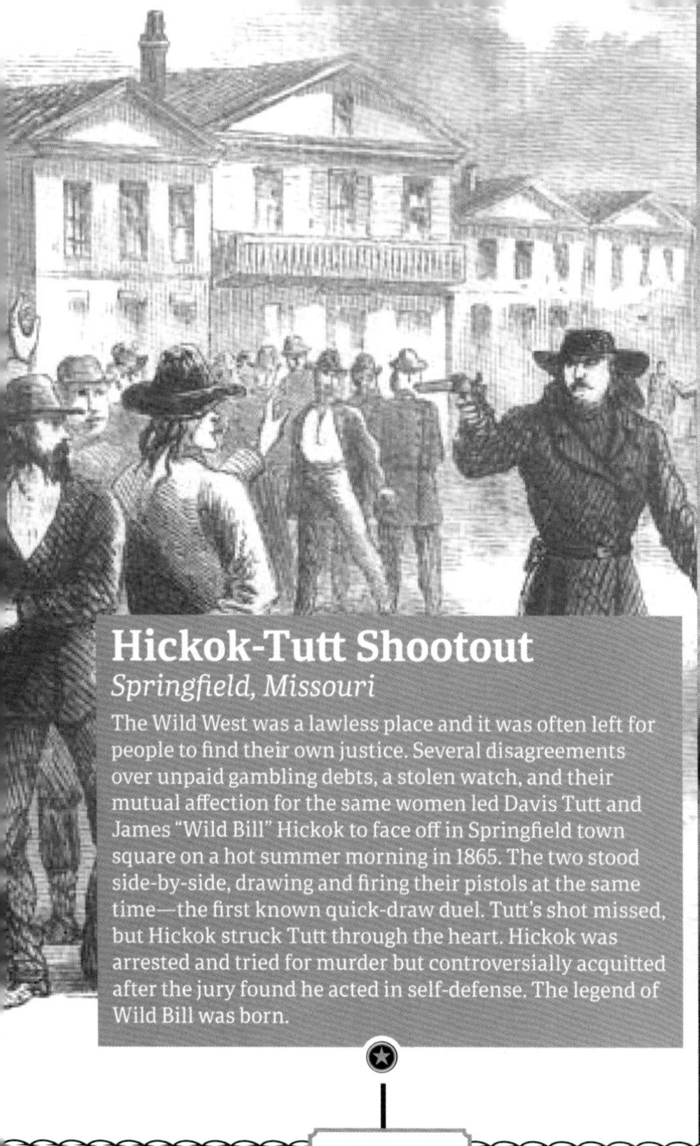

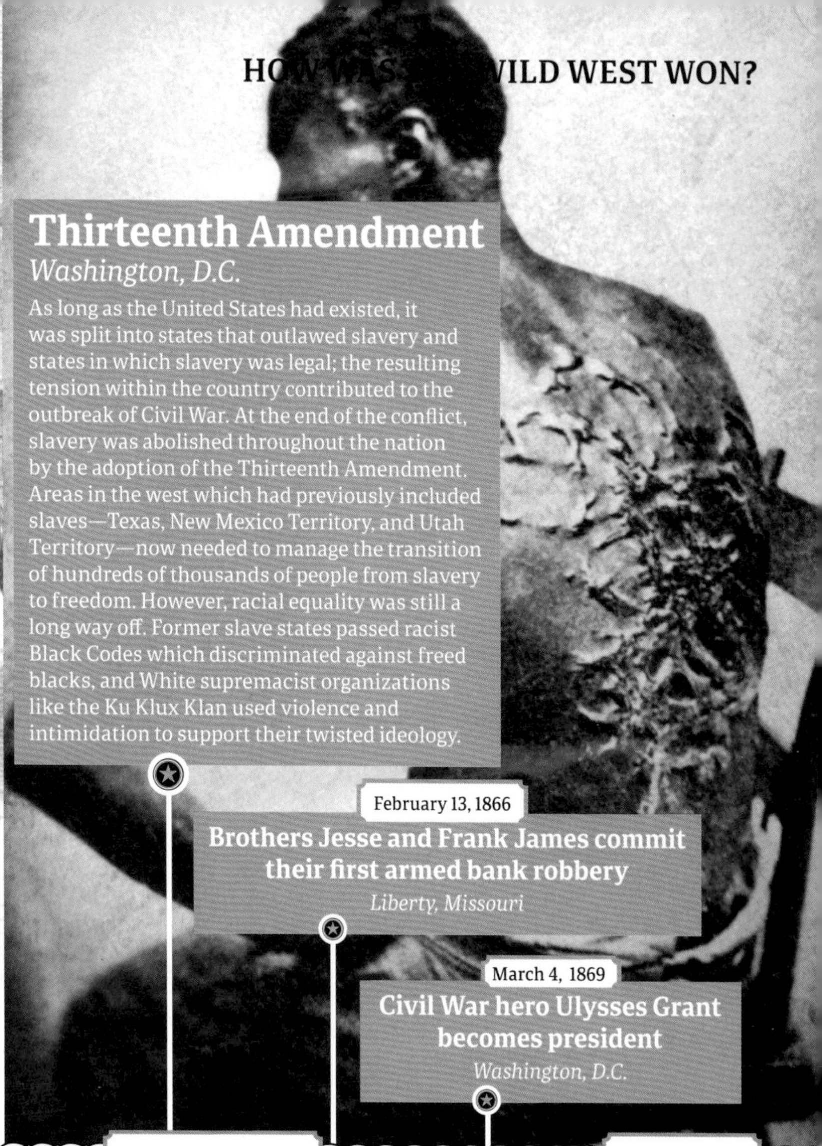

## Hickok-Tutt Shootout
### Springfield, Missouri

The Wild West was a lawless place and it was often left for people to find their own justice. Several disagreements over unpaid gambling debts, a stolen watch, and their mutual affection for the same women led Davis Tutt and James "Wild Bill" Hickok to face off in Springfield town square on a hot summer morning in 1865. The two stood side-by-side, drawing and firing their pistols at the same time—the first known quick-draw duel. Tutt's shot missed, but Hickok struck Tutt through the heart. Hickok was arrested and tried for murder but controversially acquitted after the jury found he acted in self-defense. The legend of Wild Bill was born.

## Thirteenth Amendment
### Washington, D.C.

As long as the United States had existed, it was split into states that outlawed slavery and states in which slavery was legal; the resulting tension within the country contributed to the outbreak of Civil War. At the end of the conflict, slavery was abolished throughout the nation by the adoption of the Thirteenth Amendment. Areas in the west which had previously included slaves—Texas, New Mexico Territory, and Utah Territory—now needed to manage the transition of hundreds of thousands of people from slavery to freedom. However, racial equality was still a long way off. Former slave states passed racist Black Codes which discriminated against freed blacks, and White supremacist organizations like the Ku Klux Klan used violence and intimidation to support their twisted ideology.

**February 13, 1866**
**Brothers Jesse and Frank James commit their first armed bank robbery**
*Liberty, Missouri*

**March 4, 1869**
**Civil War hero Ulysses Grant becomes president**
*Washington, D.C.*

July 21, 1865

December 18, 1865

May 10, 1869

**April 15, 1865**
**Abraham Lincoln is assassinated by a Confederate sympathizer**
*Washington, D.C.*

## Transcontinental Railroad
### Promontory Summit, Utah Territory

The ceremonial driving of a golden spike into the ground in Utah Territory officially opened the first Transcontinental Railroad to through traffic. Travel across the United States was now quicker and more comfortable, and migration to the west increased as the risks posed by the journey were reduced. However, the railroad cut across migration paths on the Great Plains and had a catastrophic effect on the buffalo population. Railroad companies initially employed buffalo hunters to help feed the laborers building the line, then whole herds were wiped out to prevent them blocking the line—some companies even offered buffalo hunting by rail, where hunters could shoot from the comfort of a train carriage.

## Powell Geographic Expedition
*Nevada*

In reaching the confluence of the Colorado and Virgin Rivers in Nevada, John Wesley Powell's small party of explorers completed the first passage by White men through the entirety of what they called Big Canyon. Despite losing one of their three boats and having four out of ten men leave the expedition—including three who walked away just two days from their final destination and were never seen again—the three-month mapping of the vast river valley was a great success. Powell returned for a second expedition two years later, this time giving his destination a new name: Grand Canyon.

## Colt .45
*Hartford, Connecticut*

No self-respecting frontiersman would have left the house without his revolver, and more than any other the Colt .45 was the gun that won the west. The "Peacemaker" became an instant favorite from its introduction in late 1873 due to its balance and ergonomic design and, by the end of the century, nearly 200,000 had been shipped to customers for $17 by mail order. The six-shooter was the preferred sidearm of gunmen on both sides of the law, including Wyatt Earp and Jesse James, and was used in some of the most notorious shootouts, battles, duels, and murders of the Wild West.

August 30, 1869

March 1, 1872

1873

December 1872

## Buffalo Bill appears on stage for the first time
*Chicago, Illinois*

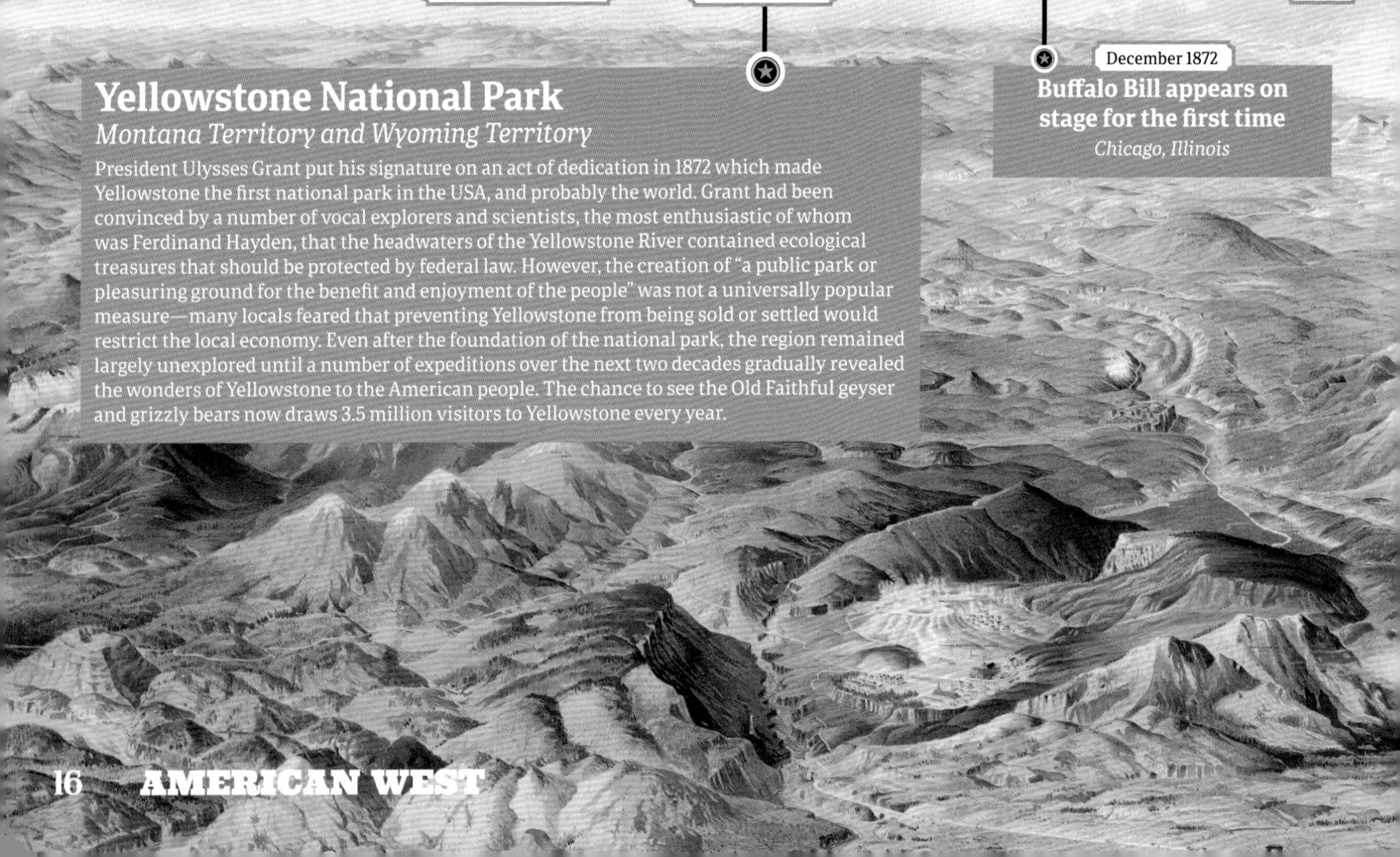

## Yellowstone National Park
*Montana Territory and Wyoming Territory*

President Ulysses Grant put his signature on an act of dedication in 1872 which made Yellowstone the first national park in the USA, and probably the world. Grant had been convinced by a number of vocal explorers and scientists, the most enthusiastic of whom was Ferdinand Hayden, that the headwaters of the Yellowstone River contained ecological treasures that should be protected by federal law. However, the creation of "a public park or pleasuring ground for the benefit and enjoyment of the people" was not a universally popular measure—many locals feared that preventing Yellowstone from being sold or settled would restrict the local economy. Even after the foundation of the national park, the region remained largely unexplored until a number of expeditions over the next two decades gradually revealed the wonders of Yellowstone to the American people. The chance to see the Old Faithful geyser and grizzly bears now draws 3.5 million visitors to Yellowstone every year.

**August 2, 1876**

**Wild Bill Hickok is shot and killed while playing cards**

*Deadwood, Dakota Territory*

**November 24, 1874**

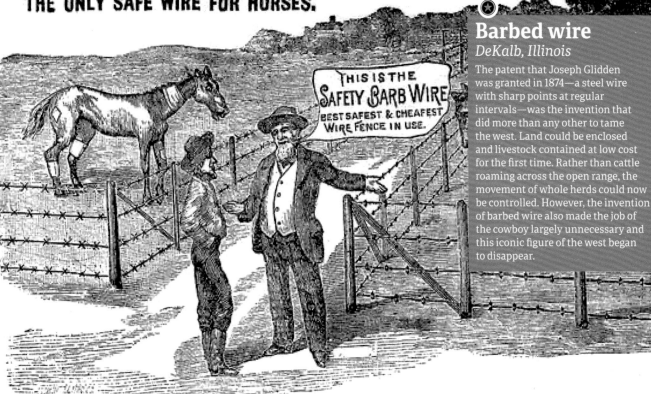

THE ONLY SAFE WIRE FOR HORSES.

THIS IS THE SAFETY BARB WIRE BEST SAFEST & CHEAFEST WIRE FENCE IN USE.

# Barbed wire
## *DeKalb, Illinois*

The patent that Joseph Glidden was granted in 1874—a steel wire with sharp points at regular intervals—was the invention that did more than any other to tame the west. Land could be enclosed and livestock contained at low cost for the first time. Rather than cattle roaming across the open range, the movement of whole herds could now be controlled. However, the invention of barbed wire also made the job of the cowboy largely unnecessary and this iconic figure of the west began to disappear.

Protect your Stock by using **SAFETY BARB WIRE.**
We Base our claim of Superiority on the Safety to Stock, Superior Quality of Material

# Battle of the Little Bighorn
## Little Bighorn River, Montana Territory

During a Sun Dance ceremony at Rosebud Creek, Lakotan leader Sitting Bull had a vision of "soldiers falling into his camp like grasshoppers from the sky." Later that month, his vision came true. The US Army was planning to force the Lakota, Cheyenne, and Arapaho back to their reservations and away from the Black Hills, where prospectors had discovered gold. George Armstrong Custer, a Civil War veteran who commanded the 7th Cavalry, spotted the Native American encampment and decided to attack immediately—a big mistake. Stern defense drove the cavalry back and Custer was surrounded, retreating to a hill with around 210 men. Not one of them survived the next wave of Lakota and Cheyenne warriors. However, although Little Bighorn is famous as the site of Custer's last stand, it was also the location of the Native Americans' last stand. The tribes scattered as US reinforcements arrived; Sitting Bull escaped to Canada, many others returned to the reservations, and the Black Hills were forcibly ceded to the US.

### September 5, 1877
**Crazy Horse, a Lakota veteran of Little Bighorn, is fatally stabbed while under military guard**
*Fort Robinson, Nebraska*

### June 25-26, 1876

### October 26, 1881

### April 28, 1881
**Billy the Kid escapes from prison, where he is awaiting execution**
*Lincoln County, New Mexico Territory*

# Gunfight at the OK Corral
## Tombstone, Arizona Territory

Tombstone was typical of many frontier towns—it grew rapidly after the discovery of silver in the local area and law enforcement struggled to cope with the bandits and criminals who flocked to the town. A feud developed between town Marshal Virgil Earp and a gang of cattle and horse smugglers known as the Cowboys, with repeated threats made by both sides. Things came to a head when Earp, with his brothers Morgan and Wyatt and temporary policeman Doc Holliday, attempted to disarm five Cowboys in a narrow street close to the rear entrance of the OK Corral. A gunfight followed during which 30 shots were fired in 30 seconds, killing three Cowboys and wounding Virgil, Morgan, and Doc Holliday. The gunfight was largely forgotten until it was resurrected as the subject of a Hollywood blockbuster, and has now come to symbolize the brutality and danger of frontier justice.

# WANTED
## DEAD OR ALIVE

BELIEVED TO BE
JESSE JAMES AN
HIS BAND OR TH
YOUNGERS.
THESE MEN ARE
DESPERATE.

## Assassination of Jesse James
*St. Joseph, Missouri*

By the 1880s, former Confederate soldier-turned-robber Jesse James was living in fear. Driven into hiding by a $5,000 bounty for his capture, he was living in Missouri with his wife, Zerelda, and two brothers, Charley and Robert Ford. What James didn't know was that the Ford brothers had decided to betray him. When James put down his pistols to dust a picture, Robert saw his chance. He drew his own pistol and fired, hitting James in the back of his head. The Ford brothers were arrested for murder but pardoned by the state governor within a day, and another infamous anti-hero of the Wild West passed into legend.

**REWARD**

THIS NOTICE TAKES the PLACE of ALL PREVIOUS REWARD NOTICES.
CONTACT SHERIFF, DAVIESS COUNTY, MISSOURI

JULY 26, 1881

and
Union Pacific Railro
Agency

## Surrender of Geronimo
*Skeleton Canyon, Arizona Territory*

For over three decades, a medicine man had led raids against Mexico and the United States as part of the long-lasting Apache campaign to resist being moved onto reservations by the new White settlers. Geronimo finally surrendered to First Lieutenant Charles Gatewood, one of the few US soldiers with whom he had some respect, in 1886. The US government took no chances with their new prisoner—he had, after all, previously surrendered twice before fleeing to resume a life of raiding. This time, Geronimo and his followers were kept under close supervision at US forts in Florida, Alabama, and Oklahoma. He became something of a celebrity, appearing at the St. Louis World Fair in 1904 and meeting President Roosevelt in 1905. Geronimo died in 1909, having been both a prisoner and a celebrity for the last 23 years of his life.

June 24, 1889

### Butch Cassidy robs his first bank
*Beaver, Utah Territory*

April 3, 1882 — May 19, 1883 — September 4, 1886 — June 2, 1890

March 7, 1888

### William Temple Hornaday estimates that there are fewer than 300 buffalo left in the wild
*Great Plains*

FAMILY SCHEDULE—1 TO 10 PERSONS
Eleventh Census of the United States.
SCHEDULE No. 1.
...ATION AND SOCIAL STATISTI
State :
1890

| A.—Number of Dwelling-house in the order of visitation. | B.—Number of families in this dwelling-house. | C.—Number of persons in this dwelling-house. | D.—Number of Family in the order of visitation. | E.—No. of Persons in this family. |
|---|---|---|---|---|
| INQUIRIES. | 1 | 2 | 3 | 4 | 5 |
| Christian name in full, and initial of middle name. | | | | |
| 1 Surname. | | | | |

## LL'S WILD WEST
### UGH RIDERS OF THE WORLD.

## Buffalo Bill's Wild West show
*Omaha, Nebraska*

As the western frontier began to close, a few pioneers began to see the potential for profit by portraying the Wild West on stage. Among the first was William "Buffalo Bill" Cody, a former buffalo hunter-turned-showman. He formed his own circus-like attraction, Buffalo Bill's Wild West, which toured throughout the US and Europe, combining reenactments of historical events with displays of sharp-shooting and horsemanship. Many notable figures joined the troupe, including Sitting Bull, Calamity Jane, and Annie Oakley. The story they peddled was a romanticized view of the western frontier, leading to the development of many half-truths that are now indelibly linked with the Wild West.

## Western frontier is closed
*Washington, D.C.*

Following the eleventh US Census, exactly 100 years after the first, Superintendents Robert Porter and Carroll Wright announced that there was no longer a western frontier of the United States beyond which there was unsettled territory. The United States had claimed and settled the entire landmass from Boston to Los Angeles and New Orleans to Seattle. The era of the Wild West was over. However, it was an age of expansion that had come at a great cost. The same census recorded a total of 248,253 Native Americans living in the United States, down from 400,764 identified in the census of 1850.

BUFFALO BILL
WILL APPEAR
AT EVERY PERFORMANCE

| 16 | Profession, trade, or occupation. | | |
| 17 | Months unemployed during the census year (June 1, 1889, to May 31, 1890). | | |
| 18 | Attendance at school (in months) during the census year (June 1, 1889, to May 31, 1890). | | |
| 19 | Able to Read. | | |
| 20 | Able to Write. | | |

# BUILDING THE FRONTIER

# FROM REVOLUTION TO REBIRTH

## The American Revolution turned a group of European colonies into a federation of (largely) independent states

Words by Robert Walsh

"Give me liberty or give me death!" Even today, the general perception of the American Revolution is of committed freedom fighters opposing a tyrannical king, almost a black-and-White affair. Events like the "shot heard round the world," the British defeat at Yorktown in 1781, and the signing of the Declaration of Independence are well-remembered to this day. Founding Father Patrick Henry's fiery rhetoric to the Second Virginia Convention in 1775 delivered one of history's most quoted lines.

But this isn't quite as accurate as it might seem—the real story is far more complex than that. Colonial desire for westward expansion (and resentment of the British curbing it) was one of many factors that eventually led to war.

The American Revolution saw the birth of a new nation and the military defeat of its former colonial master. That wasn't the original intention. Initially, the First Continental Congress demanded only greater autonomy for American colonies within the British Empire. They weren't demanding full independence at first, just a greater say in their own internal affairs. Not until 1775 did the Second Continental Congress vote for independence, and by then the Revolutionary War was underway.

King George III wasn't a tyrant, either. The monarch saw the situation as challenging parliamentary rule in England's American colonies, not as a pretext for suppressing dissent and increasing his personal power. If anything, George III wanted to pacify the colonies with minimum bloodshed, not brutally bring them to heel.

For decades, colonists had been learning the practicalities and procedures of self-government. To effectively run the 13 Colonies as colonies, nevermind a loose coalition of largely independent states, much decision-making lay in the hands of colonial officials. They were obliged to implement policy decisions made by parliament, but day-to-day governance was largely in their power. They learned government on the job, and in time, it paid off.

Over time, an increasing spirit of independence grew among many colonists. It wasn't so much explicit support for independence from Britain, but more of a feeling that the colonies could govern themselves. They effectively already did. As frustration with London grew (and London in turn took an increasingly harder line towards its American colonies) an increasingly large, vocal lobby formed favoring full independence in fact, not just in spirit. As the second United States president John Adams later put it: "The Revolution was effected before the war commenced. The Revolution was in the hearts and minds of the people."

Colonial desire for unfettered expansion existed long before it actually happened. Independence existed as an idea before becoming a possibility, never mind a reality. The skills, experience, and desire to end British rule existed long before the Revolutionary War and Declaration of Independence.

Over time, attitudes hardened on both sides. Many British politicians saw the Continental Congress as upstart rebels and traitors to the crown. George III took a reasonable personal position, wanting limited discussion and possibly reform while never allowing the colonists to forget that they were British subjects. Publicly, however, he supported the position of parliament—the colonies were British territory subordinate to Parliament, and they would remain so. The colonists were British subjects whether they liked it or not. They would submit to British rule, peacefully or otherwise.

# IN CONGRESS,
## JULY 4, 1776.

# A DECLARATION
### BY THE
# REPRESENTATIVES
### OF THE
# UNITED STATES OF AMERICA,
### IN GENERAL CONGRESS ASSEMBLED.

WHEN in the Course of human Events, it becomes necessary for one People to dissolve the political Bands which have connected them with another, and to assume among the Powers of the Earth, the separate and equal Station to which the Laws of Nature and of Nature's God entitle them, a decent Respect to the Opinions of Mankind requires that they should declare the Causes which impel them to the Separation.

We hold these Truths to be self-evident, that all Men are created equal, that they are endowed by their Creator with certain unalienable Rights, that among these are Life, Liberty, and the Pursuit of Happiness :—That to secure these Rights, Governments are instituted among Men, deriving their just Powers from the Consent of the Governed, that whenever any Form of Government becomes destructive of these Ends, it is the Right of the People to alter or to abolish it, and to institute new Government, laying its Foundation on such Principles, and organizing its Powers in such Form, as to them shall seem most likely to effect their Safety and Happiness. Prudence, indeed, will dictate that Governments long established should not be changed for light and transient Causes; and accordingly all Experience hath shewn, that Mankind are more disposed to suffer, while Evils are sufferable, than to right themselves by abolishing the Forms to which they are accustomed. But when a long Train of Abuses and Usurpations, pursuing invariably the same Object, evinces a Design to reduce them under absolute Despotism, it is their Right, it is their Duty, to throw off such Government, and to provide new Guards for their future Security. Such has been the patient Sufferance of these Colonies; and such is now the Necessity which constrains them to alter their former Systems of Government. The History of the present King of Great-Britain is a History of repeated Injuries and Usurpations, all having in direct Object the Establishment of an absolute Tyranny over these States. To prove this, let Facts be submitted to a candid World.

He has refused his Assent to Laws, the most wholesome and necessary for the public Good.

He has forbidden his Governors to pass Laws of immediate and pressing Importance, unless suspended in their Operation until his Assent should be obtained; and when so suspended, he has utterly neglected to attend to them.

He has refused to pass other Laws for the Accommodation of large Districts of People, unless those People would relinquish the Right of Representation in the Legislature, a Right inestimable to them, and formidable to TYRANTS only.

He has called together Legislative Bodies at Places unusual, uncomfortable, and distant from the Depository of their public Records, for the sole Purpose of fatiguing them into Compliance with his Measures.

He has dissolved Representative Houses repeatedly, for opposing with manly FIRMNESS his Invasions on the Rights of the People.

He has refused for a long Time, after such Dissolutions, to cause others to be elected; whereby the Legislative Powers, incapable of Annihilation, have returned to the People at large for their Exercise; the State remaining in the mean Time exposed to all the Dangers of Invasion from without, and Convulsions within.

He has endeavoured to prevent the Population of these States; for that Purpose obstructing the Laws for Naturalization of Foreigners; refusing to pass others to encourage their Migrations hither, and raising the Conditions of new Appropriations of Lands.

He has obstructed the Administration of Justice, by refusing his Assent to Laws for establishing Judiciary Powers.

He has made Judges dependent on his Will alone, for the Tenure of their Offices, and the Amount and Payment of their Salaries.

He has erected a multitude of new Offices, and sent hither Swarms of Officers to harrass our People, and eat out their Substance.

He has kept among us, in Times of Peace, Standing Armies, without the Consent of our Legislatures.

He has affected to render the Military independent of, and superior to the Civil Power.

He has combined with others to subject us to a Jurisdiction foreign to our Constitution, and unacknowledged by our Laws; giving his Assent to their Acts of pretended Legislation:

For quartering large Bodies of armed Troops among us:

For protecting them, by a mock Trial, from Punishment for any Murder which they should commit on the Inhabitants of these States:

For cutting off our Trade with all Parts of the World:

For imposing Taxes on us without our Consent:

For depriving us, in many Cases, of the Benefits of Trial by Jury:

For transporting us beyond Seas to be tried for pretended Offences:

For abolishing the free System of English Laws in a neighbouring Province establishing therein an arbitrary Government, and enlarging its Boundaries, so as to render it at once an Example and fit Instrument for introducing the same absolute Rule into these Colonies:

For taking away our Charters, abolishing our most valuable Laws, and altering fundamentally the Forms of our Governments:

For suspending our own Legislatures, and declaring themselves invested with Power to legislate for us in all Cases whatsoever.

He has abdicated Government here, by declaring us out of his Protection and waging War against us.

He has plundered our Seas, ravaged our Coasts, burnt our Towns, and destroyed the Lives of our People.

He is, at this Time, transporting large Armies of foreign Mercenaries to compleat the Works of Death, Desolation, and TYRANNY, already begun with Circumstances of Cruelty and Perfidy scarcely paralleled in the most barbarous Ages, and totally unworthy the Head of a civilized Nation.

He has constrained our Fellow Citizens, taken Captive on the high Seas, to bear Arms against their Country; to become the Executioners of their Friends and Brethren, or to fall themselves by their Hands.

He has excited Domestic Insurrections amongst us, and has endeavoured to bring on the Inhabitants of our Frontiers, the merciless Indian Savages, whose known Rule of Warfare, is an undistinguished Destruction of all Ages, Sexes, and Conditions.

In every Stage of these Oppressions we have petitioned for Redress, in the most humble Terms: Our repeated Petitions have been answered only by repeated Injury!—A Prince, whose Character is thus marked by every Act which may define a TYRANT, is unfit to be the Ruler of a FREE PEOPLE!

Nor have we been wanting in Attention to our British Brethren. We have warned them from Time to Time of Attempts by their Legislature to extend an unwarrantable Jurisdiction over us. We have reminded them of the Circumstances of our Emigration and Settlement here. We have appealed to their native Justice and Magnanimity, and we have conjured them by the Ties of our common Kindred to disavow these Usurpations, which would inevitably interrupt our Connexions and Correspondence. They too have been deaf to the Voice of Justice and of Consanguinity. We must, therefore, acquiesce in the Necessity which denounces our Separation, and hold them, as we hold the rest of Mankind, Enemies in War; in Peace, Friends.

We, therefore, the REPRESENTATIVES of the UNITED STATES OF AMERICA, in GENERAL CONGRESS assembled, appealing to the SUPREME JUDGE of the World for the Rectitude of our Intentions, do, in the Name and by the Authority of the good People of these Colonies, solemnly Publish and Declare, That these United Colonies are, and of Right ought to be, FREE AND INDEPENDENT STATES; that they are absolved from all Allegiance to the British Crown; and that all political Connexion between them and the State of Great-Britain, is, and ought to be totally dissolved; and that as FREE AND INDEPENDENT STATES, they have full Power to levy War, conclude Peace, contract Alliances, establish Commerce, and to do all other Acts and Things which INDEPENDENT STATES may of Right do. And for the Support of this Declaration, with a firm Reliance on the Protection of DIVINE PROVIDENCE, we mutually pledge to each other our LIVES, our FORTUNES, and our SACRED HONOR.

*Signed by* ORDER *and in* BEHALF *of the* CONGRESS,

## JOHN HANCOCK, PRESIDENT.
ATTEST, CHARLES THOMPSON, SECRETARY.

IN COUNCIL, JULY 17th, 1776.

ORDERED, That the Declaration of Independence be printed; and a Copy sent to the Ministers of each Parish, of every Denomination, within this STATE; and that they severally be required to read the same to their respective Congregations, as soon as divine Service is ended, in the Afternoon, on the first Lord's-Day after they shall have received it:—And after such Publication thereof, to deliver the said Declaration to the Clerks of their several Towns, or Districts; who are hereby required to record the same in their respective Town, or District Books, there to remain as a perpetual MEMORIAL thereof.

In the Name, and by Order of the COUNCIL,

A true Copy Attest, JOHN AVERY, Dep. Sec'y.

R. DERBY, Jun. President.

SALEM, MASSACHUSETTS-BAY: Printed by E. RUSSELL, by Order of AUTHORITY.

The 1773 Boston Tea Party has become almost iconic, the most famous expression of colonists' increasing frustration with British rule

Slaveowner, land speculator, and orator, Patrick Henry is forever known for saying "Give me Liberty or give me Death!"

When General Cornwallis surrendered at Yorktown in 1781, it wasn't the end of the American Revolution—it was really the beginning

Within the colonists themselves, there was also division between those who wanted to pursue greater autonomy and those who were advocating full independence. Some were prepared to fight for independence if necessary, while others were ready to fight for Great Britain. These divisions were often bitter and frequently personal.

Abraham Lincoln later said that a house divided will not stand. Initially, the colonists were divided and some of them remained so. After signing the Declaration of Independence, Benjamin Franklin is said to have described the need for unity in the bluntest of terms: "We must all hang together or, most assuredly, we will all hang separately!"

By no means were all colonists anti-British and pro-Independence—in fact, many supported increased taxation and the colonial status quo. At the same time, others opposed taxation and supported increased autonomy but rejected outright the idea of full independence. Still prepared to support England, they viewed working for independence as treason against the crown.

The Loyalist faction comprised approximately 20 percent of the colonist population in North America and their loyalty to England even led some of them to enlist in the British Armed Forces, joining the Royal American Regiment. Others didn't

enlist but still fully supported the defeat of the Continental Army and the suppression of the burgeoning independence lobby.

At the end of the war, relatively few Loyalists remained to take advantage of independence and whatever opportunities it might offer. Leaving behind their homes and much of their wealth, some 80,000 were never to return. As a matter of fact, some couldn't return as the more prominent Loyalists were often banished on pain of death if they ever came back. Some went to Britain while the majority practiced their own form of expansion. Going north in large numbers, they helped build the English-speaking community in Canada, then recently acquired by the British.

Samuel Adams, an organizer of 1773's legendary Boston Tea Party, summed up the common attitude towards Loyalists: "If ye love wealth better than liberty, the tranquility of servitude than the animating contest of freedom, go from us in peace. We ask not your counsels or arms. Crouch down and lick the hands which feed you. May your chains sit lightly upon you, and may posterity forget ye were ever our countrymen."

During the 12 years prior to the Revolutionary War, there had been many differences of opinion and conflicts between colonists and their rulers in parliament. Expansion or, to be exact, London limiting

colonists' rights to do so, was one of them. The Royal Proclamation of 1763 set out specifically to limit colonial expansion west of the Appalachian Mountains and in doing so it further inflamed local resentment of government from London.

The 1763 Proclamation made sense to London, but it angered a great many colonists. The Western frontier could be lightly garrisoned (at considerably reduced expense to the Treasury) and the Native Americans could be largely left to themselves. What London didn't foresee was the enormous resentment that it would generate among the pro-expansion lobby. Many colonists—especially those who were ambitious and hungrily seeking status and wealth—were infuriated at any restrictions at all on western expansion. It handicapped their commercial growth and was imposed from afar by a colonial master whose autocratic approach they increasingly distrusted and resented.

Most of all, the colonists resented having to pay for the British troops posted to the border regions to enforce the proclamation. Some 10,000 soldiers were positioned along the frontier and London mandated that the £250,000 annual cost be paid by the colonists. Many colonists and land speculators, already resenting having expansion interfered with from afar, were furious at being

The Sugar Act, meanwhile, created a captive taxable market for colonial products. The tax, though indirect, partially offset the cost of British troops stationed in the American colonies and the West Indies. Anyone caught smuggling taxable products would be tried in vice-admiralty courts, not local colonial ones, because local courts often condoned smuggling and acquitted smugglers. To the colonists it looked far more like London side-lining local officials and the beginnings of a larger power grab from across the ocean. Relations between the ruling elite in London and the colonists, already strained, declined still further.

The Currency Act worsened an already bad situation, forbidding colonies to use paper money to pay debts. They could issue paper money for other purposes, but only gold and silver to repay any money they owed. As the colonies used paper money at least as much as gold and silver, the Act severely hurt the colonial economy, breeding even more anger and hostility.

All the American colonies except Delaware officially regarded the Currency Act as one of their principal grievances. At the first Continental Congress in 1774, a Declaration of Rights was issued and numerous Acts of Parliament were included as grievances. The Currency Act was one of only seven considered "subversive of American rights."

The Act's impact was more psychological than financial. It did as much as anything to convince colonists that parliament neither understood their grievances or cared about resolving them. Leading colonists, even some who'd previously thought differently, began believing they could better serve colonial interests.

It didn't end there. Further conflict emerged with 1765's Stamp Act, which required the colonies to use specially stamped paper for official correspondence, playing cards, newspaper, and all manner of other paper products. The stamp proved it had been bought through an official

## "To many, proclamation represented an English attempt to take control of the west away from the colonists"

handed the bill. Among them were George Washington, Patrick Henry, and Henry Laurens, who later became president of the Continental Congress.

To many, the proclamation represented an English attempt to take control of the west away from the colonists, further concentrating power in London. With British rule ended, some thought, westward and southern expansion could begin. With expansion would come the chance to make their fortunes or increase what they already had.

Until war began in 1775, the proclamation was hard to enforce and frequently ignored, especially by non-British settlers. Many considered it a hindrance and an imposition. If it couldn't be enforced effectively then it could be ignored, up to a point, but for unrestricted expansion British policy had to change. If British policy wouldn't change, British rule had to end, and 1764 didn't improve matters. First the Sugar Act (also called the American Revenue Act or American Duties Act) was passed, then the Currency Act. The former was an obvious revenue-raiser for London, replacing the unsuccessful Molasses Act of 1733. Granted, it halved the molasses tax, but it was more strictly enforced. It also listed other products that could only be legally exported to Britain.

## Expansion and the Pioneer Spirit

### Expansion became imperative after independence—material needs, security, and culture dictated it

Today's United States grew out of a cluster of former colonies, each wanting to retain its own independence, albeit within a loose confederation of states. None wanted to be too subordinate to central government, seeing little difference between a monarch and an overly powerful president.

For both material and cultural reasons, expansion was pretty much inevitable. With the war's end in 1783, mass immigration began. Increased demand for work, land and natural resources made expansion the most obvious option. In turn, mass immigration provided the manpower for expansion.

Revolution-era Americans were risk takers with independent minds, and their need to expand was matched by a genuine desire to do so. A country whose Founding Fathers had left Europe searching for something better was never going to just sit back and rest on its laurels. Their descendants had just won a war to secure independence—they certainly weren't going to sit back and do nothing, either.

Security was also a factor. To the north lay Canada, a British territory. To the west lay the Louisiana Territory, a Spanish and then French possession until 1803. California and Mexico were then Spanish colonies. There was plenty of scope for European interference in American internal affairs and Americans knew it. Materially, culturally, and politically, the United States simply had to expand and secure its borders.

Many Americans of the time were more than ready to endure great hardship and risk to expand into the West

## The Early Move West

### Westward expansion flourished after the Revolutionary War, but it really began decades earlier

Western expansion began long before the 13 Colonies began fighting for their independence—immigrants had already pushed as far west as the Blue Ridge Mountains in present-day West Virginia. Most, however, had headed south into the fertile Shenandoah Valley. The period between 1730 and 1750 saw large numbers of German and Scottish-Irish immigrants flooding into present-day West Virginia, North Carolina, and South Carolina. Still more were rapidly populating what later became Ohio, Tennessee, and Kentucky.

A British proclamation in 1763 expressly forbade movement west of the Appalachian Mountains, but it was poorly enforced and largely ignored. Immigrants continued to head west, even during the Revolutionary War. After the British defeat and the Treaty of Paris formally ended the conflict, the comparative trickle of pioneers became a veritable flood.

After the war, immigrants spread through fertile farmland and forests around the Appalachians and the Mississippi River. By 1810, Ohio, Kentucky, and Tennessee were no longer barren wilderness. Towns, industry, and commerce were spreading, in turn attracting yet more immigrants. By 1830, Indiana, Mississippi, Alabama, Illinois, and Missouri had achieved statehood and joined the Union, so rapid was postwar expansion. The wild frontier was slowly being tamed.

George Washington was a general, Founding Father, and the first US president. He also wanted western lands regardless of the 1763 proclamation

The Royal Proclamation of 1763 did little to halt westward expansion, but it did a great deal to inflame colonial passions

## "After the war, however, the lure of owning land and building profitable businesses drew thousands of settlers westward"

government agent (the only legal vendors) and that the tax had been paid. This was direct taxation, something never before attempted, and all of it went into London's coffers. Many colonists were outraged.

Direct taxation didn't exist in the American colonies at that time. In fact, it wasn't until the American Civil War that the Federal Government finally imposed income tax. Until then, individual states could tax their citizens and pass it on to the government, but Congress and the Federal Government were denied other means to directly tax the American people. The British taxing the colonists and keeping it all for themselves further inflamed the fury. It also linked to another issue central to colonial frustration with British rule.

### No Taxation Without Representation

Parliament, responsible in colonial eyes for their many grievances, was now collecting taxes from the colonies while denying them direct representation in parliament itself. Unlike the British constituencies that had a Member of Parliament each, the American colonies lacked any at all.

To many in the blossoming independence movement, this was intolerable, clearly flouting 1689's Bill of Rights that guaranteed their personal freedoms. To some it smelled strongly of dictatorship—they were free people who were being forced to subsidize a tyrannical ruler without any right to resist. That inflamed colonial attitudes toward British rule at least as much as British efforts to restrict colonial expansion into the west.

Before the Revolutionary War, the urge to expand had existed, but expansion itself had remained relatively small. After the war, however, the lure of owning land and building profitable businesses drew thousands of settlers westward. Expansion west offered opportunities for profit and gain

Colonists originally wanted greater autonomy within the British Empire. Not until 1775 did the Second Continental Congress vote for independence

The faster western expansion developed, the quicker American commerce found itself growing. By the same token, the quicker it grew, the more British commerce could profit from it—it very much suited the interests of both the British and the Americans to foster close diplomatic and commercial links. The Treaty of Paris was as much a business deal as a peace agreement.

If Britain could outwit its European rivals, Shelburne reasoned, it would benefit both countries enormously. It would also restore some of Britain's international credibility, which had been damaged by military defeat in the Revolutionary War. That it also infuriated the French, Dutch, and Spanish probably didn't escape Shelburne's notice, either. The Treaty of Paris—and separate British treaties with Spain, France, and the Dutch Republic—saw America's former wartime allies effectively sidelined. Britain, once the colonial ruler, now became the United States' primary trading partner. Or, as disgruntled French Foreign Minister Vergennes ruefully said: "The English buy peace rather than make it."

Looking back, Britain probably had bought peace, but only at enormous cost in casualties, money, resources, prestige, and the loss of their American colonies. The Treaty of Paris was perhaps as much a business deal as a peace treaty, but it was also a model of clever, adept diplomacy that ended up benefitting both the British and Americans in equal measure. Had the British handled prewar diplomacy as well as the Treaty, the American colonies might have remained British considerably longer. As it was, they didn't. A bloody, protracted war, defeat, and a new nation were the results.

Britain's prewar ambition to curb American enterprise became largely irrelevant after Yorktown and the Treaty of Paris. Now Americans and no longer colonists, western expansion became both possible and inevitable. The series of detested prewar taxes, proclamations, and regulations aimed at restricting American trade and expansion were also gone. London's efforts had only stimulated the desire for political, geographic, and economic expansion, not curbed it. In doing so, albeit unwittingly and unwillingly, British intransigence did as much as the rebellion of the 13 colonies to alter the course of history.

long since exhausted in the stable, secure, more "civilized" east. To really prosper, many Americans and immigrants thought, they had to risk traveling west and enduring all of the frontier hardships in the hope of striking it rich.

All told, independence and subsequent expansion meant enormous change at almost every level of American society. The population grew through mass immigration; increasing population helped spur increasing expansion. One part of American society, though, didn't change.

## Slavery

Slavery had been legal before the war and remained so afterward. For slaves, the only real change was where they were bought, sold, and put to work as the United States expanded across North America. At a time when slavery was viewed very differently, it made economic sense.

Slaves themselves were a lucrative commodity until the end of the American Civil War in 1865, and employers often preferred owning workers for a one-off fee rather than employing them on a weekly wage. As expansion spawned vast

commercial development, unskilled labor became increasingly in demand and as more states developed across the South through the first half of the 19th century, the economy there came to depend largely on slave labor. It would remain so until the defeat of the Confederacy in 1865.

Ironically, the Confederate states cited states' rights as part of their cause. If states' rights were trampled by Abraham Lincoln, they believed, they would declare independence in 1861 as their revolutionary forefathers had in 1776. However, it would be the British who, after the Americans themselves, benefitted most from postwar expansion to the west. The Treaty of Paris in 1783 has been described as "exceedingly generous" to the Americans, but it was also highly lucrative to the British at the same time.

Prime Minister Lord Shelburne wisely saw the United States as a new nation rich in resources with huge potential for expansion, but the country also needed a major trading partner. Many Americans preferred trading with the British, and so trade resumed relatively quickly between the two nations that had once been enemies.

# DISCOVERING THE AMERICAN WEST

They ventured across the country through unknown terrain, facing danger and discovery at every turn. This is the journey of Lewis and Clark

Words by Jonathan Hatfull

When the Revolutionary war ended in 1783, the founding fathers had grand ideals of what the vast continent had to offer, but little notion of its sprawling landscape and what lived there. It was an incredible wilderness full of possibilities and dangers, from which Meriwether Lewis and William Clark had no guarantee of a safe return.

The shape of the young American nation would change drastically when Napoleon Bonaparte offered to sell the French territory of Louisiana, a colossal area of 1,332,530 square miles that would double the size of the USA. President Thomas Jefferson worked quickly to negotiate the Louisiana Purchase for $15 million in 1803, and he knew exactly what he wanted from it. He was desperate to know if there was a Northwest Passage that would connect the Mississippi and the Pacific Ocean, thus greatly increasing trading possibilities, and he had secretly asked Congress to approve and fund the expedition six months before the purchase was officially announced.

The president already had the perfect leader for the expedition. Jefferson's secretary, Meriwether Lewis, was a military veteran in excellent physical shape with a keen interest in the study of wildlife, and his loyalty and dedication were unquestionable. Lewis immediately began to prepare, taking lessons in navigation and absorbing every piece of available information about the geography and people of the region. However, even with all his study, he knew there would be myriad surprises ahead.

Lewis invited his former commanding officer, William Clark, to join him as co-captain, a move that partly stemmed from the diplomatic aspect of the voyage. They would be the ones to convey to the many Native American tribes on their way westward that they were now living under new masters—a difficult conversation they hoped would be smoothed over with gifts, including a specially minted coin and some demonstrations of superior firepower. Clark's experience as a soldier and frontiersman combined with Lewis's strong leadership and diplomacy made them the perfect match, and he readily agreed.

Lewis sailed the newly constructed narrowboat from Pittsburgh down the Ohio River, and he met with Clark near Louisville, Kentucky, before setting up their winter training camp on Wood River. There would be 33 core members of the Corps of Discovery, which would finally set out on May 14, 1804 on the Missouri River.

The voyage did not get off to the best start. Discipline was occasionally poor, and on May 17, three men were court-martialled for being absent without leave. Meanwhile, Lewis was given his own warning on May 23, when he fell twenty feet from a cliff before managing to stop his fall with his knife, just barely saving his own life. There was no margin for error, and the brooding, solitary Lewis was reminded that wandering alone was a dangerous habit. Of course, that would not stop him.

The weather was fine, but it was hard going, with the fierce Missouri River frequently needing to be cleared to allow the boats free passage, and mosquitoes, ticks, and illness proving to be a growing problem. It was during this summer that the expedition suffered its only fatality, when Sergeant Charles Floyd died of appendicitis. However, Lewis' journeys into the woods provided them with an abundance of new discoveries. A meeting with the Oto and

Lewis and Clark were joined on their expedition by Sacagawea

Missouri Native Americans on August 3 went very well, with speeches and exchanges of gifts getting the reception Lewis and Clark had hoped for. Another successful meeting was held on August 30, this time with the Yankton Sioux, and the Corps of Discovery entered the Great Plains in early September. It was here that the natural history aspect of the mission really began, as never-before-seen animals roamed. Beasts that seem archetypally American today (elk, bison, coyotes, and antelope, for example) were a new discovery by these awestruck men from the east. But the animals weren't the only ones who called this land home, and the expedition was about to be reminded that, to some, they were trespassing.

Although every encounter with Native American tribes had been peaceful so far, tensions quickly ran high when they met the Teton Sioux (now known as the Lakota Sioux) near what is now South Dakota, in September. The travelers had been warned that this tribe could be unfriendly, and it seemed that conflict was inevitable following a series of difficult meetings and demands for one of their boats. Crisis was averted thanks to the intervention of their chief, Black Buffalo, although Clark's diaries show that all was not forgiven, referring to them as, "vile miscreants of the savage race."

They traveled on northwards, reaching the Mandan settlements (a heavily populated area with more people calling it

A 1954 U.S. Postage Stamp featuring Lewis and Clark

home than Washington, D.C. at the time) at the end of October. Quickly, they began work on their winter camp, Fort Mandan, as the cold weather bit harder than the men had ever experienced. It was here that they made one of the most important decisions of their voyage. They hired the French-Canadian Toussaint Charbonneau, a fur trader, and his 16-year-old Shoshone wife Sacagawea as interpreters. Lewis and Clark were heading to the mountains, and although they had no idea quite how colossal the range was, they knew they would need horses. Native speakers would be invaluable for trade as well as safe passage. Sacagawea gave birth to her son, Jean Baptiste (nicknamed Pomp by Clark), during the winter, and many credit this woman and her child accompanying the travelers with being the reason they were treated so hospitably by tribes they met on the rest of the journey.

Having sent a small group back to St. Louis with samples of their findings, the Corps of Discovery set out again on April 7. They made excellent time through unexplored country, and it became clear that bringing Sacagawea was a wise decision indeed. Not only did she help them to forage, showing them what was edible and what wasn't, she also had the presence of mind to rescue important papers when a boat capsized. Then, at the start of June, everything nearly fell apart. They had reached a fork in the Missouri

River, and Lewis and Clark had to make a choice. If they chose poorly, they would be taken completely off course, and it was an incredible relief when they reached the waterfalls they had been told they would find if they were on the right track. However, the right track was not an easy path to take, and the Great Falls were another colossal challenge. There was a constant threat from bears and rattlesnakes, and several crewmembers were ill.

They would have to go the long way around, 18 miles over difficult terrain, carrying everything that they needed. There was no way back. Incredibly, the crew pulled together and accomplished this amazing feat. It's a testament to the spirit of these men, their awareness of the importance of their mission, and the leadership of Lewis and Clark that the only thing lost on this brutal detour was time, and the dream of Lewis' iron-framed boat, which simply did not work.

Time, of course, was of the essence. Despite making the right choice at a second set of forks, winter was coming and there were still mountains to climb. They needed to reach the Shoshone tribe and trade for horses if they were to have any hope of reaching their goal, and as they grew closer, Sacagawea helped to navigate through the territory of her youth. However, finding the tribe proved to be difficult, and Lewis and a scout broke off from the group while Clark continued with the rest of the party up the river. Another crushing blow was delivered when Lewis saw the full extent of the mountains they would have to cross. There was no Northwest Passage through the Rocky Mountains.

Finally, they found the Shoshone, who had never seen anyone like these strangers before. Sacagawea acted as an interpreter, and, while speaking, realized that the tribe's chief, Cameahwait, was her brother. This amazing stroke of luck secured the horses needed for their mountain crossing, after two weeks spent resting at the Shoshone camp.

In September, they began their mountain crossing at the Bitterroot Range with a Shoshone guide named Old Toby. The weather was against them, Toby lost his way for a while, and the group faced the very real possibility of starvation over two agonizing weeks. They finally found their way to the settlement of the Nez Perce on September

Lewis and Clark's journey westward would lead them along the Missouri River

Lewis, Clark, and their guide, Sacagawea, in the Bitterroot Mountains (present-day Idaho)

Sacagawea's knowledge of the route ahead was invaluable to Lewis and Clark's expedition

# "They had reached a fork in the Missouri River, and Lewis and Clark had to make a choice. If they chose poorly, they would be taken completely off course"

23, who decided to spare the lives of these wretched, starving travelers. In fact, they were incredibly hospitable, sheltering them for two weeks and even teaching them a new way to build canoes. Their first downstream journey may have seemed like a blessed relief, but the rapids were fantastically dangerous, and they were watched with great interest as they made their way down the perilous waters. Once again, they overcame the odds.

On November 7, Clark was convinced that he could see the Pacific, writing, "Ocean in view! O! The Joy... This great Pacific Ocean which we have been so long anxious to see. And the roaring or noise made by the waves breaking on the rocky shores (as I suppose) may be heard distinctly." He was sadly mistaken. They were 18 miles away, and it would take more than a week in bad weather to reach Cape Disappointment on November 18. Clark wrote that the, "...men appear much satisfied with their trip, beholding with astonishment the high waves dashing against the rocks and this immense

ocean." They had reached the Pacific; their mission was accomplished. Lewis and Clark decided to take a vote on where to build their winter camp, which is believed to be the first time in recorded US history that a slave (York) and a woman (Sacagawea) were allowed to vote. The winter was tough, as endless rain dampened their spirits, but in March they set out to return, using Clark's updated map. Their journey home may have been shorter (a mere six months), but had its own dangers, including a violent encounter with Blackfeet Indians that resulted in two killings. They finally arrived in St. Louis on September 23, 1806, almost two and a half years after setting off.

Lewis, Clark, and the Corps of Discovery had gone where no White man had gone before. The discoveries they had made, from plant life to animals (grizzly bears, bison, bighorns, wolves, and more) to the Native American tribes they met, helped to bring a greater understanding of the nation to Washington, and they changed the shape of the burgeoning United States of America.

## Life After the Voyage

### What became of the intrepid pair once they returned

Lewis and Clark were hailed as national heroes, and President Thomas Jefferson was eager to show how pleased he was, giving both men political appointments. However, in the case of Lewis, these new honors did not help him to find any peace. He struggled with his duties as governor of Louisiana and frequently gave in to his dark moods and burgeoning alcoholism. It ended in tragedy when, on his way to Washington on October 12, 1809, Lewis shot himself.

Clark's life makes for much happier reading. He worked as an agent for Indian affairs and was married in 1808, before becoming the governor of the Missouri Territory for ten years. Despite his harsh words for the Lakota Sioux after their nearly violent encounter, Clark became renowned for his fair treatment of Native Americans (with some accusing him of being too sympathetic). He also cared for the child of Sacagawea after she and Toussaint left young Jean Baptiste (the baby Clark had called Pomp) in his care. He continued to raise Jean Baptiste after Sacagawea's death in 1812, and the young man would later travel to Europe and the German court.

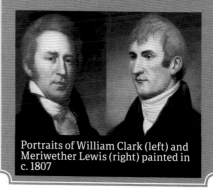

Portraits of William Clark (left) and Meriwether Lewis (right) painted in c. 1807

# On the Trail

## Track the intrepid explorers' journey across the Louisiana Territory

**01. Camp Wood** May 14, 1804
This is where they begin preparing for the expedition. Supplies are gathered, men are trained, and the importance of the voyage is emphasized. Some disciplining is required before they go.

**02. Lakota Sioux** September 25, 1804
While they've experienced several peaceful encounters with tribes, the Corps of Discovery has a fraught encounter with the Lakota Sioux on the river near what is now Pierre, South Dakota. Without the interference of the tribe's chief, this could have been the end for all.

**03. Fort Mandan** October 1804—April 1805
They arrive at the Mandan-Hidatsa settlement and prepare their winter camp, named Fort Mandan. Lewis and Clark arrange for discoveries and journals to be sent back, and Sacagawea joins them.

**04. The Unknown Fork** June 1, 1805
The expedition reaches another crucial decision when they find an unexpected fork in the Missouri. It's a gamble, but they know that they have made the correct choice when they see the Great Falls.

**05. Great Falls** June 13, 1805
They had been told about a great waterfall, but having been confronted with the five cascades of the Great Falls, Lewis and Clark realize that going around over ground will be long and arduous.

**06. Three Forks** July 22, 1805
The Three Forks of the Missouri are uncharted when the expedition reaches this point. They know that if they end up taking the wrong fork, crossing the mountains will become increasingly perilous.

**07. The Shoshone** August 17, 1805
Sacagawea is reunited with her people when the search for the Shoshone is over. Lewis and Clark need her to negotiate for horses, and they have a stroke of luck when Sacagawea's brother is the chief.

**08. Bitterroot Mountains** September 23-October 7, 1805
Accompanied by a Shoshone guide, the expedition sets out into the mountains. They are ill-prepared for such a long journey through the Rockies and face horrible weather and the possibility of starvation.

**09. Nez Perce** 23 September—October 7, 1805
They find their way out of the mountains and into villages of the Nez Perce Indians. The locals take pity on the starving, bedraggled men, and help them to prepare for the final stage of their journey.

**10. Fort Clatsop** November 24, 1805-March 23, 1806
The Corps of Discovery finally arrives at the Pacific Ocean. They take a vote as to where to build their winter camp, and dream of home while Lewis works on a new and improved map.

Preparation

Recruitment

Exploration and Homecoming

Indian Reservation

## Notable Discoveries

### Grizzly bear

The grizzly bears were far bigger than any they had seen before. It took more than ten shots to bring down a single bear when they faced one.

### Prairie dogs
Lewis and Clark found these critters fascinating, particularly the way in which they lived in connected burrows (described as "towns").

### Bison
The explorers were not prepared for the experience of seeing Bison in the wild. Lewis wrote of a friendly calf that was only scared of his dog.

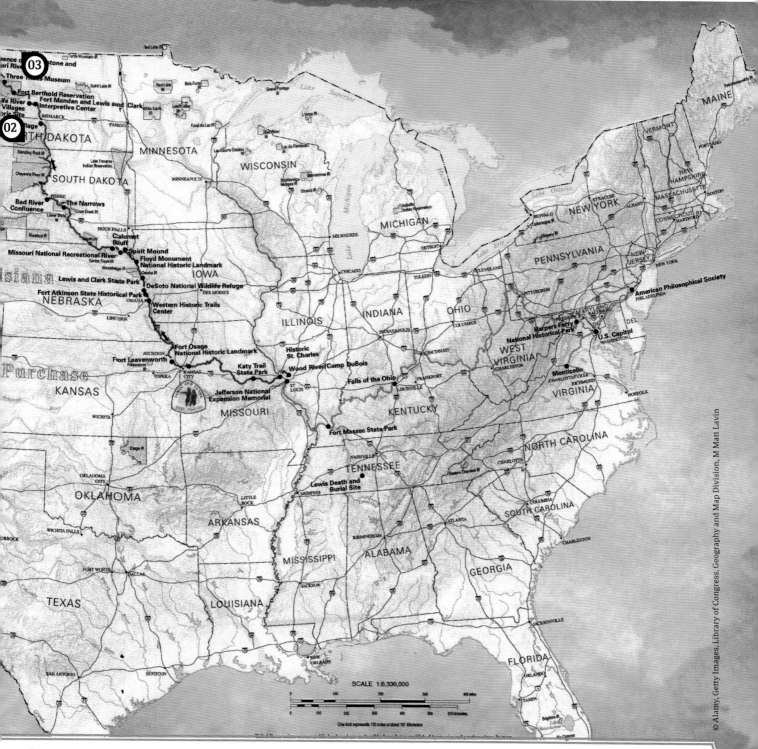

SCALE 1:6,336,000

One inch represents 100 miles or about 161 kilometers

© Alamy, Getty Images, Library of Congress, Geography and Map Division, M Matt Lavin

### Coyote

Described as "a prairie wolf," Lewis and Clark heard these creatures howling at night. They were familiar to Europeans, but unknown to the men.

### Silver sagebrush

First seen in October 1804, the sagebrush, now known as Artemisia cana, was described as an "aromatic herb," and it spread through great swathes of the West.

### Indian tobacco

As a tobacco grower, Lewis took interest in the two species he encountered on the trip, taking notes on how the Arikaras tribe grew and harvested their crops.

### Douglas firs

Towards the end of the voyage, they saw a variety of fir trees, with Lewis doing his best to describe six in his journal, including the Douglas fir.

# MOUNTAIN MEN

## Join the hardy pioneers who lived and died in the wilderness beyond the western frontier

Words by Scott Reeves

Before the Wild West there was the wilderness west—enormous swathes of land that were unknown and unexplored, a vast blank canvas on maps between the colonies of the East and the seaboard of the West. Americans believed it was their manifest destiny to expand across the continent, but if they were to do so a band of tough and robust pioneers would need to blaze a trail for them.

Many of these mountain men found their way west courtesy of the fur trade. Disappearing beyond the frontier for weeks, months, and years at a time, the fur trappers would return with cartloads of beaver furs and tales of vast rock formations, great salt lakes and jets of hot water that spurted from holes in the ground.

In their quest for the finest furs and the biggest hauls, these pioneers of the West discovered the quickest and safest paths, cutting their own roads to allow their mules to travel to the annual trade rendezvous. Mountain men were often the first White face seen by Native tribes, and sometimes also the last as they fought skirmishes with the warriors who resented White men encroaching on their land.

When the fur trade began to decline in the 1840s, the mountain men found their skills were still in demand. Hardy folk who wanted to settle in the West wanted experienced travelers to take them safely across the mountains and plains. Goldrushers wanted to know the quickest routes to California and Montana to make their fortunes. Politicians in Washington, D.C. sent the US Army to fill in the gaps on maps, and nobody was better qualified to help than the mountain men.

From early American exploration to those who helped to settle the far west, meet six mountain men who helped to push back the frontier.

## Daniel Boone 1734-1820

### Best known for: Being the first frontier hero

Born to a Quaker family in the colony of Pennsylvania at a time when the American frontier was defined by the Appalachian Mountains, Daniel Boone soon became proficient with a rifle and was a skilled hunter. After marrying and starting a family in North Carolina, Boone would disappear into the wilderness for weeks and months at a time, returning from his long hunts with furs and pelts to trade. During these trips, he discovered easy routes through the mountains, crossing into territory never seen by the White colonists.

Faced with growing financial pressures, 34-year-old Boone decided to take on a longer and more dangerous hunt than ever before—a two-year expedition in Kentucky, the largely unexplored but fertile land beyond the Appalachians. Despite being taken captive by the Native Shawnee, Boone returned to hunt in Kentucky in 1772, while in 1773 he uprooted his entire family in a failed attempt to settle Kentucky—one that saw Boone's eldest son killed by the hostile Natives.

In 1775 Boone tried again—this time plotting a route through the Cumberland Gap that would become known as the Wilderness Road. By the end of the year, Boone was living with his family in Kentucky in a small town named after him: Boonesborough. He continued to range far from home despite the interruption of the American Revolution and repeated conflicts with the Shawnee. By the time of his death, inspired by popular accounts of his adventurous life, hundreds of thousands of settlers had followed the Wilderness Road to join Boone in Kentucky.

Boone became the first frontier hero when an account of his life was printed in 1784 to encourage settlers to Kentucky

## Jedediah Smith 1799-1831

### Best known for: Mapping the West

Despite being born in New York state, Jedediah Smith had a desire to see the far west of the new United States. By the age of 23 he was living in the frontier town of St. Louis, Missouri, responding to an advertisement to join a new fur trading company set up by William Ashley and Andrew Henry. Smith was selected to be one of Ashley and Henry's "enterprising young men" and tasked with trapping along the Missouri River. Such was Smith's success in trapping furs that he was later offered a partnership in the fur company.

Smith's first expedition to the West saw him discover the South Pass through the Rocky Mountains. Subsequent expeditions went further, twice pushing on into California, although he was received there with suspicion by the Mexican governor. His return journeys from the Pacific coast saw him cross the Great Basin Desert at the height of summer and take a northerly route through Oregon, both pioneering journeys.

Smith was not just a fur trapper; he was well aware of the value of his expeditions to the nation as a whole. He was quick to write to John Eaton, the Secretary of War, to disclose the location of the South Pass through the Rockies, unlike previous trappers who had used the route but kept it secret for their own gain. Smith also kept detailed notes and maps, making observations on the nature, topography, and geology of the West, shining a light on the region for the first time.

Smith kept his hair long to hide a scar on the side of his head, the result of a grizzly bear attack that almost cost his life

## Joseph Meek
## 1810-1875

### Best known for: Being a trapper-turned-politician

For over a decade, Joseph Meek roamed the Rocky Mountains as a trapper working for the Rocky Mountain Fur Company. He was a skilled trapper, but not immune from the dangers of the lifestyle—at just 19 years old his trapping party was scattered by a band of Blackfoot warriors, leaving Meek alone and wandering to safety through Yellowstone.

However, Meek was a little late to the trapping game compared to many of his contemporaries, and the fur industry was already in decline. In 1840, Meek decided to stop trapping and tag along with a party of settlers on the Oregon Trail. Unlike many of his fellow mountain men who struggled to adapt to a sedentary life, Meek set up home in the Tualatin Valley and threw himself into civilizing the land. Aware that more and more people were moving to the area, Meek was a key mover in the creation of a provisional government at the Champoeg Meetings, setting up a political structure to provide leadership and administer the increasingly busy area.

Following a Native attack that killed 14, including Meek's 10-year-old daughter, Meek traveled to Washington, D.C. and met with James Polk. Meek persuaded the President to take control of Oregon, making it a federal territory in 1848, and was rewarded with the post of Federal Marshal. The former mountain man who had lived in the lawless wilderness beyond the frontier was now charged with bringing it under the control of the

Meek had the advantage of being the cousin by marriage of President Polk, giving him access to the most powerful man in the land

## Kit Carson
## 1809-1868

### Best known for: Being the superstar mountain man of dime novels

Carson rushed across the entire continent to deliver news of both the Californian revolt and gold strike to the president

Kit Carson knew that the life of a saddler's apprentice was not for him and ran away with a caravan of traders at the age of 15. He did whatever job he could do to scrape together a living–cook, driver, miner–until finally drifting into the life of a fur trapper.

Carson repeatedly came up against hostile Native tribes and seemed to revel in his reputation as an Indian fighter. He took his first Native scalp on his first trapping trip at the age of 19 and continued to take every opportunity to wipe out the Native people, even mercilessly wiping out a smallpox-struck Blackfoot village in 1838.

A fateful encounter on a steamboat in 1842 saw Carson first meet the man who would help him become nationally famous. John Frémont was a major in the US Army tasked with mapping the West, and he hired Carson to act as his guide. Over the next four years the two pathfinders mapped the Oregon Trail, the artery that pumped settlers into the West, and investigated the Mexican province of Alta California, helping to stir up the Bear Flag Revolt which led to California being annexed by the USA.

Frémont's positive reports of Carson's conduct and bravery made the mountain man's name known on the east coast, after which his life was seized upon by writers of cheap, dime novels who churned out exaggerated tales of his explorations and violence towards Natives to make Carson the pulp-fiction superstar of his day.

## Jim Bridger
## 1804-1881

### Best known for: Abandoning Hugh Glass

Bridger was forgiven by Hugh Glass, who accepted that the young trapper was placed in a difficult situation

One of the most widely traveled mountain men, Jim Bridger began his adventures as one of Ashley and Henry's youngest fur trappers at the age of 18. Over the course of the next 46 years Bridger was a pioneer who explored much of the West—he was among the first to view the natural wonders of Yellowstone and to find the Great Salt Lake.

He was instrumental in guiding US Army map-making parties, taking the Stansbury Expedition over what would become known as the Bridger Pass in the Sierra Madre Mountains in 1850 and guiding another expedition to Jackson Hole and the Grand Tetons. He also found the Bridger Trail, an alterNative and safer route to the gold fields of Montana that was used by countless prospectors.

However, Bridger will always be known as the man who abandoned Hugh Glass, especially after the tale was given the Hollywood treatment in *The Revenant*.

After Glass spooked a female grizzly bear with two cubs and was badly mauled, two of his comrades, Bridger and John Fitzgerald, volunteered to stay with Glass until he died and bury his body. They didn't—perhaps scared away by Native Arikara warriors, perhaps just fed up with waiting—they abandoned Glass to face his expected death alone. But he didn't die, and Glass faced a tortuous and painful 200-mile trek to safety without any supplies and a confrontation with the men who abandoned him.

# Jim Beckwourth
## c. 1798-c. 1867

**Best known for:** Being the most prominent Black mountain man

Jim Beckwourth was born into slavery; his mother was a slave and his father her master. Freed in his mid-twenties, Beckwourth sought his fortune with the new fur trappers plying their trade westwards of Missouri. Beckwourth spent eight or nine years living with the Native Crow tribe, still trapping furs but also taking part in Crow raids against their Blackfoot enemy—and occasionally against Whites too.

Beckwourth left his Crow wives and returned to White society in 1837, joining the US Army to fight against the Seminoles in Florida, then setting up trading posts in Colorado. He tagged along with the California Gold Rush, opening a store in Sacramento to supply the forty-niners with food and tools, but being a shopkeeper didn't put an end to his wanderings—in 1850 he discovered the Beckwourth Pass through the Sierra Nevada Mountains, and the following year he found an alterNative route: the Beckwourth Trail.

Towards the end of the Civil War Beckwourth rejoined the US Army to help conduct operations against Cheyenne and Apache Natives. However, controversy struck when up to 163 friendly Cheyennes were killed in the Sand Creek Massacre despite camping on land suggested by an Army officer and prominently displaying the stars and stripes and a White flag. The incident spoiled Beckwourth's previously good standing with the Cheyenne and marked a sad conclusion to a roving life largely spent improving relations between Whites settlers and Native tribes.

Beckwourth was accepted by the Crow nation because he was mistaken for the lost son of a chief and rose to become a chief himself

# FIVE WAYS TO DIE IN THE WEST

IF THE GRIZZLIES DON'T GET YOU, YOUR SO-CALLED FRIENDS WILL—THERE WERE FEW MORE DANGEROUS OCCUPATIONS THAN BEING A MOUNTAIN MAN

## Grizzly bear

Hugh Glass was not the only victim of a grizzly attack—Jedediah Smith was maimed for life by a protective bear mother and Kit Carson was chased up a tree, while countless others did not escape with their lives.

## Disease

No matter how strong a mountain man was, if he contracted one of the diseases that ran rife in the unsanitary frontier towns, his chances of survival were slim. Cholera, diphtheria, smallpox, tuberculosis, and whooping cough were just a few of the deadly illnesses that thrived with the lack of decent medical care.

## Native Americans

Relations between the mountain men and the Native tribes on whose land they roamed were usually tense and often outright violent. One of many killed was Jedediah Smith, who was surrounded by Comanche warriors after leaving his caravan to look for water.

## Exposure

Perhaps the most feared method of death, mountain men needed to be able to live alone in the wild and cope with both the cold of the mountains and the heat of the plains—the survival of Hugh Glass was an extreme illustration of their phenomenal bushcraft.

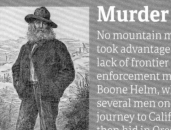

## Murder

No mountain man took advantage of the lack of frontier law enforcement more than Boone Helm, who killed several men on his journey to California, then hid in Oregon robbing and killing more victims. He was even prepared to eat human flesh when short of food in the wilderness.

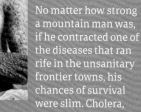

# A PROMISED LAND

## During the days of westward expansion, a Great Awakening of religious fervor swept through the American frontier

**Words by Mike Haskew**

They came by the thousands, drawn to an event like nothing they had ever seen. The American frontier was a harsh, unforgiving environment, yet it was full of promise, and these pioneering settlers had come to hear words of commitment, fulfillment, redemption, and, ultimately, salvation.

The flower of the second "Great Awakening" was beginning to blossom, and the camp meeting at Cane Ridge, Kentucky, held in early August 1801, brought 10,000 to 20,000 people together to hear the word of God preached, to be baptized, and to receive God's grace, turning as they could from lives of sin.

Hosted by the Presbyterian Church, one of several Protestant denominations committed to spreading the Christian Gospel, Cane Ridge was the catalyst for the camp meeting phenomenon that swept the woodlands and prairies of the American frontier in the years of westward expansion across the North American continent as settlers crossed the Appalachian Mountains and poured into largely unknown territory. The Methodists were at Cane Ridge as well, and the preaching of several ministers in different venues, the singing of hymns and the serving of communion marked the event as pilgrims spilled out of the meeting house and across adjacent lands, their numbers swelling.

The second Great Awakening found fertile ground on the American frontier, as the uncertainty of life and the constant tug of death were daily experiences. Assurances were welcome—particularly those of the intrepid ministers of the Lord Jesus Christ. By the early 1800s,

Protestant evangelism was not a new concept. In fact, a first Great Awakening had occurred decades earlier in the 1730s and 40s in Great Britain and its 13 North American colonies. During that time, evangelical Anglicans and Methodist followers of John Wesley found their voices, while the Presbyterians, Congregationalists, and Baptists devoted their energies to spreading the Christian message and the "conversion of the entire world." New missionary societies were formed, resources were devoted to the American colonies, and the foundation was laid for expansion of the faith.

The second Great Awakening shaped the social and cultural development of the American frontier as individuals were led to devote themselves to Christian principles and the Protestant denominations spread their influence in the young land. The practices of "revival" of the faith and "rebirth" of the individual in the Holy Spirit gained wide enthusiasm and attendance. At the same time, a wave of "democratization" continued among the Protestant denominations. Federal and state governments declined to sponsor or endorse a particular religion, and the Church lost its ability to coerce attendance or financial support from the faithful. The tenets and practices of the established Churches were challenged. For Methodists, Wesley's principle of reaching the people where they lived and worked involved reaching beyond the walls of the church building itself and going to the people wherever they were—preaching to any and all who would listen.

The movement was not limited to camp meetings, though, as new congregations were often formed in the

Francis Asbury was an early leader of the Methodist Church in America and a prolific circuit rider

This tribute to frontier religious leaders includes Presbyterian Barton W. Stone, right, an organizer of Cane Ridge in 1801

A preacher exhorts a large crowd during one of many camp meetings on the American frontier

wake of a revival and fresh perspectives on the relationship between mankind and God were shaped during the period. Among the most profound of these was the idea that "all men are created equal," as put forth in the Declaration of Independence, and the concept that every person could be "saved" and had access to the mercy and salvation of God. Of course, the implications of this notion are obvious. In an America where there were thousands of slaves, how could the Church and the true Christian reconcile one institution with the other?

Churches themselves struggled with changing perspectives, and there were splits among the believers. A schism between the Congregational and Presbyterian Churches even predated the second Great Awakening. Theological debate was energized throughout the frontier, and the Churches sometimes banded together to advance the cause while there were other instances of differing approaches to the ministry.

The Methodists, for example, employed itinerant circuit riders, preachers who traveled through towns and settlements in a district and ministered to the needy in multiple congregations. The Presbyterian and Congregational Churches agreed to the Plan of Union of 1801, allowing mutual support as either group could hire ministers from the other and providing flexibility as to discipline, either the Congregational polity or the Presbyterian session of ruling elders. Baptists chose generally to minister through established Churches and brought 10,000 new souls into their fold in the span of just three years. Everywhere, the numbers of professed Christians grew rapidly, and in 1816 the American Bible Society was organized with the sole purpose of supplying Bibles to the frontier.

The phenomena of the camp meeting and the revival became the most prominent means of reaching the unchurched. The human drama of confession, redemption, and salvation as witnessed during these events brought more people to the altar. Rooted in the Scottish Presbyterian tradition, the camp meeting was often the scene of spectacle as worshipers danced, rolled on the ground, shook, shouted, and sang hymns with boundless enthusiasm. Although Cane Ridge is remembered as one of the largest such meetings, preachers held these events by the hundreds across the frontier. In the summer of 1811 alone, the Methodists held 400 camp meetings.

Inevitably, there were detractors. Historian Philip Schaff observed one such event and wrote in 1849, "There is a stamping and bouncing, jumping and falling, crying and howling, groaning and sighing, all praying in confusion, a rude singing of the most vulgar street songs, so that it must be loathing to an educated man, and fill the serious Christian with painful emotions."

Perhaps unwittingly, however, Schaff had touched the essence of the second Great Awakening. The power of religion was evident in shaping the perspective of the people in all aspects of their lives, including their treatment of their fellow man, their definition of sin, their belief in a life after death and the solace it provided amid the hardships of the frontier, and most profoundly the organization and mission of the Church itself.

# "The power of religion was evident in the shaping of their lives, including their treatment of their fellow man"

With the second Great Awakening, the idea that the clergy was the intercessor with God for the common man dissipated. No longer was the clergy considered a separate, elite class among Christians. Logically, the opportunity for a personal relationship with God presented itself, and then came the shattering concept of personal freedom and liberty that transcended religion and daily life simultaneously, giving rise to the very ideals that are inherent in the American way of life to this day.

A century and a half after the second Great Awakening, Nathan Hatch, a professor at the University of Notre Dame, called Methodism "the most profound religious movement in American history, its growth a central feature in the emergence of the United States as a republic." The Methodist circuit riders became such a familiar part of the frontier way of life that settlers themselves popularized the saying that the first human sound to follow the "tunk" of the pioneer's axe was the friendly "Hello!" of the Methodist circuit-riding preacher. Francis Asbury, the first American bishop of the Methodist Episcopal Church, is believed to have covered an average of 5,000 miles a year on horseback as a circuit rider.

The momentum of the second Great Awakening also served as evidence for Americans that they might, in fact, be the chosen people of God. Harkening back to the early days of colonization, victory in the Revolutionary War and subsequent movement westward on the crest of the wave of Manifest Destiny, the American people also believed their growing prosperity proved to the world that their nation was blessed. Author Herman Melville said: "We Americans are the peculiar, chosen people— the Israel of our time; we bear the ark of liberties of the world."

Although the Protestant political voice had long been prominent in American politics, the second Great Awakening strengthened it. Nevertheless, the issues of the day—particularly the question of slavery—sowed dissent among the faithful, from the cities in the north and east to the plantations of the South and the frontiers of the West. By 1845, the three largest Protestant denominations in the United States, Presbyterian, Baptist, and Methodist, had fractured into northern and southern branches over slavery, and many of them remained divided for the next century.

Some historians point to a third Great Awakening beginning around 1850, during which the growth of the Protestant Churches in the US had matured and the denominations were perceived as a political and social force in the cities. In effect, the evolution of religion on the frontier had become a paradox. While offering stability and assurance to the pioneering people of the Trans-Appalachian West, it had also introduced radical concepts of relations between mankind and God, as well as between fellow human beings, destabilizing the social status quo.

A newfound freedom of religious thought and expression also gave rise to new religious perspectives during the mid-18th century. New sects of believers emerged, including spiritualists; the Millerists, followers of William Miller who believed the second coming of Christ was imminent and expected his return sometime between 1843 and 1844; the Mormons, followers of Joseph Smith who migrated westward beyond the Rocky Mountains; and the Shakers.

Religion on the American frontier shaped the character of the westward movement and settlement of the North American continent. The result was a uniquely American viewpoint and identity regarding the nature of religion in daily life, the subsequent campaigns in favor of morality and virtuous living, and the political influences of the faithful as the nation wrestled with emerging social and cultural issues that persist, at least in part, to this day.

## The Mormon Movement

### Persecuted on the frontier, members of the Church of Jesus Christ of Latter-Day Saints moved westward

Founded by Joseph Smith in 1830, the members of the Church of Jesus Christ of Latter-day Saints, or Mormons, were victims of suspicion and hatred on the frontier because of their peculiar beliefs, communal, lifestyle and practice of polygamy. The Mormons were persecuted and essentially driven from the territories of the Midwest, including Ohio, Missouri, Illinois, and Iowa. As a result, they sought a "new Jerusalem" where they might practice their faith without fear.

In 1847, the Mormons set out westward, crossing the Great Plains and the Rocky Mountains. That summer, after traveling hundreds of miles, they came to the flatlands beside the Great Salt Lake and decided to settle there. By 1850, nearly 5,000 Mormons had come to the area, and their settlement in the desert began to take root. Although they had sought isolation, the Mormons were inevitably caught up in the general westward movement of Americans, the tumult of the Mexican War, and later disputes with the US government. By 1896, however, the state of Utah, largely the creation of the Mormons, had joined the Union.

Members of the Mormon faith pull up stakes and abandon Illinois for the promise of religious freedom in the West

The Battle of the Alamo in 1836,
decisive in expansion southwest into
today's state of Texas

# FROM SEA TO SHINING SEA

## After the Treaty of Paris ended hostilities with the British in 1783, Americans looked West to expand their new nation

Words by Robert Walsh

Expansion was the dream of many Americans, albeit a nightmare for the Native American population and deeply unpopular with the Mexicans. Since the founding of the original colonies in the 1600s, colonists had a desire to spread wherever they saw an opportunity. That desire had long been inhibited, if not halted, by British colonial policy, war, and practical concerns like manpower and logistics.

Unofficially, an expansion had been happening for decades, long before the 19th century saw the United States extend from sea to shining sea. Even before the Proclamation of 1763, the Revolutionary War, and 1783's Treaty of Paris, settlers had been spreading west, legally or otherwise.

The Proclamation of 1763 had been intended to keep settlers east of the Appalachians but, poorly enforced and often ignored, it only managed to fuel the existing resentment among colonists of British colonial policy.

With British rule ending after Yorktown in 1781, American and immigrant settlers could attempt further expansion without colonial intervention. They lost no time doing so. Many Americans and their politicians were keen on nation-building, which was extremely difficult without territorial expansion.

Within 25 years of the Treaty of Paris, 1803's Louisiana Purchase doubled the size of the United States almost overnight. Expansion southwest created the Republic of Texas in 1836, becoming the Union's 28th state in 1845.

Expansion to the north, particularly in the Oregon Territory, had been accomplished by a series of treaties with the British. The early 1840s would be the springboard for unrivaled expansion through both diplomacy and war.

The death of President William Henry Harrison in 1841 carved out an opportunity for maverick Vice President John Tyler, who was an expansionist. Tyler, sworn in almost immediately, became America's longest-serving president never to have been elected.

In 1842, Tyler's secretary of state, Daniel Webster, signed the very popular Webster-Ashburton Treaty, defining the border between Maine and Britain's remaining North American territory, later present-day Canada.

Other provisions included joint use of the Great Lakes, an extradition agreement for some crimes, reaffirming the Rocky Mountains border established in 1818, the border between Lake Superior and the Lake of the Woods, and finally ending slave trading on the high seas. Britain had already abolished slavery, the US hadn't.

The Webster-Ashburton Treaty proved very popular in the US. Before, long Tyler started eyeing another potential prize; the Republic of Texas. Before resolving the Texas issue, though, the Oregon question came first. Oregon had been a thorny issue for some time. The British held part of it, but American expansion and popular opinion wanted all of it.

In 1846 the Oregon Treaty settled rival American and British claims to the Oregon Country, comprising present-day Oregon, Washington State, Idaho, parts of Montana, and Wyoming, along with a portion of British Columbia.

President James Polk, elected on an expansionist platform in 1844, wanted to satisfy American demands for control of the entire Oregon Territory by revoking

## "The US, despite Mexico's complaints, had done little to curb 'filibusters' provoking trouble in Mexican territories"

the treaty of 1818. The 1846 treaty didn't give America full control, a line being drawn along the 49th parallel instead, but compromise suited both sides.

Britain had other concerns besides Oregon and so did the US, specifically deteriorating relations with Mexico. America and Mexico were on the brink of war over the Republic of Texas joining the Union. While the 1846 agreement over Oregon was peaceful, expansion to the southwest wasn't.

One of Tyler's first major political moves was campaigning to annex Texas. Since defeating Mexican dictator General Santa Anna, Texas had been an independent nation. Tyler, wanting it under American control, started laying the foundations for annexation. He launched a propaganda campaign implying the British intended to take it, abolish slavery, and send American cotton farmers home. That, Tyler claimed, would seriously damage the southern economy.

His appeals to expansionist and nationalistic sentiments worked wonderfully. His appeals to pro-slavery and pro-annexation opinion proved especially popular down south. President Polk was equally keen, as was Sam Houston, former Governor of Tennessee and in 1844, and the president of the Republic of Texas.

In 1845 Houston was elected to the US Senate partly for helping the former Republic of Texas become the Union's 28th state. Texas joining the Union suited expansionists perfectly, expanding American territory in a strategically important region. It also provoked the Mexican-American War in 1846.

This pleased many Americans, but displeased a great many Mexicans. Texas—being former Mexican territory—meant tensions still existed between Mexico and the United States. Years before Texan independence, American businessmen, adventurers, and colonists had been entering what had been northern Mexico. As their numbers grew so had the Texan independence movement. The US, despite Mexico's repeated complaints, had done little to curb these "filibusters" provoking trouble

in Mexican territories. The loss of Texas had further wounded Mexican pride, but the Mexican War proved vastly more damaging.

In February 1845, the US Senate and House of Representatives voted to annex Texas. Mexico had never recognized the Republic's independence, also declaring it an act of war if Texas joined the Union. When Texas, explicitly ignoring Mexico's warnings, did so in December 1845, the stage was set for open war. The war itself was brief and bloody, greatly expanding the United States and humiliating Mexico.

President Polk had tried to buy parts of present-day California and New Mexico in 1845. Part of his offer to Mexico had been defining the Rio Grande as the southern border of the United States. Mexico had refused, leaving the US southern border undefined and disputed. US troops were sent there in large numbers, further antagonizing Mexico.

Now Texas had become the 28th state, Tyler, new secretary of state John Calhoun, and the expansionist lobby were unapologetic and unrepentant. Texas had joined the Union, they said, and Mexico would have to fight to get it back. With the support of the expansion-minded Polk, Tyler, and Calhoun, the US Army would ensure any fight would fail.

A series of bloody battles followed; Fort Texas, Palo Alto, Resaca de la Palma, Tabasco, Cerro Gordo, Churubusco, Monterey, and many others. Mexican troops won some battles but not the war. They were repeatedly beaten as US troops kept pushing forward. Mexico City fell in September 1847.

With the Treaty of Guadalupe-Hidalgo signed on February 2, 1848, the US gained about 8,000 square miles of what had been Mexican territory.

Texas was now US soil along with California, Nevada, Utah, and parts of New Mexico, Colorado, Wyoming, Arizona, Oklahoma, and Kansas. Some Mexican land not previously within the new State of Texas also changed hands and the Rio Grande now marked the new US-Mexico border. That war may have officially ended, but skirmishing between Mexicans and Americans lasted considerably longer.

Politically, militarily, and territorially, the Mexican War was a triumph for the United States. It wasn't universally popular, though. Protests were mounted and many US Army officers felt it was a "bad" war they didn't believe should have been fought.

John Tyler's unexpected presidency was to kick-start westward expansion, beginning with Texas

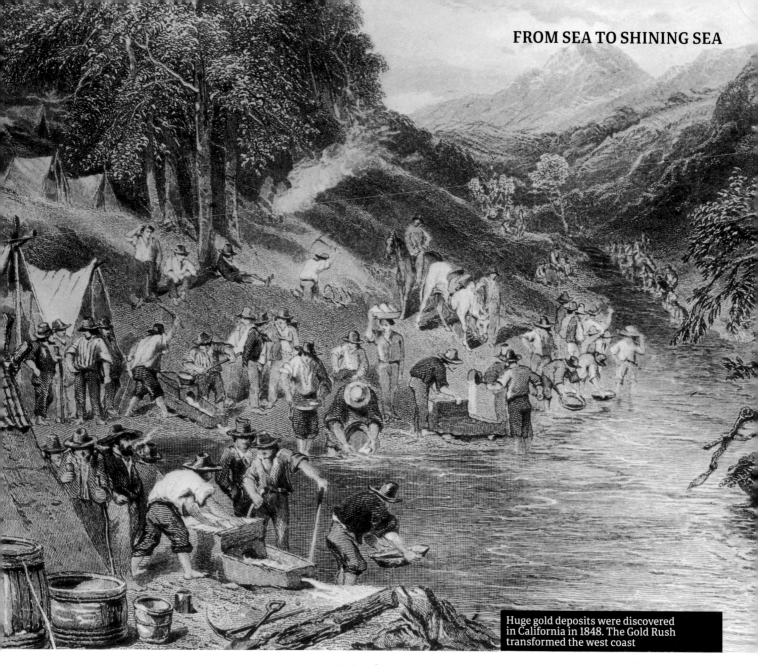

Huge gold deposits were discovered in California in 1848. The Gold Rush transformed the west coast

# Expansion, a Divine Right

### Many Americans came to believe expansion was their birthright, preordained by God

As America's population expanded, so did the need for living space and natural resources. Americans also needed an ideological reason to push west, something more substantial than a purely material need. From material need, political rhetoric, and religious ideals came action: America progressively expanded west.

The doctrine didn't come to be called 'Manifest Destiny' until the 1840s, but the idea existed long before then. The name came from the July-August 1845 issue of the *Democratic Review*, apparently coined by editor John O'Sullivan. It also appeared in the *New York Morning News* (which was also edited by O'Sullivan).

The idea was simple. God intended democracy and capitalism to be spread across the entire North American continent. American settlers were the people chosen by God to do it by whatever means were available. The wants or needs of indigenous people were at best a secondary priority.

In today's less-religious times it's hard to imagine just how powerful a call that was. Coupled with political machinations, it certainly had a potent effect on American thinking.

According to one advocate, it was: "Our manifest destiny to overspread the continent allotted by Providence for the free development of our yearly multiplying millions."

Americans believed the drive west was their manifest destiny preordained by God

# The Louisiana Purchase

## Westward expansion involved military action and bloodshed, but diplomacy and money also played their part

By the early 1800s, westward expansion was beginning. Military conquest played its part, but one of the largest moves west involved money rather than blood. Louisiana had been Spanish territory until secretly ceded to France in 1801. Alarmed by the French move but wanting to avoid war, the United States didn't conquer Louisiana; they bought it. In doing so, they effectively doubled the size of the United States as it was.

This proved more difficult than expected. The United States simply didn't have the money to buy it and no income tax then existed to raise funds. The alterNative was a bond issue via private investors and bankers.

US government bonds were offered through the financial centers of London and Amsterdam, then among the most powerful money markets. Barings, one of England's oldest merchant banks, was heavily involved. Hopes of Amsterdam also played a significant role.

What had been the Louisiana Territory rapidly evolved. In 1803 it was a huge, unmapped wilderness of over 1.5 million square miles, forming much of the USA's western frontier. Today, 13 present-day US states, in whole or part, exist within what was one of history's largest peaceful land transfers.

The Louisiana Purchase was vast, costing almost 600 billion dollars at today's prices

## "The Transcontinental Railroad and Homestead Acts were crucial to expansion and a major source of conflict with Natives"

Ulysses Grant, later elected president in 1869 after his stunning run of victories in the American Civil War, was one of them. Then a junior officer in the 4th Infantry Regiment, Grant later described Mexico as a "most evil war" and cynically criticized its motives:

"We were sent to provoke a fight, but it was essential the Mexicans should commence it."

In Mexico, Grant met one of his superiors, Robert E. Lee, who distinguished himself during the Mexican War and led the Confederate forces in the Civil War. When discussing terms for surrendering Lee's Army of Northern Virginia at Appomattox in 1865, Lee didn't remember meeting Grant despite their encounters across many Civil War battlefields.

Grant's West Point classmate James Longstreet, later one of Lee's most able Confederate deputies, also went to Texas. Texas joining the Union and the US Army arriving in large numbers was all the provocation Mexico (and certain Washington politicians) required.

Grant also encountered another officer who would play a major part in his later successes, William Tecumseh Sherman. Sherman would also play a major part in the future of the Native Americans, to their deepest regret.

Like Grant and mutual adversaries Lee and Longstreet, Sherman's star had risen high during the Civil War. Gifted, ruthless, and steadfastly refusing to be drawn into politicking, he succeeded Grant as commanding general in 1869 when Grant was elected president.

He remained commanding general until 1883. As he had during the Civil War, Sherman advocated total war against the latest opponents of American expansion, the Native Americans. The bloodiest phase of the American Indian Wars was about to begin.

The Mexican War was also brought within US borders areas occupied by Natives, including the fierce Apache and Comanche tribes. Like their Sioux, Cheyenne, and Cherokee brethren, the Apache and Comanche were prepared to fight any attempt by Americans to take their land and natural resources and frequently did. Among them was one of the most famous Native American warriors, then a little-known brave named Geronimo. The US Army would get to know him better over the next 40 years.

The Transcontinental Railroad and Homestead Acts were crucial to expansion and a major source of conflict with Native Americans. Construction began at Sacramento, California in January 1863 and Council Bluffs near Omaha, Nebraska in July 1865. The two lines met at Promontory Summit, Utah on May 10, 1869.

Funded with a combination of private capital and public bond issues, the Transcontinental Railroad also received astounding land grants from the Federal Government. In total it received over 450 million square miles from state and Federal governments.

A 400-yard corridor for the track and trackside buildings extended from

General William Tecumseh Sherman led operations against Native Americans

The 1848 Treaty of Guadalupe Hidalgo ended the Mexican War, adding over 600,000 square miles to the United States

Sacramento to Council Bluffs with a further ten miles on both sides of the track split into alternating sections. Odd-numbered sections were owned by the railroad companies, the Federal Government retaining the even numbered. The railroad companies raised further funds by selling their sections, although there were strings attached.

If unable to sell the land granted them within three years, the railroad companies had to sell it back to the government at $1.25 an acre. If they didn't repay the bonds, including their six percent interest rate, the government would own all railroad property outright. Pressure was on from the start. The Native Americans were in the way.

The Modoc War, the Great Sioux War of 1876, and the Nez Perce War were bloody campaigns with regular Native clashes and punitive expeditions by Sherman's troops. As the railroad and frontier expanded west, clashes worsened, especially between Natives and those pushing the "iron horse" through Native lands.

The Homestead Acts also caused conflict, offering settlers the chance to apply for free tracts of land mostly west of the Mississippi River. In total, some 270 million acres were simply given to applicants provided they'd never taken up arms against the United States, had lived there for the required period, and actively worked their land.

All that was needed to prove they'd done so was an affidavit from a witness. Needless to say, there were always witnesses available for a price. Applications themselves often came from frontmen for large cattle barons who posed as ordinary citizens. In areas where water was scarce, a frontman could apply for land with the only water source for miles, not to build a farm as they claimed, but to deny water supplies to rival cattle operations.

The Homestead Acts were periodically amended, increasing the size of individual land grants and adding new criteria to make appropriating land easier. The system was virtually unregulated, open to rampant abuse and corruption, and it was very seldom that anything meaningful was done to curb these abuses. Speculators and large businesses used it ruthlessly, attempting to corner sources of oil, minerals, and timber.

Over time, the Homestead Acts further eroded traditional Native American lands, simply handing them to settlers. That Native Americans had been there first wasn't seen as important. If it was, the importance lay in getting them out rather than letting them stay.

Native Americans feared their traditional way of life was starting to disappear as expansion swallowed their lands. To a large degree, their traditions and culture were also consumed. Treatment of Native Americans, then and now, remains uncomfortable for many Americans today. It caused lasting discomfort for Grant as well.

Grant's time in Mexico had been dispiriting for him. Already opposed to the Mexican War, he loathed the way White settlers often treated Native Americans. In one letter to wife Julia, he made his feelings clear in typically blunt language: "My opinion is that the whole race would be harmless and peaceable if they were not put upon by the Whites."

Whether Grant was right we'll never know, but the Natives undoubtedly were put upon and Sherman was among those most responsible. He pursued them as harshly as he had Confederates during the Civil War. That didn't make him universally popular in Washington.

As the pioneers and Transcontinental Railroad started driving west, they came into increasing contact (and conflict) with Native American tribes. Sherman's job was to protect the settlers and railroad from "hostiles," as they were then called. His methods differed little from his "march to the sea" and burning of Atlanta in 1864.

The Natives would submit peacefully or be subdued militarily as the frontier moved. The Indian Removal Act of 1830, allowing forcible relocation of Native Americans along the "Trail of Tears," had only been the beginning. Any tribe resisting Sherman faced harsh treatment including punitive raids on their camps and destruction of their property and means of survival.

As Sherman's troops burned homes and destroyed crops during the Civil War, they inflicted the same on the Natives after it. Eradicating the buffalo on which many Natives depended wasn't Sherman's official policy, but he certainly endorsed it. Sherman saw his job as protecting settlers and the railroad, subduing the opposition regardless of Native casualties.

As Sherman himself said during the Civil War: "War is cruelty. There's no use trying to reform it; the crueler it is, the sooner it will be over."

Not everybody agreed. Despite his avowed dislike of politics, Sherman's tenure as commanding general made him powerful enemies. Secretaries of war John Rawlins and William Belknap had, in Sherman's opinion, appropriated too much of the commanding general's power and influence for themselves. Another foe was even more powerful; old comrade-in-arms and now president, Ulysses Grant.

Sherman's attitude to war hadn't changed, but neither had Grant's toward the Native Americans. When Sherman's brass-knuckled tactics angered humanitarians, they found common ground with President Grant. That put Grant in a very difficult personal and political position.

Sherman's attitude to criticism, especially from politicians and the press, wasn't helpful. In 1874 he moved his headquarters from Washington, D.C. to St. Louis, Missouri, visiting D.C. only when absolutely necessary. There, he felt, he was less subject to meddlesome civilians and politicians. He only returned to Washington, D.C. in 1876 when new secretary of war, Alonzo Taft, promised him greater authority to act as he saw fit.

That didn't dampen criticism of Sherman's total war policy from the public, press, and politicians, but it did mean he

could continue as he wanted to. St. Louis was far from Washington's restrictions and politicking while the Indian Office and Department of the Interior also lent a hand.

Their policies were aimed at weakening the independence of Native tribes, in turn making them increasingly dependent on the Federal Government for their survival. Natives could be defeated by Sherman's troops or assimilated relatively peacefully into American society, but not free in their traditional sense. Grant, though still entirely opposed to a war of extermination, had hardened his attitude to settler-Native relations since Mexico:

"No matter what ought to be the relations between such settlements and the aborigines, the fact is they do not get on together, and one or the other has to give way in the end."

Sherman, as two-fisted as ever, reportedly wrote: "All Indians who cling to their old hunting grounds are hostile and will remain so til they are killed off."

Rampant corruption also played its part. Many local officials within the Indian Office and Department of the Interior were corrupt. They offered Natives limited rations of rotten food seldom meeting their needs and often less than agreed. They took bribes from land speculators and settlers when arbitrating disputes to further deprive Natives of their traditional settling places and hunting grounds.

Ironically, while pursuing total war against the Natives, Sherman also despised corruption and wholesale swindling by Indian agents and local officials. But it didn't stop him from continuing punitive expeditions wherever possible and reorganizing frontier forts for maximum effect. For Native Americans the choice remained simple; assimilation and submission or destruction and defeat.

It remains a bitter irony that their greatest battlefield victory at Montana's Little Big Horn in 1876 was perhaps the downfall of the Native Americans (or Plains Indians as they were then called). Civil War hero George Armstrong Custer's attack on a Native encampment on June 26, 1876 has since been cited as an epic military blunder and Custer himself blamed for the defeat.

At the time it was widely, some say falsely, portrayed as a massacre perpetrated by savages bent on death and destruction. The annihilation of the Seventh Cavalry's troops

The Louisiana Purchase came during the third term of President Thomas Jefferson

under Custer provided the anti-Native and expansionist lobbies with all the impetus they needed to pursue ruthless policies openly. It also stifled criticism of Sherman's tactics, giving him a freer hand than ever before.

After Little Big Horn, the US Army pursued Natives with a fury. The Natives, some sensing defeat and others looking just to survive, found themselves scattered all over North America. Many went with Sitting Bull to Canada, remaining there as fugitives until forced out by the British.

At first, Sitting Bull lived among around 5,000 followers in present-day Saskatchewan. Provided they committed no crimes and caused no trouble, they were told they would be protected from the US Army and given food to help them survive. Their safe haven didn't last very long.

Canadian authorities became fearful of intertribal conflict, annoyed that some of Sitting Bull's younger followers misbehaved, and wanted the area cleared for their own White settlers. His request for a permanent reservation refused, Sitting Bull's people were first encouraged and then forced to surrender. Their government rations were eventually stopped, making surrender or starvation their only options.

Sitting Bull and his remaining followers, now less than 200, re-entered the US, surrendering at Standing Rock in May 1881. Sitting Bull died there on December 15, 1890,

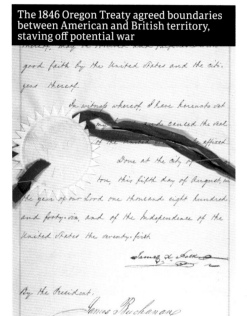

The 1846 Oregon Treaty agreed boundaries between American and British territory, staving off potential war

An 1883 photograph of Sitting Bull

## The Monroe Doctrine

**US President James Monroe aimed to remove European colonialism in America, North or South**

Like Manifest Destiny, the Monroe Doctrine existed as an idea long before being given a name. Monroe had first expounded it in the early 1820s, but not until the 1840s was the actual document named after him. It was largely written by future president, John Quincy Adams.

Unrest and political turbulence had made Monroe nervous. By December 1823, almost all Spanish and Portuguese colonies were on the verge of independence. Monroe saw the potential for huge regional instability in years to come. With this instability, Monroe also saw the potential for trouble.

Monroe's Doctrine sought to curb what he viewed as foreign powers meddling in the Americas. Any foreign power trying to take control of any independent state in North or South America would therefore be deemed as being "unfriendly."

That said, the doctrine specified that if foreign powers refrained from meddling in the Americas then the United States wouldn't meddle either with existing European colonies or the internal affairs of any European countries.

The Monroe Doctrine has long outlived its namesake. Subsequent presidents have quoted it and enforced it, including Ulysses Grant, Franklin Roosevelt, John F. Kennedy and Ronald Reagan. Revised and reinterpreted several times in different ways, it remains an important US policy.

A founding father and Revolutionary War veteran, President Monroe is remembered for the foreign policy doctrine named after him

shot by police there to arrest him in case he joined the Ghost Dance movement.

Two weeks after Sitting Bull died, US troops committed the Massacre at Wounded Knee. Over 300 Natives are said to have died. Founder of the Ghost Dance movement Wovoka, who claimed to have seen a vision of Jesus Christ returning as a Native American, had numerous followers.

They'd gathered at Wounded Knee to perform the Ghost Dance in the hope, according to Wovoka's teaching, of reversing their fortunes. If performed correctly the Ghost Dance would see White settlers vanish from Native lands and the almost-extinct buffalo return in large numbers. Their deceased Native ancestors would also come back.

Some Whites, especially Indian agent James McLaughlin, saw a large gathering of Natives as an imminent attack. McLaughlin's hawkish response and ignoring military objections led to disaster. Hundreds of Natives died when they were cornered by a larger US Army force under Colonel James Forsyth and Major Samuel Whitside. The troops responsible were Custer's old unit.

His old comrade Crazy Horse, legendary for his bravery at the Little Big Horn, had fared no better. Imprisoned at Camp Robinson in present-day Nebraska, he was fatally wounded on September 5, 1877 while allegedly resisting imprisonment. It's long been suggested that Crazy Horse was actually murdered and the crime covered up.

Geronimo was a little luckier. Although never a chief, he'd led numerous war parties against the US Army. He'd also surrendered three times only to leave his Reservation and fight again. His battles with the United States had begun in 1848, leading Apache warriors against US troops and settlers. Since then he'd been a regular thorn in their side.

He finally surrendered in September of 1886. Geronimo was never allowed to return to his homeland. Born near Turkey Creek in present-day New Mexico, Geronimo died on February 17, 1909 at Fort Sill, Oklahoma, still officially a prisoner of war. The great era of domestic expansion was over and America had changed forever.

If the Standing Rock Reservation, site of Sitting Bull's death, sounds familiar today, it should. It's currently the site of protests against the Dakota Access Pipeline intended to go through Native land. The pipeline has drawn protests from environmentalists, but especially from Native Americans in Iowa, North Dakota, and South Dakota.

It seems that far from having improved since the end of the expansionist era, relations between modern America and its indigenous peoples remain contentious to this day.

# THE INDIAN REMOVAL ACT

President Andrew Jackson's controversial legislation removed tens of thousands of Native Americans from their own land. The exodus became known as the Trail of Tears

Words by Owen Williams

By 1830, the number of White settlers desiring to move into Native-occupied territory, and the clamor of their demands, prompted the US government to take drastic action in favor of its electorate. The "solution" to the problem arrived at under the presidency of Andrew Jackson was the Indian Removal Act, which would uproot the "Five Civilized Tribes" (Choctaw, Seminole, Muscogee/Creek, Chickasaw, and Cherokee) from their lands in the deep south of America and displace them hundreds of miles to new territories further west.

Prior to the act, the five tribes had been assured of their right to remain east of the Mississippi as long as they toed certain lines of European society, such as adopting Anglo-European cultural behaviors and practices, and converting to Christianity. Jackson, however, called an end to this era in his State of the Union speech in 1829, arguing that nobody can stand in the way

President Andrew Jackson, painted in 1824 by Thomas Sully. Jackson was incumbent in office for almost the entire Removal period

of "progress," and that relocation was the only way to prevent the Natives' otherwise inevitable annihilation. According to his proposal, Natives could only observe self-rule in federally designated reservations west of the Mississippi, and would be forcibly escorted to those lands.

The act was passed in the senate on May 28, 1830, after much acrimonious debate; although in the end, only the maverick congressman Davy Crockett voted against it. Over the course of the subsequent 20 years, the Five Tribes were "escorted" on foot to their new destination in Oklahoma by local militia forces. Many resisted, leading to wars before the Natives could be subdued and marched on their way again. Disease was rife, environmental conditions were severe, and the Natives were subject to constant attacks en route, meaning that thousands died without seeing the end point of their arduous and unjust journey. The European Americans inherited 25 million acres of land, little caring about the appalling price.

# THE CHOCTAW

The Choctaw were the earliest of the Five Civilized Tribes to be evicted from their lands in Alabama, Arkansas, Mississippi, and Louisiana, following the Indian Removal Act. Their relocation was managed in three stages between 1831 and 1833—although some Choctaw refused to leave and their uprooting continued throughout the rest of the 19th century and into the 20th.

The Choctaw nation had come together in the 17th century from the remnants of other tribes that had occupied lands in the Deep South of America for many thousands of years. A lot of Choctaw had fought for George Washington's army during the American Revolutionary War, and in the politically fraught times that followed, the Choctaw generally sided with the nascent United States Government (or at least, never took up arms against it; they even fought with the US against the Creek Indians in 1813). This spirit of cooperation, however, didn't garner them any special treatment or privileges. Jackson visited them in 1820 as a commissioner representing the United States in a treaty negotiating the boundaries of Choctaw lands. He decided to resort to blackmail, bribery, and threats to get his way. The 1820 Treaty of Doak's Stand saw the Choctaw ceding half their land to the US Government, and agreeing to work towards US citizenship, which would only be granted once they were deemed "civilized and enlightened." But a decade later with Jackson now in office, those remaining rights were lost, and the final 11 million acres of traditional Choctaw land exchanged for 15 million in what is now Oklahoma in the Treaty of Dancing Rabbit Creek. It was the Choctaw's final significant land cession treaty, and the first under the Removal Act. Chief Greenwood LeFlore was almost immediately deposed by the Choctaw for signing the treaty, and succeeded by his nephew, George W. Harkins.

Following the treaty, the Choctaw divided into two distinct groups: the Choctaw Nation who undertook the trek to Oklahoma, and the Choctaw Tribe, who stayed behind in Mississippi. Those 5,000 or so who held out were granted US citizenship, but endured legal conflict, harassment, intimidation, and violence at the hands of the European Americans who wanted them gone (by 1930 only about 1,600 were still there). The 15,000 who left, meanwhile, had to contend with the brutal winter of 1830-31 and a cholera epidemic in 1832. About 6,000 Choctaw died on the journey.

In the years that followed, most Choctaw supported the Confederacy during the American Civil War, largely due to the promise of a state under Indian control. In World War I, the Choctaw were the first of the US Army's famous codetalkers (their language, as far as the enemy was concerned, an unbreakable code). Today they are the third largest of the remaining Native American tribes.

George W. Harkins replaced his uncle Greenwood LeFlore as Choctaw chief in 1830

Two Choctaw tribes are descended from the relocated Choctaw bands: the Jena Band and the Mississippi Band

US Marines search for Seminole warriors in the Everglades during the Second Seminole War

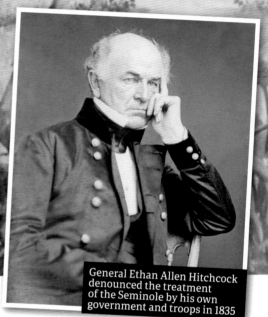
General Ethan Allen Hitchcock denounced the treatment of the Seminole by his own government and troops in 1835

# THE SEMINOLE

The Seminole had settled in the Florida area in the early 18th century. As a people they were a culture made up of offshoots of the Creek, Choctaw, and other tribes. Their name is derived from the Spanish *cimarrón*, meaning "wild" or even "runaway." Under the Indian Removal Act they were to be settled in Creek territory west of the Mississippi and be folded back into the Creek tribe. They put up fierce resistance to this, however, fearing that the Creek—who considered them deserters—would take it upon themselves to be aggressively unwelcoming to the Seminole people. They had fought Andrew Jackson's initial incursions into Florida in a prolonged conflict between 1816 and 1819. However, the Removal Act sparked the Second Seminole War, which raged from 1835 until 1842.

The specific treaty detailing the proposed removal of the Seminole was the Treaty of Payne's Landing. The seven chiefs of the Seminole had traveled to the new Oklahoma reservation and reportedly signed documents agreeing that it was acceptable. But on returning to Florida the chiefs retracted their apparent consent, saying they had been coerced and bullied into compliance. Even some US Army officers supported this claim. Nevertheless, the Treaty was ratified in April 1834, giving the Seminole three years to vacate the land. When the Seminole refused to recognize the treaty, Florida prepared for conflict.

The 28th of December 1835 saw the Dade Massacre, where 110 American soldiers under the command of Major Francis Dade were ambushed and killed by Seminole Warriors. US Major Ethan Allen Hitchcock, who found the bodies, wrote that it was a wholly avoidable tragedy brought about by "the tyranny of our government." Further skirmishes took place in the subsequent months at Fort Brooke, Fort Barnwell,

Camp Cooper, Fort Alabama, and Fort Drane, none of which resulted in the defeat of the Seminole: several of the forts even had to be abandoned by the American troops. It eventually took a force of 9,000 US marines, navy, and militia, under the command of Major General Thomas Jesup, to subdue an Indian resistance that had never numbered more than 1,400 warriors. A truce was reached following the Battle of Hatchee-Lustee in January 1837. Hundreds of Seminole surrendered at this point, but those few who did not kept the conflict going until August 1842.

The last act of the war was the capture of Chief Tiger Tail (one of the Seminole leaders during the Dade Massacre) and the killing of his small band of holdouts. Tiger Tail died in New Orleans before he could be transported to Oklahoma. Most of the Seminole resigned themselves to removal, although a hundred or so remained in the Florida Everglades and were left alone on an-ad-hoc reservation of their own. They remain the only tribe never to relinquish their sovereignty or sign a peace treaty with the US.

Seminole Chief Osceola

# THE CREEK

Indigenous to the Southeastern Woodlands of the United States, the Creek had been the first Native Americans to be considered "civilized;" they were the first of the Five Civilized Tribes. That's perhaps surprising given their history of resistance and conflict with the US. They had seen their lands ceded to the US by the British following the American Revolution, and had fought alongside the Cherokee against the White settlers of Tennessee during the Cherokee-American Wars of the late 1700s.

The outbreak of the Creek War in 1813 was a series of conflicts between the Creek's Red Stick faction and American militias. There were several Red Stick attacks on American forts, including a famous massacre at Fort Mims, Alabama in August. Creek men, women, and children were slaughtered in retaliation for an atrocity at Tallushatchee in November of the same year. General Andrew Jackson finally put down the rebellion at the Battle of Horseshoe Bend in March 1814. The Creek signed the Treaty of Fort Jackson in August, ceding 23 million acres of land in Georgia and Alabama to the US

Government. The war effectively undid all the work of previous Creek generations who had attempted to coexist peacefully with the European-American settlers. The antipathy Jackson developed for the Creek during the conflict would be carried into his presidency.

By the time of the Indian Removal Act, there were still about 20,000 Creek in Alabama. Their lands had been divided into individual allotments, and the terms of 1832's Treaty of Cusseta actually gave them the choice of remaining in situ (and submitting to state laws) or relocating to Oklahoma with financial compensation for doing so. In practice, however, staying in place was never really an option. Illegal occupation of Creek lands by settlers was widespread, with US authorities largely turning a blind eye. The increasingly impoverished and desperate Creek resorted once again to attacking the interlopers, leading to the short-lived Second Creek War of 1836. It ended with the forced removal of the Creek by troops under the command of General Winfield Scott. In mid-1837 about 15,000 Creek were first rounded up into internment camps and then driven from

Members of the Creek Nation, photographed in 1877

their land for the final time. About a quarter of them died on the arduous journey west to Oklahoma.

Subsequently, the Creek were divided in their loyalties during the American Civil War, with some supporting the Confederacy and others siding with the Union. President Abraham Lincoln initially rewarded the loyalists with increased government aid, but the actions of the rebels meant a new treaty was required in 1866. Under its terms, the Creek lost further territory, with part of the Creek reservation given over to recently emancipated slaves.

Chief Red Eagle surrenders to Andrew Jackson following the Battle of Horseshoe Bend in 1814

# THE CHICKASAW

The Chickasaw are closely related to the Choctaw. Their oral history recalls their settling in Mississippi in prehistoric times, and the two peoples separated into distinct tribes sometime in the 17th century. Their first contact with Europeans was when the Spanish explorer Hernando de Soto encountered them in 1540. After several disagreements, they attacked his entourage and he swiftly moved on. They allied with the British in 1670 (a period that often brought them into conflict with the Choctaw), and with the newly formed United States in the Revolutionary War. Subsequently, they tended always to side with the US and its government, even as their rights and lands were eroded.

The treaty securing their removal west was that of Pontotoc Creek in 1832. A previous attempt had failed in 1830, when the Chickasaw had baulked at the poor quality of the land they were being offered in Oklahoma. But two years later, with the encroachment of the European-American settlers onto their valuable Mississippi territories, and an epidemic of whiskey addiction, they began to feel their culture was being overwhelmed and on the point of being wiped out. An indication of their desperation at this point is that they ended up ceding their Mississippi lands to the government on merely the promise of new land being found for them.

Uniquely among the Five Civilized Tribes, they were also persuaded to pay for their own migration. They used the financial compensation they received for their Mississippi lands to buy a part of the Choctaw tribe's new Oklahoma territory. The American Senate ratified the agreement between the Chickasaw and the Choctaw in the 1837 Treaty of Doaksville—unusual for an internal matter between Native Americans.

The Chickasaw's migration west began in 1837 and continued into the following year. Just under 5,000 Chickasaw made the journey, which was accomplished relatively successfully compared to the trails of tears the other four tribes endured. Instead, their privations began on arrival, when most Chickasaw, rather than gaining their own new district on former Choctaw land as was originally arranged, were interned in temporary camps in Choctaw towns and government supply depots. Poverty, addiction, internal political disputes, and attacks from other tribes were rife, and it would be another 15 years before the tribe was finally settled in a dedicated Chickasaw territory.

The Chickasaw formally separated from the Choctaw, emerging as a new Chickasaw Nation in 1856. In the Civil War they joined the Confederacy. By 1907, following the defeat of the Five Tribes' petition for statehood, the Chickasaw were a powerless minority in their own lands. The 20th century saw a revival in their fortunes, however. They were officially recognized as a Nation again in 1983.

The Chickasaw leader Holmes Colbert represented the tribe politically after the Civil War

A rising of the Chickasaw people, angry at mistreatment, is suppressed by the United States Cavalry

The Cherokee are pictured here removing west

President Martin Van Buren succeeded Andrew Jackson and enforced the Cherokee Removal

# THE CHEROKEE

Incursion on Indian land by European-American settlers had always been due to its particular desirability, whether for perfect farming conditions, mineral deposits, or both. In the case of the Cherokee's land in Georgia, however, there was a very specific reason: gold. The Georgia Gold Rush, in which thousands of prospectors descended on Cherokee land in search of their fortune, began in 1829, preceding the more famous California Gold Rush by 20 years. The Cherokee, who had inhabited the land since prehistoric times,

Elizabeth Brown Stephens was one of thousands of Cherokee on the Trail of Tears. This photograph was taken in 1903 when she was 82

were quickly overwhelmed. The State of Georgia, far from supporting its indigenous people, was desperate to get them out of the way.

Even by the previous standards of the Indian Removal Act, the treaty that uprooted the Cherokee was dubious in its morality and legality. The Treaty of New Echota was accepted neither by the tribal leaders nor the majority of the Cherokee people, but was nevertheless enforced in 1838 by Andrew Jackson's successor, Martin Van Buren. Sadly, a new president didn't mean a change in Native American fortunes. Having refused to recognize the terms of the deal, the Cherokee were first herded into internment camps for several months, before being forcibly marched from their lands by militia troops. Twelve wagon trains, each comprising about a thousand Cherokee, began the arduous trek in the winter of 1838. Their various routes encompassed trails through Kentucky, Illinois, Tennessee, Mississippi, Arkansas, and Missouri. Most of the Cherokee traveled barefoot.

Malnutrition, disease, pneumonia, and exposure were rife on the journey. The summer in the camps had been one of blistering heat and severe drought, and

the winter of that year was freakishly cold, making progress brutally slow (the 60 miles between the Ohio and Mississippi rivers alone took three months). The risk of the Cherokee bringing sickness to populations meant their journey was made even longer than it might have been, since they were forbidden from passing through towns or settlements and had to go around them. When they reached the Ohio river, they were charged a dollar a head by the ferryman who usually only charged 12 cents. On the long wait to cross the river, many Cherokee died from exhaustion and starvation. Some were even murdered by locals.

The Cherokee finally reached their destination in Oklahoma in the early months of 1839. Between the internment camps and the journey itself, the estimated death toll was between 4,000 and 6,000.

Today, the Cherokee are the largest Native American group in the US, but the shameful ethnic cleansing of them and the other Civilized Tribes has not been forgotten. The 2,200-mile Trail of Tears National Historic Trail was opened in commemoration in 1987. The Five Tribes finally received a formal apology from the US Government in 2008.

# RIDING THE OREGON TRAIL

Journalist and politician Horace Greeley famously stated "Go west, young man." He had no idea just how arduous and dangerous a trip he was suggesting

Words by Robert Walsh

Alfred Bierstadt painted hundreds of scenes of 19th-century America, including The Oregon Trail, Emigrants crossing the Plain

The Oregon Trail is another hallmark of the Old West. Between the mid 1830s and the completion of the First Transcontinental Railroad in 1869, some 400,000 people used it, vastly accelerating expansion of the western frontier. Starting as a motley collection of dirt tracks passable only on foot or horseback, it grew into a spider's web of wagon trails, way stations, forts, and towns linking numerous Midwestern states.

Starting out in Missouri, at its peak the trail linked Iowa, Kansas, Nebraska, Colorado, Wyoming, Utah, Idaho, and Oregon itself with California, where it linked up with the California Trail among others. Some of today's major roads still follow parts of the trail.

Originally the trail was the domain of trappers and hunters. At its peak, however, it was used by explorers, ranchers, hunters, trappers, pioneers, missionaries, and businessmen, all hoping to start new lives and perhaps make their fortunes. Whatever it was they were looking for, many would find death and tragedy instead.

Some reached their destinations safely and even prospered. Others arrived, but achieved little other than surviving the trip, while some simply gave up on their original destinations, settling down along the way rather than continue. For the rest, only death awaited them. Hostile Natives, disease, starvation, outlaws, and accidents left graves marking the Oregon Trail like milestones.

The Great Migration of 1843 was a particular high point, some 1,000 people departing aboard a huge wagon train. After reaching Fort Hall, Idaho they were told by their guide that, from then on, the trail was impassable to wagons and they should use pack animals instead. Their leader, Marcus Whitman, disagreed. He and many of the pioneers believed that a wagon trail could be made, if necessary by clearing forest and leveling a track as they went. Whitman and his followers were right.

They managed to cut a route through Oregon's heavily forested Blue Mountains before meeting the then-impassable obstacle of Mount Hood. Bypassing the mountain, sending the wagons down the Columbia River and the animals via the Lolo Pass, almost all of the travelers successfully arrived in the Willamette Valley in October 1843. The Oregon Trail had been created.

One of the largest groups to use it was the Mormons. They came in their thousands to live together as a homogeneous group. Early Mormon settlers were responsible for finding suitable places, then building farms and homes to accommodate their brethren as they arrived. Mormons came from all over the country, their leader Brigham Young choosing the Salt Lake Valley in Utah as their main base. Some Mormons, however, settled in other places. One of them, store owner and newspaper publisher Samuel Brannan, settled in California and was to cause a massive rise in traffic via the trail. It was Brannan's newspaper, the California Star, that publicized a momentous discovery—gold.

The 1848 California Gold Rush was another major source of travelers. With such huge amounts seemingly there for the taking, people traveled from all over the world seeking their fortunes. Those traveling from Europe and wanting to avoid a risky boat journey round Cape Horn or via Panama used the trail to reach their destination. With endless wild stories of gold so plentiful it could simply be picked up from riverbeds and streams, many thousands headed for California. "Gold fever" proved even more contagious than cholera.

In 1849, cholera also struck the US. Thousands died on the trail west, especially along the Platte River between 1849 and 1855 during the "epidemic years." With little understanding of how cholera spread or how to treat it, parts of the trail were natural breeding grounds. Kansas, Nebraska, and Wyoming were the last resting places for many who sought fame and fortune, with their unmarked graves left lining the trail.

The most basic essentials for trail travelers were food, water, and transport. Transport involved horses, pack mules, oxen, and wagons. However, each of these modes of transport had their own particular difficulties. Mules weren't the most cooperative of creatures, especially carrying loads of over 100 pounds up steep hills and through mountainous country. Horses and oxen had to be shod. Wagons needed to be repaired on the trail, requiring spare parts and tools for the job.

Water had to be found along the way, which was not always possible—nor was it necessarily safe. Finding rivers, ponds, and streams was sometimes difficult for travelers. Finding water that was safe for drinking and cooking was even harder. With little knowledge of waterborne diseases and large numbers of people living with poor sanitation, cholera was a constant threat.

Fort Laramie was an important staging post for pioneers along the trail. This memorial commemorates those who died on the trail

## Trail Truths

The eastern section of the Oregon Trail linked to the California, Mormon, and Bozeman Trails, all major routes.

One of the busiest departure points for the Oregon Trail was St. Joseph, Missouri, home of the Pony Express.

Lacking their own supplies of fresh fruit and vegetables, travelers ate trailside fruits and berries to ward off scurvy.

The trails were commonly used for mass cattle drives, ranchers moving livestock wherever the best prices were found.

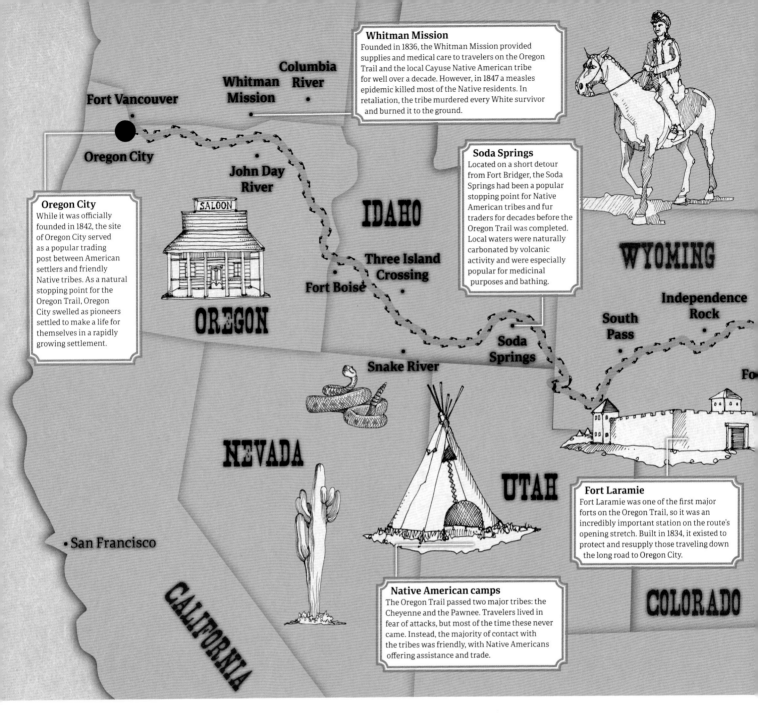

**Whitman Mission**
Founded in 1836, the Whitman Mission provided supplies and medical care to travelers on the Oregon Trail and the local Cayuse Native American tribe for well over a decade. However, in 1847 a measles epidemic killed most of the Native residents. In retaliation, the tribe murdered every White survivor and burned it to the ground.

Columbia River

Whitman Mission

Fort Vancouver

Oregon City

John Day River

**Soda Springs**
Located on a short detour from Fort Bridger, the Soda Springs had been a popular stopping point for Native American tribes and fur traders for decades before the Oregon Trail was completed. Local waters were naturally carbonated by volcanic activity and were especially popular for medicinal purposes and bathing.

IDAHO

WYOMING

**Oregon City**
While it was officially founded in 1842, the site of Oregon City served as a popular trading post between American settlers and friendly Native tribes. As a natural stopping point for the Oregon Trail, Oregon City swelled as pioneers settled to make a life for themselves in a rapidly growing settlement.

SALOON

Three Island Crossing

Fort Boise

OREGON

Independence Rock

South Pass

Soda Springs

Snake River

NEVADA

UTAH

Fo

San Francisco

**Fort Laramie**
Fort Laramie was one of the first major forts on the Oregon Trail, so it was an incredibly important station on the route's opening stretch. Built in 1834, it existed to protect and resupply those traveling down the long road to Oregon City.

**Native American camps**
The Oregon Trail passed two major tribes: the Cheyenne and the Pawnee. Travelers lived in fear of attacks, but most of the time these never came. Instead, the majority of contact with the tribes was friendly, with Native Americans offering assistance and trade.

COLORADO

CALIFORNIA

Food was basic. Meat could be bought before departure and hunted along the trail, where it could be found. Hardtack biscuits, salted pork and bacon, beans, dried fruit, pickles, bread, and rice were staple supplies. To make meals less monotonous sugar, tea, coffee, dried vegetables, and small amounts of spices and maple syrup supplemented their diet. If a wagon train got lost or scattered by, say, a Native raid, entire wagon trains could starve out on the plains. For this reason, experienced guides were well worth their exorbitant fees.

The right clothes and equipment were vital. Warm clothing for cold weather, several pairs of boots as two or even three pairs would wear out on the trail, guns for hunting

and protection, tents and bedding, candles and lanterns, books, paper and pens for keeping diaries and records of the journey, spare leather and tools for running repairs of saddles, bridles and boots, soap for washing, and so on. Tobacco was a popular item for smoking and for trading with friendly Natives and other travelers. Basic cooking equipment was also essential. As the amount of necessary supplies increased, so did the number of wagons and mules needed to haul them.

Travelers often discarded equipment if it couldn't be repaired or they lacked the means to transport it. If a wagon was irreparably damaged, essential supplies were taken off and redistributed among

other wagons and pack animals. If there was no space left, then supplies were simply dumped by the trailside. Many travelers foraged among the abandoned wagons and supplies of their predecessors, carrying off whatever they found useful. "Waste not, want not" and "finders keepers" became rules of the long road west.

One factor helped or hindered travelers more than any other—money. Stores, wagons, animals, weapons, supplies, and guides all had to be paid for unless they could be bartered. As demand increased, so did prices. Groups of travelers often pooled their money to pay for everything, keeping the rest in a strongbox for security. It didn't always work. Native raiding parties might

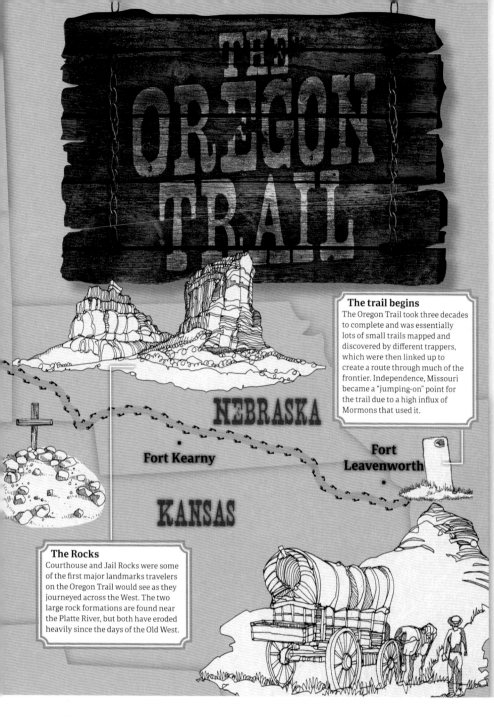

# THE OREGON TRAIL

**NEBRASKA**

**Fort Kearny**

**KANSAS**

**Fort Leavenworth**

### The trail begins
The Oregon Trail took three decades to complete and was essentially lots of small trails mapped and discovered by different trappers, which were then linked up to create a route through much of the frontier. Independence, Missouri became a "jumping-on" point for the trail due to a high influx of Mormons that used it.

### The Rocks
Courthouse and Jail Rocks were some of the first major landmarks travelers on the Oregon Trail would see as they journeyed across the West. The two large rock formations are found near the Platte River, but both have eroded heavily since the days of the Old West.

## Women of the Frontier
### Men and women viewed life on the frontier differently...

Women and men seem to have had very different attitudes to and experience of expanding the western frontier. While men often viewed the journey as an adventure and were more likely to risk it if they thought the rewards worth the risks, women were less eager. They often saw it as threatening a stable, ordered, more comfortable way of life.

Many women kept diaries and journals describing the hardships of the trail and their sadness at losing so many along the way. They also often found their life on the trail far more demanding, physically and mentally, than they had expected.

That said, it did give women the chance to break traditional stereotypes. In an environment where everybody had to contribute something, women often found themselves in roles they hadn't previously experienced, something resembling equality. The social scene out West was also different. In the California goldfields, for instance, women could run their own businesses and often did.

The pioneer experience often changed men's view of women and women's view of themselves. It wasn't actual equality, but it was certainly a path not only to the West, but toward a freer, less restrictive existence.

make off with a wagon train's entire stake. Outlaws might also attempt to rob a wagon train, law enforcement being limited in most places and practically nonexistent in others.

Like the Pony Express, the decline of the Oregon Trail was marked by the encroaching Transcontinental Railroad. Riding the trail was arduous, dangerous, and costly. Traveling from the east coast to the west by rail was cheaper, safer, faster, and less uncomfortable. A journey taking eight months via the Oregon Trail could take eight days via train, usually without catching cholera, being robbed by outlaws, or scalped by Natives.

With the railroad converging on Promontory Summit, Utah from both east

and west, the days of the Oregon Trail were increasingly numbered. As the railroad advanced towns and cities grew along its route, allowing travelers to stop and continue their journeys in relative safety if they chose to, further lessening the need for the old trails.

By the 1870s the Oregon Trail had had its day. Railroads and stagecoaches had replaced wagons and pack mules. Of approximately 400,000 people who traveled along it, as many as 21,000 died. But, obsolete though it was, it was the Oregon Trail that had opened the route west.

Independence Rock, Wyoming, was an important point on the trail west

# JAMES POLK: AMERICAN CONQUEROR

## Meet the forgotten eleventh president who shaped the United States into a continental giant — but hastened its fall into civil war

Words by Dominic Green

The United States of America, the song "America the Beautiful" says, runs "from sea to shining sea," east to west from the Atlantic Ocean to the Pacific. The country also runs from the 49th Parallel, much of which marks its northern border with Canada, to the Rio Grande, which forms its southern border with Mexico.

These boundaries were the creation of many ordinary Americans, especially the settlers who established themselves on Mexican land in Texas and British-claimed land in the Oregon Country in the Pacific Northwest. But the formation of the nation as the modern colossus bestriding two great oceans was the diplomatic and military feat of the country's often overlooked eleventh president, James Knox Polk.

It was he who successfully asserted American claims against Britain in the Oregon Country, securing the northwestern corner of the nation without firing a shot. He also sent an army to Mexico City and forced the Mexican Republic to surrender all of its territory north of the Rio Grande.

But Polk's presidency was only a brief triumph. His inability to understand that slavery was a danger to the Union accelerated America's path to the catastrophic Civil War in 1861.

In Pineville, North Carolina, Polk was born in a simple log cabin in 1795, the first child of Samuel and Jane Polk, who could trace their family origins to Presbyterian emigrants from Ireland. At the baptismal font, it apparently emerged that Samuel had doubts about Presbyterian theology so his firstborn son went unbaptized. Nevertheless, his mother, a strict Calvinist, imbued him with staunch religious principles of hard work, self-discipline, and an unquestioning faith in predestination, the belief that God has already decided what will come to pass.

But it was Polk's grandfather Ezekiel who ordained the future of the family's lives. In 1803, when Polk was eight years old, Ezekiel, like a biblical patriarch, led some of his family on a pilgrimage into the wilderness.

They settled in the frontier country at Maury County, Tennessee, and three years later, Samuel and his family joined them.

Polk was a sickly child and life was hard. In 1812, he underwent an operation for urinary stones—the anesthetic was brandy—which may have left him sterile.

The Polk family soon dominated the political life of this new society in the woods. As Samuel's business interests grew, he became a county judge. He also befriended another influential judge, Andrew Jackson, the future hero of the War of 1812 and eventual president of the United States. After studying at the University of North Carolina, Samuel's son began practicing law at Nashville, Tennessee, in 1820. Polk's first brief was to defend his father against a charge of public brawling. Samuel allegedly paid a token $1 fine.

In 1822, Polk stood for the Tennessee House of Representatives as a Democrat and won by a huge margin. Jackson supported his political career, causing the two to spark an alliance that would endure for the rest of Jackson's life. Polk played the "Young Hickory" to Jackson's gnarled "Old Hickory." Months later, Polk also made another strategic alliance (possibly with Jackson's encouragement) by marrying Sarah Childress, the accomplished but strictly religious daughter of one of Tennessee's leading families.

> "He also sent an army to Mexico City and forced the Mexican Republic to surrender all of its territory north of the Rio Grande"

Polk was the United States' last strong president before the outbreak of the Civil War

## The Creed of Expansion

### The original roots of the now-famous term, "Manifest Destiny"

In 1845, as President Polk steered the United States towards a stand-off with Great Britain in the Oregon Country and a war against the Republic of Mexico, the journalist John O'Sullivan wrote that it was "our manifest destiny to overspread the continent allowed by Providence for the free development of our yearly multiplying millions."

Since then, the words "manifest destiny" have served as shorthand for the ideas that drove the expansion of the United States. This process ensured the rise of the nation as a global power in the last decades of the 19th century, but it also accelerated the slide towards the Civil War and the decimation of the Native Americans.

Polk's party, the Democrats, was the party of expansion and slavery. The opposition, the Whigs, were looking for abolition as they feared that expansion would tip the political balance of the United States away from the cities of the northeast, and instead towards a society of slave-holding farmers in the west.

For the Whigs, talk of manifest destiny was a corruption of the noble principles on which the American republic had been founded, and a reflection of the dangerous populism of Andrew Jackson and his protégé, James Polk. Yet the United States had been founded by Puritans who, like Polk's mother, believed in the religious predestination of their society. The idea of manifest destiny, like the later belief in American exceptionalism, was a reflection, ugly or not, of the country's origins.

Manifest Destiny personified assists the frontiersmen in American Progress by John Gast

**Rather than a "dark horse" candidate, biographer Walter Borneman argues that Polk was actually a tenacious workhorse**

**A career politician, was it really unexpected that he would run for president?**
The idea of Polk as a "dark horse" is a political myth. Polk was one of the most seasoned and accomplished politicians of his day, someone who had designs to follow Jackson to the White House from the very beginning of his political career. In the Tennessee legislature, seven terms in Congress, including two as Speaker of the House, and as governor of Tennessee, Polk always had his eyes on the bigger prize. He was a viable candidate for vice president in 1840 and was positioning himself for the same in 1844. The letters that go back and forth between Polk and his campaign managers show how much he maneuvered and sought the nomination.

**Was Polk blind to the tensions over slavery?**
Polk was definitely not blind to the rising tensions between the North and South over slavery — he was himself a slave owner — but he generally chose to ignore, or at least downplay, these ties. For example, he was very careful as president to keep his ownership of slaves and a Mississippi plantation quiet. Many historians have claimed that Polk's expansionist policies were tied to his promotion of the expansion of slavery, but I don't believe this is true. Polk was motivated largely by the example of Jacksonian America and manifest destiny to expand across the continent. He pushed this agenda for reasons of trade with the Pacific and to counter British and Spanish interests in North America far more than any idea of expanding slavery.

**Why is Polk not better remembered?**
The major reason is that Polk was a slave-owning Southerner whose legacy got pushed aside in the wake of the Civil War. I have always thought it interesting to speculate which side Polk would have come down on had he lived to see the war. Many assume that he naturally would have supported the Southern cause as a result of his inherited plantation but his strong Unionist tendencies — clearly in the mold of Andrew Jackson — may well have kept him on the side of the North. Perhaps he might even have kept Tennessee in the Union.

**Walter Borneman is the author of Polk:** *The Man Who Transformed America and the Presidency.*

An 1861 painting depicting the move westwards

## "Polk deployed his experience as a party politician, skilfully maneuvering through nine ballots at the party convention of 1844"

A year later at the 1824 elections, Jackson won the popular vote but failed to get a clear majority from Electoral College. The House of Representatives instead chose John Quincy Adams as president but he had come second in both the popular vote and the Electoral College.

Jackson and his supporters alleged underhand dealings by Adams and his supporters. When Polk came to Washington, D.C., as a Tennessee Congressman in 1825, he took up Jackson's cause, calling for the abolition of the Electoral College and echoing Jackson's agrarian populist policies. These depicted the small farmer as the true American pioneer, and the urban, eastern establishment as a corrupt elite.

When Jackson won the 1828 election, Polk became one of his closest advisors. As Jackson's voice in the House of Representatives, he rose quickly, learning how to manipulate the legislative machinery of committees and procedures as he went. In 1838, with a presidency in mind, he returned to Tennessee and won the governorship. But he was unable to master the Tennessee House.

The economy was still weak after the Panic of 1837 — a recession caused in large part by Jackson's policies — and in 1840, Jackson's presidential successor, Martin van Buren, lost the White House to the rival Whig party. The Tennessee legislature voted against Polk's requests for expensive programs of education and infrastructure, and his Jacksonian proposal to strengthen state banks against financial panics instead of giving additional powers to a national bank. In 1841, Polk lost the governorship. He stood once more in 1843, only to face failure once again.

Still, Polk had positioned himself to inherit the nomination as van Buren's running mate in the 1844 elections. Polk was a diplomat in a Washington where political differences still led to duels, and where the issue of slavery was threatening to split the North and South. In a Jacksonian style, he also aligned himself with the issue that would force slavery to the top of the agenda by the end of the 1840s — the territorial expansion of the United States.

In 1836, the White settlers of Mexican-ruled Texas declared their independence. Jackson, then the president, had recognized the rebels but Mexican threats of war had prevented him from annexing the self-proclaimed Republic of Texas. Meanwhile, Britain, which had defeated the United States little over two decades earlier in the War of 1812, was courting Texas.

The Texans were slaveholders while the British, having recently eradicated slavery, used their navy to become patrons of abolition. If the United States allowed Texas to fall into British or Mexican hands, it would become an obstacle to expanding west. But if America absorbed Texas as a pro-slavery state, it would exacerbate tensions between the South and the North's abolitionist majority. Tensions would also rise if Texas was absorbed without slavery, as it would become a haven for escaped slaves. Polk, too, was a slave owner — he had inherited twenty slaves and a cotton plantation on his father's death in 1827. The right to hold slaves was protected in the American Constitution, but he underestimated slavery's potential as an issue capable of dividing the Union. He believed that expanding the country was a more pressing affair and one that, if realized, could unite opinion around an expanded ideal of the nation.

The Whigs and Democrats were both divided over Texas. When the Whig nominee, Kentucky's Henry Clay, declared that he was against annexing it, so did van Buren. Jackson, who favored the plan, now pushed for Polk, presenting him as the only nominee capable of uniting the party and winning the presidency. In turn, Polk deployed his experience as a party politician, skilfully maneuvering through nine ballots at the party convention of 1844, and took his chance.

"Who is James Polk?" became the Whigs' election cry. He was the first "'dark horse" candidate but he only appeared to emerge from nowhere. In reality, he was actually an experienced administrator, materializing from within a party in crisis, as Abraham Lincoln would as the Civil War loomed. Yet while Lincoln would become the candidate of a party on the edge of civil war, Polk won the 1844 election as a unifier.

The American population was doubling in every generation and now equaled that of Great Britain. This baby boom created a rapid momentum of industrial growth in the established states in the east and a constant flow of settlers to the west. The country now possessed the means and numbers to fulfil the dream of the founding fathers—a United States from the Atlantic to the Pacific. To Americans it seemed History and God had

# The Making of the United States

### The Florida Cession, 1819
In 1810, when West Florida declared its independence from Spain, President James Madison sent in the troops. Spain did not accept this conquest until 1819, when the Adams-Onís Treaty finally settled all American and Spanish claims in North America. Six months later, Spain annulled part of the treaty by recognizing the independence of Mexico, creating new boundaries.

### The Louisiana Purchase, 1803
In 1800, the French leader Napoleon Bonaparte tried to reestablish the French Empire in the Louisiana Territory. Three years later, the administration of President Thomas Jefferson bought the 1.9 million-square-mile territory from the French government for 50 million Francs ($11.25 million) and the cancellation of debts worth 18 million Francs ($3.75 million).

### Treaty of Paris, 1783
The Treaty of Paris, in which Great Britain recognized the independence of its former American colonies, established the United States of America as 13 states, with an eastern border on the Atlantic Ocean and a northern border with British-ruled Canada. Its western border was the eastern bank of the Mississippi River.

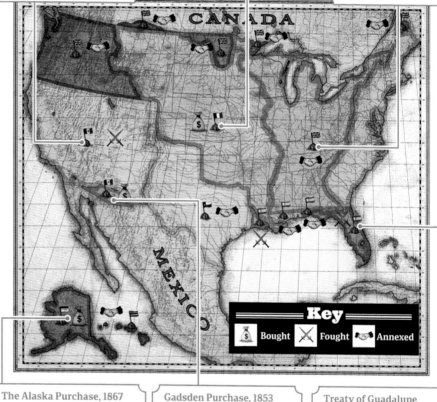

**Key**
💰 Bought   ✕ Fought   🤝 Annexed

### The Alaska Purchase, 1867
In 1867, Secretary of State William Seward signed the Alaska Purchase, buying more than 550,000 square miles of territory in Alaska from the Russian Empire. The Russians, realizing that Alaska was militarily indefensible, sold it for $7.2 million — about two cents an acre.

### Gadsden Purchase, 1853
In 1853, the US paid $10 million to the Republic of Mexico for over 29,000 square miles of territory in what is now southern Arizona and southwest New Mexico. The US wanted land for a transcontinental railroad and the Mexican government needed money.

### Treaty of Guadalupe Hidaglo, 1848
Imposed on Mexico by the Polk administration, the Treaty of Guadalupe Hidalgo expanded the borders of the US towards the Rio Grande, with the accession of Texas, and the Pacific Ocean, and the acquisition of California.

Polk's inauguration featured in the Illustrated London News

## The Unequal War for Mexico

### 100,000 AMERICAN
### JUST OVER 30,000 MEXICAN
TROOPS FOUGHT THE WAR

### 73,260
(NEARLY THREE QUARTERS)
of the American troops were militia volunteers

ALMOST
### 14,000
AMERICAN SOLDIERS DIED
90% OF THEM FROM DISEASE

### 25,000
MEXICAN SOLDIERS ARE ESTIMATED TO HAVE DIED

The US Navy's Pacific Fleet had
### 10 SHIPS

### THE US GAINED
### 500,000+
SQUARE MILES OF TERRITORY

### MEXICO LOST
MUCH OF ITS TERRITORY
AND RECEIVED
### $15 MILLION
(ONLY HALF WHAT IT WAS ORIGINALLY OFFERED)

---

predestined that the nation would become a global power.

The outgoing president, Andrew Tyler, tried to push a resolution for the annexation of Texas through the Senate with Polk's help. Taking office as the eleventh president, and the youngest up to that point at the age of forty nine, Polk pledged to complete the annexation of Texas, to defend slavery as a constitutional right, and to protect the claims of American settlers in the Oregon Country, which extended from the northernmost border of Mexico at the 42nd Parallel to the 54th.

Britain and the United States both claimed the territory — Britain through the expeditions of Captain Cook and George Vancouver, and America through the land explorations of Lewis and Clark as well as the voyages of Robert Gray. Neither country wanted a conflict. In 1818, they agreed to administrate the land together but the influx of settlers in the 1840s tipped the demographic balance towards an American majority and patriotism rose accordingly.

When Polk spoke of annexing the Oregon Country, the British threatened war. Polk, calculating that they were more interested in good trade relations, proposed dividing it, extending the Canadian-American border eastwards to the Pacific. Britain would get Vancouver Island but would concede the future state of Oregon.

Polk had called Britain's bluff and he now called it again in Texas — but he didn't read his adversaries' intentions correctly. In December 1845, he signed a resolution annexing the land, then sent an envoy to Mexican president José de Herrera with an offer to buy New Mexico and California for $30 million. Polk expected de Herrera to sell but he refused.

While exploring the idea of sponsoring a coup in Mexico, Polk sent General Zachary Taylor and 3,500 troops to the Nueces Strip—an area on the northern bank of the Rio Grande claimed by Texas and Mexico — in early 1846. He instructed his general to provoke the Mexican Army and by May, word had reached him that American soldiers had been killed and captured on the Strip. Polk accused the Mexicans of having "shed American blood on American soil," even though Taylor had provoked the conflict. Congress voted for war.

Naturally, pushing the United States' frontier forward meant pushing back Great Britain's ambitions—the British claim to California dated to Sir Francis Drake's landing at "New Albion" during his circumnavigation of the globe. To pre-empt possible interference, Polk sent his troops to occupy Santa Fe, the capital of New Mexico,

### "Taking a riverboat destined for New Orleans, he ignored rumors of cholera, despite several passengers dying"

Read all about it! War News From Mexico by Richard Caton Woodville, Sr., from 1848

The US Army takes control of Mexico City in 1847

and Los Angeles, which allowed him to declare the seizure of California.

In September 1847, Mexico City fell to the United States and Polk imposed the terms of Mexico's defeat via the Treaty of Guadalupe Hidalgo. Texas was to become the 28th member of the Union and the Rio Grande its southern border.

Mexico also ceded a vast tract of land — known as California — in the west and its northern border touched the southern border of the American half of the Oregon Country. It included almost all of the future states of Arizona, Nevada, and Utah, large parts of Wyoming and Colorado, and half of New Mexico. In return, America paid Mexico $15 million — less than half the amount that Polk had offered before the war — and agreed to settle claims amounting to $3.25 million by American citizens against the government of Mexico.

Texas entered the Union in 1845 as a slave-holding state. Soon after, Iowa entered as a "free" (non-slavery) state in 1846. California, its population suddenly increased by the Gold Rush that began just a week before the annexation in 1848, entered the Union in 1850 as another free state. Nevada became a free state just before the elections of 1864, its admission potentially hurried through because Lincoln wanted to ensure a Republican majority in Congress.

The expansion of the United States south and west exacerbated tensions over slavery — its already divided political parties disagreed over whether the "peculiar institution" should be extended to the new

territories. Polk, once the master of political compromise, didn't stay in office and attempt to reconcile the pro- and anti-slavery factions. He had secured the Democratic nomination in 1844 as a compromise candidate — but the compromise was that he wouldn't run for a second term.

Yet there could be no lasting agreement on slavery. With Polk retiring from the presidency, the Democratic Party would soon split over its expansion into the newly won states. When the Democratic convention chose Lewis Cass, a strong supporter of spreading slavery, as its presidential nominee, Democrats from the northern states, who opposed expanding it, broke away. Calling themselves the Free Soil Party, they nominated van Buren as their candidate — but this split the Democratic vote and allowed the Whigs' nominee to move into the White House. The new president, sworn into office in March 1849, was none other than Zachary Taylor, the star of the Mexican-American War.

Despite his relative youth, Polk was exhausted after four years in the top job. He and his wife decided to leave Washington, D.C., in 1849 to begin a planned tour of the south of the country that was meant to end at their new home in Nashville. Instead of a triumphal return, the tour would eventually turn into a funeral march.

The Polks kept to a busy schedule of festivities as they traveled down the east coast. Never physically strong, Polk picked up a heavy cold as their tour turned west towards Alabama. Taking a riverboat

destined for New Orleans, he ignored rumors of a cholera outbreak, despite several passengers dying of the infectious disease on their journey down the Mississippi River.

When the Polks arrived in New Orleans, Polk continued to ignore swirling rumors of cholera cases in the city and insisted on honoring his invitations and his public. He and Sarah then took another ship bound for Tennessee. At one point on the journey, he fell so ill that he had to disembark and spend several days in bed on dry land. While a doctor assured him that he definitely did not have cholera, Polk kept drinking water, even during the epidemics. As Sam Houston, his fellow Tennessee Democrat, joked, Polk was "a victim of the use of water as a beverage."

The Polks quickly returned to Nashville and settled into their new home after a visit to Polk's aging mother. Polk's health rallied, and it finally seemed he was in the clear — but he suddenly declined again. He finally died at home on June 15, 1849, probably from cholera.

Polk, in the front row, third from the left, pictured with his cabinet in 1846. This was the first photo ever taken inside the White House

# CALIFORNIA: THE STATE MADE OF GOLD

How one man's accidental discovery of gold would go
on to change the face of California forever

Words by Jo Cole

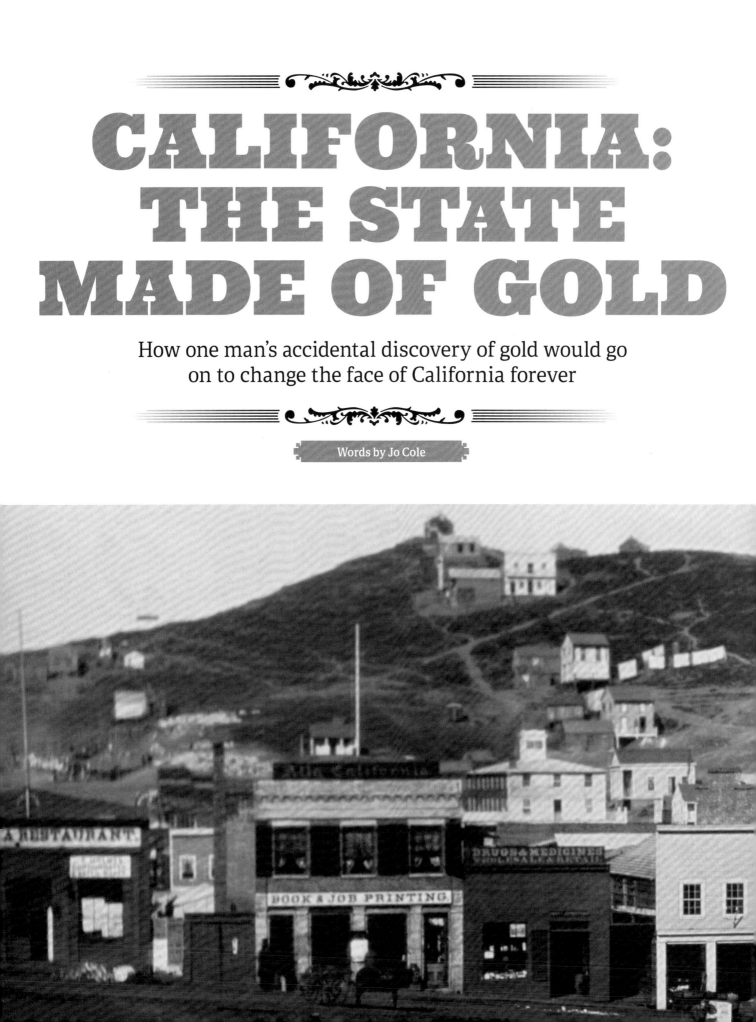

The day started pretty much like any other for James W. Marshall. A foreman employed by John Sutter in Coloma, California, he went about his task of building a tailrace for a lumber mill he was constructing for Sutter. But January 24, 1848 was not destined to be an ordinary day. During his morning inspection, Marshall noticed a piece of shiny metal. That shiny metal would turn out to be gold and Marshall's discovery would lead to a gold rush that would last from 1848 to 1855.

You might imagine that such a find would have Sutter screaming from the rooftops with excitement, but the opposite was true. Sutter had dreams of building a vast agricultural empire, and he knew that if word got out that there was gold on his land, his dream would be ruined. So he tried to keep the discovery quiet.

His plan didn't work, however. Rumors started to circulate and when businessman Samuel Brannan made the discovery public in May 1848, there was no putting the genie back into the bottle. And the news would only travel further: the *New York Herald* reported the discovery on August 19, 1848, followed by President James Polk discussing the gold in an address to Congress on December 5, 1848. It wasn't just the residents around California who wanted part of the action—by the beginning of 1849 the news had spread worldwide, causing people to gravitate west in the hope of getting rich.

The first gold-hunters to arrive were Californians, with entire families making the journey to try to gather as much gold as possible. And, at the beginning, the job was relatively easy. Tectonic forces had pushed minerals (i.e. gold) to the surface of the Sierra Nevada, water carried it downstream, and it finally settled in gravel beds along rivers and streams. This meant that gold could be found by panning in streams, or even just picking the flakes and nuggets out by hand.

The reward for the early prospectors was great. They were able to collect large amounts of gold pretty easily—even complete amateurs could gather enough to change their lives. It is thought that average daily gold finds were worth between 10 and 15 times the daily wage of a laborer.

Early prospectors also benefitted from the odd legal situation of California. In 1848, California was technically part of Mexico, but under American occupation (as part of the Mexican-American War). Although the war had ended in early 1848, causing California to become part of the US, nothing was formal. So, California was in a kind of limbo—residents existed with a gumbo of Mexican, US, and local rulings. The goldfields were theoretically on public land, but without any executive or judicial body to enforce this, it was essentially a free-for-all. Prospectors adapted Mexican mining law, where a prospector could claim a piece of land, but the claim only stood for as long as the land was being mined. Add to this the fact there were no taxes or licensing fees in enforcement, and Californian gold became a very attractive proposition.

Although 1848 had certainly seen a sizeable number of people arrive looking for gold, 1849 saw the numbers explode. All of the people around the world who had heard the news finally began arriving, from pretty much everywhere you could imagine. These settlers earned the name "forty-niners" and they changed the face of California forever.

Most were American, with tens of thousands traveling by wagon train, riverboats, or any method they could

The California state motto is Eureka!, which was what prospectors shouted when they found gold

San Francisco became a boomtown, with new businesses springing up to cater for the influx of people

## The First Gold Rush Millionaire

**Meet the man who made the first million from Californian gold**

It seems right that one of the first people to publicize the Gold Rush should also be one of its greatest beneficiaries. Samuel Brannan had many strings to his bow, but the most important in terms of the Gold Rush was businessman and journalist. He founded the California Star newspaper in San Francisco, and was one of the first to spread the word about the discovery of gold. It wasn't just because of the love of a good story, in fact he couldn't print the story because all of his newspaper staff had left to mine gold. But as owner of the only store between San Francisco and the goldfields, he bought all the gold mining supplies he could find, and then ran around San Francisco shouting, "Gold! Gold on the American River!" to drum up business. Reports have said that after paying 20 cents for each pan, he sold them for $15 each, making $36,000 in just nine weeks.

Brannan used some savvy business decisions to make his fortune

Brannan's good fortune didn't last, however. When his wife divorced him, he had to liquidate most of his real estate to pay her half of their assets. He died a poor man in 1889.

SS Central America sank off the coast of the Carolinas in 1857, with around 20 tons of Californian gold on board

The Gold Rush changed the fate of California and made a lot of people very rich

arrange. But it wasn't just Americans. Eager prospectors from China, Germany, France, Italy, Britain, Australia, and New Zealand arrived. Approximately 90,000 people made their way to California in 1849, around 40,000 of whom were from other countries. While the rewards were great upon arrival, for many, even the Americans, the journey came at great cost. For a start, most prospectors had to borrow money or use their life savings to get to California. The mainly male gold-hunters had to leave their family to fend for themselves, with women being left behind to raise children on their own and take on all the tasks their husbands would have been responsible for.

But the rewards were worth it—if the miners got there early enough. While the gold deposits in rivers were unbelievably plentiful, tens of thousands of hands soon depleted the easy gold. By 1850, most of the gold that amateurs could find had been taken, meaning more complex mining methods had to be adopted. This included techniques such as "coyoteing," which involved digging 20-42-foot deep shafts along a stream, with tunnels being dug in all directions to access deep gold deposits. AlterNatively, entire rivers would be diverted to access the gold at the bottom of the exposed river bed. By 1851, miners had also moved on to blasting areas to access rocks containing gold.

The hunt for gold had turned from being like taking candy from a baby to a far more nuanced and expensive procedure. It must have been soul-destroying to finally arrive in California after using all of your money to make the journey, only to find that you had to have professional mining skills to get any gold. This disappointment quickly turned to hostility and then to blame. American gold-hunters looked around and saw people from all over the world, stealing what they saw as their rightful gold. To try to put travelers off, the Foreign Miners Tax was introduced in 1850, which charged each foreign miner $20 a month.

Still, violent attacks erupted, most notably towards Chinese miners. While only a few hundred had made the journey in 1849 and 1850, more than 20,000 landed in San Francisco in 1852. But whatever fear the White Americans had of the Chinese coming to take over their land, the truth was most of them simply wanted to get as much gold as they could, before returning home.

Some individuals made a decent amount of money from the California Gold Rush, others made an obscene amount of money, but one of the biggest winners was California itself.

At the start of the Gold Rush, California hadn't yet been awarded the honor of statehood. When Marshall found that tiny piece of gold in 1848, California was a dusty

The environmental cost of the Gold Rush was, and still is, huge, with rivers being diverted and toxins entering the water supply

## "The mainly male gold-hunters had to leave their family to fend for themselves, with women being left behind to raise children on their own and take on all the tasks"

ex-Mexican territory with a small population and little hope. But the immigrants and gold that emerged as a result of the Gold Rush meant that California became one of only a handful of American states to be instantly awarded statehood, in 1850. But while California benefitted greatly from the discovery of gold, it was the city of San Francisco that really reaped the rewards.

In 1848, when the gold was first discovered, San Francisco had roughly 1,000 residents. At first the discovery did nothing for the city—in fact, it turned it into a ghost town because people fled to get themselves some gold. But then, it became a boomtown. As people and merchants arrived, the number of residents escalated to 25,000 by the start of 1850. To meet the needs of the arrivals, new businesses sprung up, including saloons, brothels, and boarding houses.

San Francisco became the metropolis of the Gold Rush era. Infrastructure was quickly taken care of, specifically focusing on improving transportation between California and the east coast. The Pacific

Mail Steamship Company started a regular route from San Francisco to Panama. Passengers would take the new Panama Railway (finished in 1855) across the Isthmus of Panama and then get on steamships destined for the east coast.

But it wasn't just infrastructure that blossomed. Roads were built, as were churches and schools. Agriculture began on a large scale to try to meet the needs of the new settlers. In fact, for many, agriculture became the real treasure of the Gold Rush. As gold supplies slowly dwindled, those who put their time and money into agriculture profited from all the people who had traveled to and then stayed in California.

Unfortunately, the elevation of some was made on the backs of others. In the case of the Gold Rush, there were two main groups who suffered—the gold became harder to find, and the methods of finding it became more destructive, which had a lasting impact on California's environment. Where the miners would initially use pans, as the gold became harder to find, they would instead build massive dredgers for the rivers and

John Sutter's fears of the gold destroying his agricultural dreams were well founded. His workers left and his crops were stolen

This illustration by J .R. Browne shows the typical stance taken towards the Native Americans—exterminate

In the early days of the Gold Rush, prospectors could find decent deposits just by panning

Where it all began: Marshall's discovery at Sutter's Mill forever changed the face of California

streams. Water cannons would blast the side of hills to try to expose gold. Then there were the mines themselves, each shaft created by blasting out tons and tons of stone.

Hydraulic mining became popular in the 1850s and caused irreparable damage to the landscape. This consisted of a hose directing a high-pressure jet of water at gravel beds. The gravel, and hopefully the gold within it, would then pass over sluices, where the gold would settle on the bottom. The problem with this method of mining is that it caused pollutants like gravel, silt, and metals to wash into streams and rivers. It also clogged waterways in the vicinity, harming agriculture across the Central Valley. This caused tension between miners and farmers, which was resolved in 1884 with the Sawyer Decision, which called for an end to hydraulic mining. However, to this day there are still areas downstream of old hydraulic mines that aren't able to support plant life. A lot of the mining methods also released toxic substances into the environment, specifically mercury, which was used to extract gold from quartz and stone. Environmentalists are studying the damage caused to the water, with the United States Geological Survey

## Carving Out Routes

### Either along the Oregon Trail or by sea, miners had only two options to reach the state made of gold

Traveling to the gold fields was a major undertaking for most people. In terms of American travel, it was the journey from the east coast to the "Golden State" that led to the building of some serious infrastructure.

For early gold-seekers making the journey from east to west, there were only two routes to choose from. They could take the Oregon-California Trail, traveling in covered wagons. This route involved rugged terrain and some decidedly hostile territories. It took about six months to complete.

The other option was via sea. Again, taking six months, eager prospectors would sail from New York, down to South America, and then on to San Diego or San Francisco. Sitting on a boat, watching the world go by might sound appealing, but this was no luxury cruise. Travelers endured seasickness and intense boredom as well as food infested with insects. They also had to pay a significant amount for the privilege.

Neither of these routes were suitable for the important business of finding gold, so in 1850, the Panama Railway was planned. Built by private American companies, it cut across the Isthmus of Panama and was the world's first transcontinental railroad. More importantly, it slashed months off the journey.

finding unsafe levels of mercury in fish from Nevada County.

As well as the damage caused by the actual mines, the processes put in place to keep the mines going were just as destructive. For example, water was needed in the dry months, so dams were created, changing the course of rivers. Wood was needed to work the boilers at the mines, in addition to building all the artificial canal systems. This created a logging industry, which set about tearing through California's forests. But as horrendous as all of this is, the environmental damage pales in comparison to what happened to the Native Americans.

There are some phenomenal statistics when it comes to the California Gold Rush—from the 300,000 people who arrived looking for gold, to the estimated 370 tons of gold extracted in the first five years of the Gold Rush, worth tens of billions of US dollars in today's prices. Then there are the 100,000 Native Americans who died between 1848 and 1868, in what is known as the "California Genocide." Problems started pretty quickly. The vast swathes of people descending on California pushed the Native Americans out of traditional hunting areas. Fearing for their homes, they would attack miners,

only to then suffer revenge attacks on their villages. The miners had guns, so any Native American in the area would inevitably be slaughtered. Surviving an attack didn't mean you were saved, though. Because the miners had taken over traditional hunting spots, any survivors were likely to starve.

But even if a village wasn't directly targeted by miners, the silt and chemicals entering the environment as a result of mining killed fish and other vital habitats for their existence. Land was taken by farmers to help feed the miners, making it even harder for the Native Americans to survive.

The attitude towards Native Americans was brutal. The miners didn't see them as people, but as something that threatened their profit, and so would simply eliminate them. In 1850, the California Legislature passed the Act for the Government and Protection of Indians, a law that, while suggesting it will protect Native Americans, actually made it legal for settlers to use them essentially as slaves, to

adopt Native American children, and also to prevent any Native American from testifying against a non-Native in a court of law.

California's first governor, Peter Burnett, did nothing to try to improve the situation—his opinion being that what was essentially government-sanctioned genocide was all part of God's plan. He viewed the tensions between settlers and Native Americans as inevitable, leaving the Natives with two options—leave or die. The state even funded death squads, made up of vigilantes, soldiers, miners, and others, to hunt and kill Native Americans.

Despite the clear damage done to the Native American population during this time, and the apparent lack of caring on the part of the state, the government of California has recorded that only 4,500 Native Americans suffered violent deaths between 1849 and 1870. Like many other major events in the Wild West, the Native Americans suffered the consequences of the White man trying to make a better life for himself.

Chinese miners would melt gold and use it to create ordinary household goods to try to disguise their wealth from robbers

# HOW THE PATH TO THE WEST LED TO WAR

## As the United States spread westward, one question divided the nation: would the new states be Slave States or Free States?

Words by Edoardo Albert

From the dawn of the 19th century, America had been divided culturally, politically, geographically, even religiously about the issue of slavery. But the Union had been preserved by the division being equal. Half the twenty-two states comprising the United States were Free States and half were Slave States. But when Missouri petitioned to join the Union in 1819 as a Slave State, that delicate balance was threatened.

Missouri was part of the Louisiana Purchase. This was when, in 1803, the United States (at the time the country ran roughly south from the western edge of the Great Lakes) bought a vast tract of land from France. To give an idea of just how big the Louisiana Purchase was, it doubled the size of the United States, adding 828 million square miles to the republic's territory (that's nearly four times the area of Britain). The new territory was bounded by the Mississippi River in the east, the Rocky Mountains in the west, Canada in the north, and the Gulf of Mexico in the south. It was huge.

What would later become the state of Missouri was a part of the Purchase and when it had passed the population threshold, it applied for admittance to the United States. As a new state, it would be entitled to two senators in the Senate, thus upsetting the balance between Free and Slave States. As rancor grew between the opposing sides, Henry Clay, the speaker of the House of Representatives, brokered a compromise whereby Missouri entered the Union as a Slave State but, at the same time, so did Maine as a Free State. Thus the balance would be maintained. But, critically, the bill as

passed also decreed that slavery should not be allowed north of the line of latitude at 36 degree 30 minutes, with the exception of Missouri, whereas any future states south of this line would be Slave States. With this enforcement, slavery was extended westward, with the same north/south divide.

Although the Missouri Compromise made a way forward for the states, a number of American statesmen could see it sowed the seeds for future conflict. John Quincy Adams, sixth president of the United States, wrote in his diary, "Take it for granted that the present is a mere preamble—a title page to a great, tragic volume."

The issue came to the fore once more in 1849 when California petitioned to join the Union. The territory's population had rocketed following the discovery of gold in 1848, drawing in people from both the Free States, who called themselves "free-soilers," and the Slave States, who adopted the label "Chivs" (short for chivalry). Such were the continuing tensions in California over the issue that even when it joined the Union in 1850 as a Free State, nine years later two of its most eminent political representatives, Senator David Broderick and ex-chief justice of the California Supreme Court David Terry, fought a duel over their political disagreements on the issue. The men had once been friends, but had fallen out over the issue of slavery. Terry, the advocate of slavery, had taken the precaution to practice beforehand with the weapons they would be using for the duel, two Belgian .58 caliber pistols. Broderick, the free-soiler, had not.

Come the duel, Broderick's gun misfired just before the final count. Hearing the count up to three, and with his gun already

> The idea of Manifest Destiny, that it was America's duty to spread west, found its greatest support among Democrats

Battle of
Chickamauga, 1863

Victor Hugo tried to gain a pardon for John Brown. "There is something more frightening than Cain killing Abel ... Washington killing Spartacus"

The duel between David Broderick and David Terry, showing Broderick's gun misfiring and Terry shooting nonetheless

## THE DAY OF OUR ENSLAVEMENT!!

A poster proclaiming Kansas a Free State despite the vote that it should accept slavery

After an anti-slavery speech, Senator Charles Sumner attacked pro-slavery Congressman Preston Brooks

having fired, Broderick made no effort to move but stood tall. Terry, knowing that his opponent had already shot, had the option to fire to miss. He didn't. He shot Broderick square in the chest. The senator died three days later. "They killed me because I am opposed to the extension of slavery and a corrupt administration," he said on his death bed.

Tensions between Free and Slave states deepened in the decade following California's accession in 1850 as a Free State. To mollify the Slave States, Congress had agreed that while California would be free, the people of the New Mexico and Utah territories would decide whether they would be Slave or Free states. The compromise also required that people in Free States help to capture runaway slaves. This led to a considerable heightening of tension between Free and Slave states, as both took up opposing positions on the moral high ground, the people of Free States objecting to being co-opted as slave-catchers while those in Slave States saw their northern brethren as flouting the law.

As America expanded westward, the issue of whether the states petitioning for accession to the Union should be Slave or Free came up more and more frequently.

Just four years after California's accession, Illinois Senator Stephen Douglas made another attempt at a solution. As Slave States had no interest in allowing new Free States into the Union, the westward expansion of the United States had stopped at the Mississippi River. To get it going again, he proposed a new bill, the Kansas-Nebraska Act, which decreed that popular sovereignty would decide the issue of whether these new states should be Free or Slave. Many of Douglas' fellow Democrats saw this as a ploy to expand slavery and they began to join with other politicians into what would become the Republican Party, united by its opposition to slavery.

What's more, when delegates came to be elected in Kansas to decide whether the state would be Free or Slave, the votes were skewed by people crossing the border from Missouri to vote for Kansas becoming a Slave State. Indeed, so widespread was the fraud that two votes were cast for every registered voter. Thus, the Kansas legislature passed pro-slavery laws. So outraged were Free State-supporting Kansans at this fraud that they began to arm themselves, creating a parallel legislature, while increasingly violent confrontations broke out between Free Staters and slavery supporters, who

SOUTHERN CHIVALR

called themselves the Law and Order Party. It was a nasty conflict in which neither side was blameless. In revenge for a murder, Free Staters burned and terrorized pro-slavery settlers, before being themselves pursued and surrounded in the town of Lawrence. In the ensuing siege, abolitionist women smuggled guns to the besieged Free Staters hidden in their petticoats. The siege was called off in the midst of a cold winter, but when the slavery supporters returned to Lawrence in the spring, they burned the Free State Hotel and threw the press of the abolitionist paper, The *Herald Of Freedom*, into the river. Back in the east, Republican-supporting papers wrote this up as the "Sack of Lawrence."

One abolitionist, a man named John Brown (1800-1859), on his way to help in the defense of Lawrence, heard that he was too late but, enraged by the events, he led a party of men to Pottawatomie Creek where they murdered five pro-slavery settlers. After what came to be called the Pottawatomie Massacre, Brown took up guerilla tactics, fighting skirmishes against pro-slavery militias.

Some historians consider these small battles the first of the Civil War. And with the notoriety Brown had acquired through his actions in

> Northern farmers did not necessarily object to slavery, but they did not want to compete with low-cost slave farms

Kansas, he was able to gather funds for his attack on Harper's Ferry in West Virginia, where he hoped to gain arms to raise a general slave revolt. The raid failed, and Brown was captured, tried, and hanged for treason. The attack so inflamed passions on either side that it all but made war inevitable. On the morning of his execution, Brown wrote, "I, John Brown, am now quite certain that the crimes of this guilty land will never be purged away but with blood."

Within eighteen months, the American Civil War began. As for the west itself, the Civil War and its aftermath transformed it. In particular, three acts signed into law by Abraham Lincoln in 1862 were to prove transformative: the Homestead Act, the Pacific Railway Act which facilitated the first transcontinental railroad, and the Morrill Act, which provided federal land to states to fund agricultural colleges, which went on to train generations of ranchers and farmers. With these laws in place, all the foundations had been laid to "win" the west. For its Native American inhabitants, it meant the loss of ancestral lands but many newly-freed slaves found homes there, settling in towns such as Nicodemus, Kansas. In the end, the Civil War not only bound North and South together, but it also brought the west into communion with the rest of the United States.

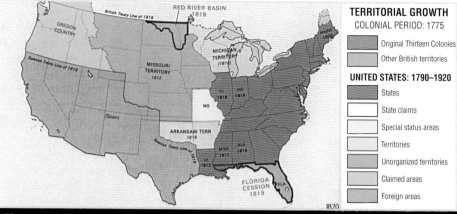

The area of the Missouri Compromise. The dark green area was to be free of slavery, while the yellow and light blue areas were to be Slave States

**TERRITORIAL GROWTH**
COLONIAL PERIOD: 1775

- Original Thirteen Colonies
- Other British territories

**UNITED STATES: 1790–1920**

- States
- State claims
- Special status areas
- Territories
- Unorganized territories
- Claimed areas
- Foreign areas

RGUMENT VERSUS CLUB'S.

## Lots of Houses on the Prairie
### How a law inspired the creation of a series of children's stories

*The Little House On The Prairie*, along with many others, was the direct result of the Homestead Act. President Lincoln signed it into law on May 20, 1862 and by its statute it allowed 160 acres of unclaimed public land to any citizen, or an immigrant intending to become a citizen, in return for a small filing fee. To gain final title on the land, the claimant had either to build a house on the land, plant crops and remain living there for five years continuously, or they could buy the land for $1.25 per acre after living on it for six months, so long as they had built a house and planted crops in that time. Between the signing of the Act in 1862 and 1900, more than 80 million acres was distributed to people moving west and building their houses on the prairies of the American West. Among them were the Ingalls family, who moved to Montgomery County, Kansas, in 1869. *Little House On The Prairie* was based on the family's experiences there.

LITTLE HOUSE ON THE PRAIRIE

LAURA INGALLS WILDER

The cover of the first edition of Little House On The Prairie

# THE WILD WEST

86

112

92

100

86

# THE HOMESTEAD ACTS AND WESTWARD SETTLEMENT

## As the United States spread westward, one question divided the nation: would the new states be Slave States or Free States?

Words by Mike Haskew

The inexorable westward migration of American settlers during the 19th century brought opportunity for many, and the US government encouraged the movement with measures making land ownership possible for millions. In 1862, Congress passed the most significant of the Homestead Acts, providing land grants to any US citizen who had never taken up arms against the nation to own a tract of 160 acres as long as they were willing to settle on the land and farm the property for at least five years. If a person was willing to pay $1.25 per acre, they could own the real estate after living there for just six months.

Prior to the Civil War, numerous measures had been introduced in Congress to promote the settlement of western lands; however, Southern legislators had successfully blocked virtually all of them, fearing that such settlement would tip the

balance of power in Congress toward those Northern advocates of a "Free Soil" policy and members of the newly formed Republican Party who encouraged individual farmers to acquire land, eventually inhibiting the spread of slavery into the new territories. One limited success was the Donation Land Claim Act of 1850 that enabled settlers to stake claims in the Oregon Territory. Settlers were eligible to receive free tracts of either 320 or 640 acres from 1850 to 1854, and later to pay $1.25 per acre to purchase land until the measure expired in 1855.

Still, most of the time homestead legislation became bogged down in disagreements. In 1858, a homestead bill was approved in the House of Representatives but failed by a single vote in the Senate. Then in 1860, Democratic president James Buchanan vetoed homestead legislation. However, once the secessionist members of Congress had

left Washington, D.C. as the Civil War began, the Homestead Act of 1862 was passed. It was signed into law by Republican president Abraham Lincoln.

Those applying for land grants were subject to relatively few requirements. Heads of households who were at least twenty-one years old were required to file an application, commit to cultivating the land, and subsequently provide proof that they had done so, although the government's verification process never became fully developed. Many subsistence farmers in east and midwestern states took advantage of the Homestead Act of 1862, as did free Blacks, growing numbers of former slaves after the Civil War, immigrants, and others. However, the measure did not spur a great migration of low-income or impoverished people from the large cities of the north and east as hoped.

Nevertheless, 15,000 claims had been filed by the end of the Civil War, and eventually 1.6 million land grants were concluded, totalling 270 million acres, approximately 10 percent of all property owned by the US government. Although land speculators often gained control of homestead grants, hoping to turn a profit on quick sales, the Homestead Act of 1862 was a catalyst for western settlement.

At the same time, Native Americans lost their lands at an alarming rate. While treaties had been concluded with the Federal Government and the Native Americans legally occupied reservations in the Dakotas, Oklahoma, and elsewhere, the encroachment of settlers continually eroded their legal

A family of homesteaders cutting wood for their stove, a routine chore in the 19th-century American West

Nine canvas tents serve as registration booths for potential homesteaders photographed on the western frontier in 1893

claims. At times, the government seemed powerless to stem settlement on Native land, and the Homestead Acts only exacerbated their plight.

The initial Homestead Act existed for more than a century, and Congress passed several measures through the years to expand its effectiveness. The Southern Homestead Act of 1866 was enacted to assist sharecroppers and tenant farmers in the post-Civil War South in owning their own land, but it was only marginally successful. Even though land was cheap, few had the money to pay associated fees. The Timber Culture Act of 1873 enabled homesteaders to claim 160 acres with the requirement that they plant trees on one quarter of the property, while an additional incentive allowed such tracts to be combined with an existing grant to total 320 acres.

Homestead-related legislation continued into the 20th century. In 1904, the Kinkaid Amendment provided larger tracts up to 640 acres to settlers in less arable regions west of the 100th meridian, particularly in Nebraska, where more land was needed to make individual farms successful. The Enlarged Homestead Act of 1909 offered larger 320-acre tracts for homesteaders willing to take on land that was difficult to irrigate and generally located in the Great Plains.

The 1916 Stock-Raising Homestead Act provided 640 acres to potential ranchers who needed land for grazing herds, and subsistence homestead provisions were included in President Franklin D. Roosevelt's New Deal of the 1930s. The last Homestead Act claim was an 80-acre grant in Alaska in the late 1980s.

## Oklahoma's Land Rush

**In 1889, thousands of settlers waited for the signal to stake claims to land in Oklahoma**

At noon on April 22, 1889, about 50,000 people were poised to stampede into Oklahoma and stake claims on two million acres of land opened for settlement by President Benjamin Harrison following the passage of the Indian Appropriations Act of that year. Inspired by the provisions of the Homestead Act of 1862, the settlers were poised to find the best land, but some individuals had chosen to enter the territory prematurely, claiming the choicest parcels before the starting time. They became known as "Sooners," while those who actively urged the opening of the land were called "Boomers." After the rush had quieted, *Harper's Weekly* reported, "At twelve o'clock on Monday, April 22nd, the resident population of Guthrie was nothing; before sundown it was at least ten thousand. In that time streets had been laid out, town lots staked off, and steps taken toward the formation of a municipal government."

Settlers rush to claim land in Oklahoma that once belonged to the Cherokee tribe of Native Americans

# FIGHT FOR SURVIVAL

## Native Americans fought desperately to retain their way of life in the face of encroachment onto their lands by White settlers

Words by William E. Welsh

The American Indian Wars in the United States of America consisted of many raids and ambushes: major clashes were few and far between. In the former, the Native American warriors were able to even the odds, but in the latter they found themselves outgunned by a foe that possessed far greater resources both in manpower and equipment. These conflicts stretched over the course of nearly three centuries, from the earliest time that European colonists arrived in America to the final decade of the 19th century.

The Native American tribes were for the most part warrior societies, with tribes fighting their neighbors for land and resources before the Europeans arrived. A major shift occurred in the way of life of the tribes of the Great Plains when they obtained horses. Spanish explorers of the 16th century brought horses to North America, and the Spaniards subsequently settling northern Mexico also had horses, some of which escaped and roamed wild throughout the southwest. The Southern Plains tribes obtained horses from wild herds and also from raids into Spanish territory in the modern state of New Mexico. By the mid-18th century, the tribes of the arid southwest and Southern Plains possessed horses, and soon afterwards the tribes of the Northern Plains had them too.

The acquisition of horses revolutionized the lives of these tribes, enabling them to conduct long-range strikes and overpower neighboring tribes that lacked horses. Although Native Americans traditionally fought with bow and arrow, tomahawks, hatchets, and knives, they soon began to obtain firearms as gifts, as well as through trading and raids.

The American Indian Wars can loosely be thought of as falling into several periods that overlap considerably depending on the cause, location, and participants in the conflict. Thus, the conflicts of the 17th and 18th centuries were an attempt by the Native Americans in the east to resist White colonial settlement. In the mid-19th century White Americans embraced the doctrine of Manifest Destiny; that is, the quest to expand across the continent and settle the lands west of the Mississippi River. The flood of migrants into US territories west of the Mississippi River sparked numerous conflicts.

The tribes of North America increasingly faced a desperate struggle for survival throughout the 19th century, during which the US Government sought to force them to live on reservations established on poor-quality land. The proud Natives resisted for as long as they possibly could, but one by one they all eventually succumbed to the military might of the US Army.

### THE COMANCHE WARS
#### (South Plains)

The Comanches that controlled the Southern Plains had the distinction of being the most warlike of the Native American tribes of the western United States. The Comanches were allies with the Kiowa, Arapaho, and Southern Cheyenne. In battle they skillfully wielded nine-foot lances and could fire six arrows in the time it took an enemy soldier to load his smoothbore musket.

At the outset of the 19th century the Comanches numbered about 30,000 in twelve loosely related groups that were splintered into as many as thirty-five different bands with chieftains. Although the Comanches raided south into Mexico, they became increasingly hostile to White Anglo-American settlers as a result of creation of the Republic of Texas in 1836.

The Comanches regularly raided Texan settlements. One such raid against a local

> "The Native American tribes were for the most part warrior societies, with tribes fighting their neighbors for land and resources before the Europeans arrived. A major shift occurred when the tribes obtained horses."

settlement known as Fort Parker on May 19, 1836, had a profound influence on the Comanche nation in the years that followed. 300 Comanches swept down on the settlement, killing the men and carrying off horses and cattle, as well as women, children, and captives. Among the captives was nine-year-old Cynthia Ann Parker. Raised by the Comanche, she married Chief Peta Nocona of the Quahadi band. Their son, Quanah Parker, would grow up to be the leader of the Comanche resistance in the 1870s.

One of the most famous events in the annals of the Comanche Wars was the Council House fight that occurred during a parlay in Austin on March 19, 1840. When the Comanches failed to bring White hostages to turn over, the Texans shot thirty-five of the Comanche delegates and took another thirty prisoner. In retaliation, Chief Buffalo Hump led 1,000 warriors on a deep strike into Texas that was known as the Great Raid. The Comanches pillaged the towns of Victoria and Linville on 6–7 August, carrying off a great deal of plunder.

After Texas became a state in 1845, the US Army constructed a string of forts along a 400-mile stretch in Texas that divided the White settlements of the east from the Comanche-controlled lands in the west. Frequent patrols helped curtail Comanche raids. Because the US Army found itself stretched thin in Texas, the Texans created a paramilitary organization known as the Texas Rangers to maintain law and order and fight the Comanches.

Beginning in the 1840s, the US Cavalry and Texas Rangers were increasingly equipped with repeating Colt revolvers and breech-loading carbines that enabled them to stay in the saddle during a firefight. At the Battle of Antelope Hills in 1858, a force of about 100 Texas rangers armed with Colt revolvers killed seventy-six Comanches along the Canadian River at the cost of only two rangers.

The Medicine Lodge Treaty of 1867 granted the Comanches and their allies exclusive rights to buffalo hunting north between the Arkansas and Cimarron rivers. However, the arrival of large numbers of White buffalo hunters threatened their existence. In response to the threat, the Comanches began attacking parties of buffalo hunters and trading posts where the buffalo were processed and shipped north to the railroad in Kansas for distribution throughout the country. Following a bloody raid by Comanches and Kiowa on a US Army wagon train on May 18, 1871 in which the warriors killed the majority of the wagon drivers, the US Army redoubled its efforts to force the Comanches onto reservations. It fell to Quanah Parker to lead the resistance. Parker's nemesis was Ranald Mackenzie, the veteran commander of the 4th US Cavalry based at Fort Richardson. Mackenzie's aim was to cripple the Comanches' ability to wage war. The ensuing Red River War of 1874–1875

saw overwhelming force brought to bear against Parker's Quahadi Comanches. By that time, the Comanche nation had shrunk to a fraction of its original size, with 2,000 Comanche living on the reservation and 1,000 "hostiles" led by Chief Parker operating in the rugged mesa of northwest Texas.

Five columns of US cavalry and infantry converged on the Comanches and their allies. The combined strength of the remaining Comanches and their allies living off the reservation amounted to only 800 warriors. The cavalry pursued the Comanches into their hiding places in the Staked Plain, a rugged tableland in northwestern Texas.

In September 1874, Mackenzie's 600 troopers located a handful of Comanche encampments in Palo Duro Canyon. Parker's men fought a rearguard action that enabled their families to escape, but Mackenzie captured their 1,400 horses. He kept some and slaughtered the rest. The loss of their horses compelled the Comanches to submit once and for all to living on the Comanche-Kiowa reservation in the Indian Territory, which is now the state of Oklahoma.

## THE SIOUX WARS
### (North Plains)

The Sioux were not a single tribe but actually several related peoples of

the same linguistic family who fell into three subgroups: the easternmost Santee Dakota, the central Yankton Nakota and the westernmost Teton Lakota. The Lakota consisted of seven bands: Oglala, Brulé, Miniconjou, Hunkpapa, Sihasapa, Oohenunpa, and Itazipcho. The Lakota, who were closely allied with the Northern Cheyenne, dominated the northern Great Plains, and four of the five major conflicts known collectively as the Sioux Wars concerned them. The five major wars between the Sioux and the US Army were the First Sioux War of 1854–1856, the Dakota War of 1862, the Red Cloud's War of 1866–1868, the Great Sioux War of 1876, and the Ghost Dance War of 1890–1891.

The First Sioux War erupted in the wake of the Grattan Massacre of August 1854. When a Lakota warrior of the Brulé band killed a cow belonging to a Mormon wagon train, Lieutenant John Grattan attempted to arrest the man by force when negotiations failed to compel Chief Conquering Bear to turn the warrior over to authorities. When Grattan ordered his men to fire with howitzers and rifles into the lodges of the Lakota, 200 warriors counterattacked, killing the twenty-nine soldiers. The war dragged on with raids and counter-raids, with the US Army ultimately prevailing.

Unlike the nomadic Lakotas, the Dakotas were farmers. In 1851 they signed over 24 million acres to the US Government in return for the promise of sizeable annuities. Nearly a decade later, the Dakotas found themselves squeezed onto two small reservations with little compensation. On the verge of starvation, the Dakotas rebelled in August 1862.

Under the leadership of Chief Little Crow, the Dakotas began massacring White settlers living in towns and farms along the Minnesota River. In September, former governor Henry Hastings Sibley led an army composed of 1,500 militiamen against the Dakotas. Of the 2,000 Dakota warriors captured, 100 were sentenced to hang. At the last minute, President Abraham Lincoln commuted the sentences of all but thirty-eight.

Red Cloud's War four years later was a reaction by the Lakotas to the creation of the Bozeman Trail, a spur of the Oregon Trail that led to newly discovered gold mines in Montana. The Lakotas were incensed because the Bozeman Trail cut through their hunting grounds in the Powder River

This image is thought to show the Potawatomi, a Native American people of the upper Mississippi River and Western Great Lakes region

# Battle of Little Bighorn

Expecting an easy victory, Lt. Col. George Custer bungled his attack against the Sioux encamped along the Little Bighorn River

**01 THREE BATTALIONS**

Seventh Cavalry Regiment commander Lt. Col. George Armstrong Custer divided his twelve companies into three battalions. Major Marcus Reno took three companies, Custer took five companies, Captain Frederick Benteen took three companies, and Captain Thomas McDougall guarded the pack train with Company B.

**04 CUSTER'S BLUNDER**

Custer led his 250 troopers two miles north in order to strike the rear of the Lakota-Cheyenne camp. He again divided his force by sending the right wing under Captain Myles Keogh north along the ridgeline, while he led the left wing north in search of a ford to reach the north end of the enemy encampment. Failing to find the north end of the vast camp, he returned to the ridge. Leaving Keogh atop Calhoun Hill, Custer attempted to lead his two companies north.

**06 RENO'S STAND**

Benteen and McDougall joined Reno, and the remaining seven companies withstood repeated attacks on the second day. When the chiefs learned that enemy reinforcements were soon going to arrive, they withdrew.

**03 RENO'S RETREAT**

Reno ordered a mounted retreat to the east bank. The survivors took up a defensive position in a shallow depression on the ridge east of the river.

**05 CUSTER'S LAST STAND**

2,000 warriors crossed the river and attacked Custer's and Keogh's five companies. Some of the warriors advanced on foot, while others remained mounted firing bullets and arrows. A successful charge overran Keogh's position. One mile to the north, Custer's wing made its last stand. The warriors surrounded Custer's men and then finished off the wounded with edged weapons.

**02 FAILED CHARGE**

Reno deployed at 3:00 p.m. After a brief charge, the men dismounted and formed a skirmish line. The Lakota warriors counterattacked in strength, forcing Reno to withdraw to a stand of timber along the river.

region of the Wyoming Territory. With the federal government preoccupied with building the first transcontinental railroad, federal officials ultimately negotiated a treaty favorable to the Lakota. A key term of the treaty was that the US Army agreed to abandon three forts along the Bozeman Trail.

Following a reconnaissance mission through the Black Hills in 1874 that led to the discovery of gold in the region's streams and rivers, miners arrived in large numbers to pan for gold even though the land was part of the Great Sioux Reservation. Efforts by the US Government to force the Lakota to sell the Black Hills failed, and the Lakota prepared to defend themselves against a major offensive by the US Army designed to subjugate them.

Maj. Gen. Phil Sheridan, the commander of US Army forces in that region of the country, devised a multi-pronged campaign against the non-reservation Lakota and Cheyenne who traveled back and forth through the Dakota, Wyoming, and Montana territories. In 1876, three columns converged on the Lakota-Cheyenne forces encamped south of the Yellowstone River in the Montana Territory. They had orders to attack Lakota and Cheyenne villages, burn their food stores, and destroy their pony herds.

The Lakotas won a significant victory against General George Crook's army at Rosebud Creek on June 17. Before the end of the month, Sitting Bull's Lakotas won a major victory over Lt. Col. George Custer's 7th Cavalry at the Battle of Little Bighorn in which Custer was slain and five cavalry companies wiped out. After the battle the Lakota and Cheyenne, people drifted east towards the Great Sioux Reservation. Determined to exact revenge, the US Army columns followed closely behind them.

Once inside the Dakota Territory, Crook's vanguard under Captain Anson Mills launched a surprise dawn attack against a Miniconjou Lakota band on September 9. The cavalrymen charged into the village firing their repeating Colt carbines and pistols. While Chief American Horse and his warriors fought from a protected position in front of a cave, Crook's main force blocked 600 Oglala and Hunkpapa followers under Sitting Bull and Crazy Horse in a nearby encampment from coming to their assistance. The battle ended in a US victory.

In January 1877, Brig. Gen. Nelson Miles, commander of the US 5th Infantry, attacked a force of Sioux and Cheyenne at the Battle of Wolf Mountain. Taking up a defensive

position, Miles' troops used their breech-loading rifles to repulse repeated charges by the screaming warriors. That same month Sitting Bull led his followers into Canada. Meanwhile, Crazy Horse and 900 Lakotas surrendered on May 6 to reservation authorities. Four years later, Sitting Bull led his people back into the United States to live on the reservation. Crazy Horse was shot on September 5 when authorities tried to arrest him for allegedly disturbing the peace. Meanwhile, the US Government began to methodically carve the Great Sioux Reservation into smaller reservations, which had names such as Standing Rock, Cheyenne Ridge, and Pine Ridge. One of the most disgraceful massacres by the US Army during the American Indian Wars occurred at Wounded Knee Creek on the Pine Ridge Reservation during the month-long Ghost Dance War. The Ghost Dance originated with the Northern Paiutes and spread to tribes in the Great Basin and Great Plains. Ghost Dance believers held that Whites would one day disappear and Native Americans would be able to live as they had before the Whites arrived.

Sitting Bull was accidentally killed when reservation police tried to arrest him on

December 15, 1890. Two weeks after that incident, a bloody melee erupted when troopers of the 7th Cavalry tried to disarm members of two Lakota bands engaged in the ghost dance.

Of the 350 Lakota warriors, women and children, 150 were killed and fifty-one wounded compared to twenty-five soldiers killed and thirty-nine wounded. Wounded Knee was the final chapter in the Sioux Wars.

## THE APACHE WARS
### (Southwest)

Living in the arid climate of the American southwest, the Apaches exhibited cunning skills as raiders. A skilled Apache could draw quickly enough to keep eight arrows in flight at the same time. When planning a raid or ambush, the Apaches carefully plotted paths of retreat beforehand. One of their hallmarks was that after striking a target in a raid, they would scatter in multiple directions to thwart pursuit and then reunite at a predetermined location.

The US Army's thirty-five-year intermittent war against the Apaches in the New Mexico Territory stemmed from an 1861 incident in which an overzealous

Illustration from Theodore Roosevelt's article on St. Clair's defeat

low-ranking army officer became embroiled in a dispute with Apache Chief Cochise of the Chiricahua band. A rancher falsely accused Cochise's warriors of theft and kidnapping. When Cochise met with Lt. Charles Bascom to inform him that the Tonto band, not the Chiricahuas, had committed the crimes, Bascom tried unsuccessfully to arrest him.

Although Cochise escaped, Bascom took other members of his party into custody. As the matter escalated, both sides executed their hostages. The Bascom Affair made the US Government aware that it needed to secure a key corridor through the mountains known as Apache Pass on the travel route connecting Texas and California. To control the route, the government built Fort Bowie next to the pass. In addition, the government began moving the various Apache bands onto reservations throughout the New Mexico Territory. One of the most squalid reservations was the San Carlos Reservation on barren flats along the Gila River. The Apaches found life on the disease-ridden reservation intolerable.

The most famous of the Apache chiefs was Geronimo of the Chiricahua band. A cunning tactician, Geronimo escaped from the San Carlos Reservation three times. War broke out when the US Army sought to clamp down on medicine man Nakaidoklini, who prophesied that dead warriors would return to assist the Apaches in overthrowing their White oppressors. When troopers of the 6th Cavalry seized Nakaidoklini at Cibecue Creek on August 29, 1881, the Apaches attacked in an attempt to free him. During the fighting, Nakaidoklini was slain.

Outraged by the American's missteps regarding Nakaidoklini, Geronimo led

seventy-four warriors into the Sierra Madre Mountains of Mexico. For two years they raided across the border into the United States with impunity. Geronimo's warriors plundered wagon trains to get arms and ammunition and ranches to get horses and food.

With the assistance of Apache scouts, General George Crook led an expedition into Mexico in 1882 in pursuit of Geronimo. In a parlay with Crook, Geronimo agreed to surrender, but on the journey back to San Carlos Reservation he managed to escape his captors. The embarrassing incident resulted in Crook's dismissal. The US Army gave his successor, Brig. Gen. Nelson Miles, 5,000 troops with which to try and capture Geronimo again. The Apache chief surrendered to Miles on September 4, 1886.

## THE NEZ PERCE WAR
### (Northwest)

Concurrent with the final victories over the Lakota Sioux, the US Army found itself outfoxed for several months by Chief Joseph, the leader of the Wallowa band of the Nez Perce tribe, in one of the most extraordinary military campaigns of the American Indian Wars.

Although the Nez Perce initially received through the Treaty of Walla Walla in 1855 a sizable reservation that included their homeland in eastern Oregon, the discovery of gold in the Black Hills of their lands doomed them just as it had the Lakota. A new treaty in 1863 obtained under fraudulent conditions reduced the Nez Perce reservation lands to one-tenth of their original size. The first treaty had already caused a rift among the Nez Perce peoples. One group

## 10 GREAT BATTLES

US Army units armed with repeating rifles enjoyed a significant advantage against Native Americans in the final battles of the American Indian Wars

### Adobe Walls
Colonel Christopher 'Kit' Carson set out with 472 men to punish Comanche raiders in the Texas Panhandle by attacking their winter camp. Facing 1,200 warriors, Carson used his howitzers to break up repeated charges by the enemy.
**1864**

View of Adobe Walls battlefield

### Wagon Box Fight
A strong force of Lakota attacked a work party on August 7, 1867, outside Fort Kearny in the Wyoming Territory. Captain James Powell ordered his men to construct a field fort from wagons, logs, and sandbags. Armed with repeating rifles, they inflicted 180 casualties on the attackers while suffering only eight casualties in a savage five-hour fight.
**1867**

|1858

### Rush Springs
Captain Earl van Dorn led 200 troopers of the crack 2nd US Cavalry in an unprovoked surprise attack against a Comanche camp in the heart of Comanche country on October 1, 1858. The troopers attacked at dawn killing men, women, and children. The Comanches suffered fifty-eight casualties and the US Cavalry lost twenty men.
**1858**

### Fetterman Fight
In a clash on the Bozeman Trail on December 21, 1866, Captain William Fetterman, under orders to protect troops constructing Fort Kearny on the Bozeman Trail, was baited into pursuing a force of mounted Sioux raiders under Crazy Horse. The Sioux surrounded and destroyed his seventy-nine soldiers.
**1866**

### Hayfield Fight
Twenty-one soldiers and nine civilians manning a defensive perimeter in a hay field near Fort C.F. Smith on the Bozeman Trail in the Montana Territory used breech-loading Springfield Model 1866 rifles to repulse several hundred Lakota and Cheyenne warriors in a fierce firefight on August 1, 1867.
**1867**

Wagon Box Fight site, near Fort Phil Kearney

abided by the treaty, while the other did not recognize it.

Brig. Gen. Oliver O. Howard issued an ultimatum to the anti-treaty Nez Perce that they relocate to the Lapwai reservation in the Idaho Territory or suffer the consequences. The five anti-treaty bands of the Nez Perce concentrated on June 3, 1877, at Tolo Lake in Idaho. Some of the more militant Nez Perce killed eighteen civilians on the Salmon River in mid-June, prompting Howard to send in the cavalry. On June 17, the Nez Perce defeated a force of 130 troops under Captain David Perry that included more than a dozen Nez Perce scouts.

Thereafter, Chief Joseph led approximately 800 warriors, women, and children on a 1,630-mile trek east through the rugged terrain of the Idaho, Wyoming, and Montana territories in which over the course of 107 days they fought seventeen skirmishes and battles with various forces of the US Army attempting to defeat them.

The Nez Perce, who were trying to join Lakota Chief Sitting Bull in Canada, were finally stopped thirty miles from the Canadian border at Bear Paw Mountain on September 30 by a combined arms force of 600 infantry, cavalry, and artillery under Colonel Nelson Miles. In his surrender speech on October 5, Chief Joseph spoke words of his weariness of fighting and the deep sadness he felt in seeing his people killed. "From where the Sun now stands I will fight no more forever," he said.

In a nod to their compassion (they refrained from scalping) and the sophistication of their tactics, General of the Army William T. Sherman had rare praise for Chief Joseph and his warriors. The Nez

A group from the North American Comanche Indian tribe discuss matters with representatives of the United States Government, some of them from the military, 19th century

Perce "displayed a courage and skill that elicited universal praise," Sherman said, noting that they had employed sophisticated tactics during their fighting march such as advance and rear guards, skirmish lines, and field fortifications.

## CONCLUSION

The Wounded Knee Massacre marked the end of the last large-scale resistance to reservation life, with only minor raids occurring sporadically thereafter. The last of these was an Apache raid against Arizona ranchers in 1924.

About one-fifth of the 5.2 million Native Americans currently live on reservations. Many live in conditions that would be unimaginable to their forbearers. The US Government has persisted in keeping those living on the reservations in a state of dependency.

The American Indian Wars produced a number of inspiring stories of courage that can be relished not just by Native Americans but by all Americans. One of the balms

Native Americans have is the knowledge that their ancestors fought to the bitter end and resisted the overwhelming military might of their adversary for as long as they possibly could. Their legacy as great warriors is acknowledged by descendants of both sides who fought during the American Indian Wars.

The death of the great chiefs had much to do with the end of the American Indian Wars. When their generation passed, each generation that followed knew less about life in a tribal setting outside of a government-administered reservation. Both Crazy Horse and Sitting Bull found reservation life utterly intolerable and died shortly after being confined to it. Geronimo, however, lived well into the new century, although not happily.

On his deathbed in 1909 as a prisoner of war in Fort Sill, Oklahoma, he shared his regrets with his nephew. "I should have never surrendered," he said. "I should have fought until I was the last man alive."

### Washita River
Lt. Col. George Armstrong Custer's 7th Cavalry attacked a Southern Cheyenne camp on the Washita River in the Native Territory. A half dozen allied tribes encamped nearby counterattacked Custer's cavalry. Custer used his fifty-three captives as human shields in order to withdraw unmolested.
**1868**

The 7th US Cavalry charging into Black Kettle's village, November 27, 1868

### Big Hole
On August 9-10, 1877, US soldiers attacked the Nez Perce during their forced march to Canada. After a dawn attack on the Nez Perce camp in the Montana Territory, the warriors conducted a brilliant rearguard action that pinned down the soldiers. Although losing eighty-nine of their tribe, the Nez Perce killed twenty-nine soldiers.
**1877**

### Big Dry Wash
Five companies of US cavalry pursued Chief Natiotish's White Mountain Apache band of sixty warriors to punish them for a raid. A sharp battle unfolded in Big Dry Wash in Chevelon Canyon on July 17, 1882, with the Apaches losing one-third of their force, including Natiotish. Outflanked by the cavalry, they withdrew.
**1882**
1882

### Beecher Island
A Sioux-Cheyenne force besieged a party of forty-nine cavalry scouts bivouacked on a river in the Colorado Territory. The scouts, armed with seven-round Spencer repeating rifles, retreated to a sandy island where they held out for nine days until relief arrived.
**1868**

A soldier offers aid to his wounded comrade after the Battle of Beecher Island

### Rosebud Creek
General George Crook's 1,300 troops were part of a three-pronged strike against the Lakota summer camp in the Montana Territory. Using friendly Crow and Shoshone scouts to survey the enemy, on June 17, 1876, Crook seized the high ground over the creek just in time to receive a powerful attack by Lakota and Cheyenne. In a rare pitched battle, the attackers nearly overran Crook's force.
**1876**

General George Crook

# THE TAMING OF THE WEST

## Discover how railways and barbed wire transformed the frontier into America's heartland

Words by Scott Reeves

On May 10, 1869, Leland Stanford picked up a hammer and bashed a five and a half inch nail into the ground. Although just one of millions of spikes used in the construction of the first transcontinental railroad, there was little doubt that this was the most special. Made from gold and engraved on all four sides, this particular nail marked the completion of the longest railway ever built.

Stanford was no mere laborer; he was president of the Central Pacific Railroad and one of the wealthy investors who had backed the venture. His prowess with the hammer was captured in a ceremony conducted in front of hordes of photographers and journalists who were there to capture the occasion. The hammer and spike had even been hooked up to cables so each strike of the hammer would be heard as a click at telegraph stations across the nation. Unfortunately the wires failed and a savvy operator had to input all of the clicks by hand instead. Regardless, the vast media interest indicated that the last spike ceremony was not just the culmination of a decade of blood, sweat, and tears; it was a moment of national importance.

The idea of a railroad connecting the east and west coasts of the United States was floated as early as 1840, less than twenty years after the continent's first railway—a 9,000-mile stretch of line designed to haul coal in the Pennsylvania mountains—had opened. The nation still only encompassed twenty-six states, with Michigan the most recent entrant and Arkansas the most westward. By the 1850s, politicians in Washington, D.C. came to see the value in a cross-country rail link and sent US Army surveying parties to the still-unmapped western territories, trying to work out the best route a railroad might take. The decision came down to two possibilities: a central route through Nebraska and Wyoming, or a southern route across Texas and New Mexico.

The railroad promised future prosperity wherever the line ran, leading politicians and businessmen to—unsurprisingly—lobby for it to run through their own patches of land. The deadlock was broken when the first shots were fired in the Civil War. When the Southern states seceded from the Union, any possibility that the railroad would run through southern territory went with them. The way was clear for the central route.

Despite the carnage of the Civil War, Congress approved the Pacific Railroad Act in 1862 and authorized bonds to be issued in order to fund its building. Two companies were created to make the railroad a reality. Union Pacific was tasked with the line from Omaha, Nebraska to Ogden, Utah, where Central Pacific would take over and deliver the line to Sacramento, California. Wealthy businessmen invested in the companies, hoping (and usually succeeding) to make a fortune. In addition to being paid to lay track with a varying rate depending on the terrain ($16,000 per 1,000 miles on the flat, rising to $48,000 per 1,000 miles in the mountains), the railroad companies were granted territorial rights along the route—in total, the area of land given to them was larger than Texas. If the companies sold the land to settlers within three years, they could keep the money.

With the promise of dollars in the bank, the Central Pacific eagerly set to work, breaking ground in January 1863. Supplies first had to be shipped from the east coast around Cape Horn to San Francisco, before being loaded onto a paddle steamer for the final stint to Sacramento. Building east from the terminus, the Central Pacific made use of Chinese laborers, many of whom had fled the Taiping Rebellion. The Union Pacific was slower to get started, not laying any track until July 1865. Its shortage of labor was solved with the conclusion of the Civil War, which freed up thousands of demobilized soldiers to travel west in search of regular work and wages.

Once both lines were under construction, the gap between them closed at a rapid rate. Small survey parties scouted ahead to plot the exact line of the track—dangerous work since

Jubilation followed the completion of the nine-year project to build the 1,776-mile Transcontinental Railroad

# "While the building of the Transcontinental Railroad was a magnificent engineering achievement, it alone did not tame the west"

Native American raiders would target the newcomers, killing them and leaving the bodies behind as a stark warning to the White men and their "iron horse." Specialized teams were tasked with tunneling through the Rocky and Sierra Nevada mountains and bridging the many streams and rivers that blocked the route, but the bulk of the workforce was responsible for the relatively unskilled job of laying the track and these workers lived in temporary towns that followed the progress of the work. Aside from the dormitories and canteens provided by the railroad companies, enterprising businessmen soon set up saloons, gambling houses, and brothels to encourage the laborers to part with their hard-earned wages. Such were the unsavory reputation of these itinerant towns that one newspaper editor referred to them as "Hell on wheels."

After years of toil, a number of construction-related deaths and a far higher number of deaths from disease in the unsanitary worker towns, the two railroads finally closed in on each other at Promontory Point, Utah. It was here that the golden spike was driven into the ground and the railroad symbolically completed.

While the building of the Transcontinental Railroad was a magnificent engineering achievement, it alone did not tame the west. The single train line running from Missouri to California may have enabled transport from east coast to west coast, but only along a narrow corridor in a country that measured some 1,500 miles north to south. What the railroad did do, however, was provide a solid foundation upon which the west was settled.

A host of smaller railroads sprouted, linking to the Transcontinental Railroad to create a true network across the west: the Hannibal and St. Joseph, Kansas Pacific, and Denver Pacific railroads provided the first true coast-to-coast railroad via the Hannibal Bridge over the Missouri River in August 1870, while the Southern Pacific ultimately provided the southern transcontinental route that was originally debated in the 1850s.

The towns and cities that grew up around the railroads became the biggest settlements of their area. Kansas City took advantage of its location as a rail hub, while Cheyenne, Wyoming was one of many towns that was established at regular intervals by the

railroad builders with the express purpose of providing fuel and water for the steam trains that were passing through.

Where the railroad engineers chose not pass through—typically many of the old mining towns in the foothills of the mountains, where pioneers had flocked to in the hope of striking a mother lode of gold or other precious minerals—the old communities found themselves isolated and cut off. Hundreds of these small towns experienced a gradual decline until the last residents moved out, leaving behind nothing but a ghost town.

The miners were, however, replaced by far more migrants to the west who hoped to make a living off the land. The coming of the railway network meant the west suddenly did not look as wild. It became far cheaper to transport goods across the country, lowering the price of supplies in the west and making cross-country trade much easier. It also became much easier for wannabe westerners to migrate to a new homeland.

The Homestead Act, passed in 1862, granted 160 acres of public land to any migrant in the west—they had to agree only to stay for five years and "improve" the untamed land, usually by making it arable. An amendment of 1866 explicitly encouraged Blacks to move west, providing work and land for the slaves freed in the recently concluded Civil War. However, migrants

The last spike ceremony marked the moment when the Union Pacific and Central Pacific railroads finally met

still had to be prepared to take on the arduous and dangerous trek on one of the migrant trails, making the long slog through mountain passes on foot or horseback.

The coming of the railroads changed all that. By 1876, the Transcontinental Express could leave New York and arrive in San Francisco three and a half days later, cutting weeks off the journey time. Tourist brochures were published to encourage interested travelers to the west, promising that they could travel quicker, safer, and in much more comfort if they used a railway carriage.

Around 40,000 families took advantage of the Homestead Act to settle in the west, and many others purchased land alongside the tracks directly from the railroad companies with the promise of their rail fare being refunded. The central belt to which they were moving, previously marked on maps as the Great American Desert, was not the utopia they were led to believe. Many of the first generation of homesteaders discovered that the weather and climate they faced in the Great Plains—blizzards in winter, tornadoes in spring, drought in summer, and devastating insect swarms in autumn—meant that there was a high risk of crops being totally lost. However, despite many returning back east, the number of farms in the USA still tripled to six million between 1860 and 1905.

Those that stuck with it were often European migrants, especially Germans, the largest ethnic group among newcomers to America in the middle of the 19th century. Between 1860 and 1890, more than three million Germans settled in the USA. Whole families were involved in the hard work of growing crops on the dry soil, with women and children just as vital to the work as the men. Relying on McCormick reapers and John Deere steel-bladed plows, growing new varieties of wheat that were more suited to the dry soil, the families tilled the land by hand and horse. To ease the burden, rural communities often banded together in social activities that also combined farming work—perhaps gathering to raising a barn for one of their community, joining together to communally husk corn, or holding a quilting bee.

Homesteaders were also supported by the National Grange of the Order of Patrons of Husbandry, an organization of farmers and their wives formed by Oliver Kelley to promote and protect farmers from exploitation by railway companies charging over the odds for transporting and storing grain. Within five years of its foundation in 1867, the Grange had 200,000 members, three years later it had

Dale Creek Bridge under construction in 1868—the wooden trestle was swiftly replaced after it swayed alarmingly when trains passed over

# It's All About the Money

## Meet the wealthy businessmen who made the Transcontinental Railroad a reality

**Asa Whitney**
One of the first to promote the idea of the Transcontinental Railroad, Whitney pushed Congress to consider the idea because it would help the United States to trade with China. However, his plan seemed so far-fetched that it garnered little support and he gave up campaigning in 1851.

**Theodore Judah**
One of the first railway engineers to work in California, Judah was convinced that a railroad through the Sierra Nevada Mountains was possible. His enthusiasm for the project won him many co-investors, although he died before the Central Pacific had laid more than a hundred-odd yards of track.

**Thomas Durant**
As vice president of the Union Pacific, Durant was prepared to tweak the rules to give him control of half the shares in the company. He also manipulated the stock market, making a great profit by buying and selling shares in other railroad companies, picking up a reputation for corruption and mismanagement.

**Leland Stanford**
A successful merchant, Stanford was one of the "big four" investors in the Central Pacific and served as governor of California during its construction. He continued diverse business interests after driving the golden spike in 1869, serving as a senator for California in Congress and founding Stanford University.

balloooned to 858,050. Members banded together to make purchases, often supplied by sympathetic Chicago wholesaler Aaron Montgomery Ward.

And if there was one product that Montgomery Ward supplied that was more important than the others, it was an innovation of the 1870s that would radically transform the west: barbed wire. This one, simple invention, patented by Joseph Glidden of Illinois, had as massive an impact on the western landscape as the railroads.

The barbed wire was required because much of the west was open range country; public land where cattle ranchers could graze their cattle for no charge. Cattle ranchers allowed their livestock to roam, bringing them together in roundups every spring and autumn so new calves could be branded, sick animals could be treated, and those destined for sale could be selected. Vast cattle drives pushed herds up to 3,000 strong across the country to the nearest railroad, where the cattle could be loaded onto the trains and taken to markets in the east. Some of the cattle drives lasted two months, with the cows being forced to move 15 miles every day. It was a way of farming that spurred the cowboy into existence in the American West. These mounted ranchers rounded up the herds and escorted them on the long drive to the railhead, working in shifts with teams of horses at their disposal to ensure that the herds were monitored twenty-four hours a day.

However, as homesteaders came into contact with cattle ranchers and cowboys, it quickly became obvious that free-to-roam cattle did not coexist happily with crop farming. The farmers made use of barbed wire, which kept out the cattle far more successfully than smooth wire or wooden fences, preventing the herds from grazing on their crops. As more and more of the west was claimed, richer ranchers who could afford to claim large parcels of land began to use barbed wire themselves to fence off their own tracts, protecting the best grazing pasture for their own herds, sometimes refusing to share water sources or cutting off roads. Typical of the new barbed wire enclosures was that of William Day, who set about erecting a massive fence that would cut off 40,000 acres of Texan grazing land in 1880, despite the opposition of many smaller ranchers who claimed that they owned sections of the pasture closed off to them.

The completion of the Transcontinental Railroad saw a crowd of up to 3,000 flock to Utah for the momentous occasion

The western section of the Transcontinental Railroad relied heavily on Chinese laborers as White migrants flocked to the mining towns

Cowboys became synonymous with the west, but the introduction of barbed wire constrained the open range they worked on

The seismic landscape and cultural changes that barbed wire brought led to small-scale conflicts across the west as settlers adapted to the new way of life. Legal efforts to stop big cattle companies from seizing large swatches of land were failing, leading to the Fence Cutting Wars. Small ranchers who still relied on the open range destroyed the fences of large ranches where they felt that public land was being misappropriated, with occasional shootouts between fence cutters and ranch guards. Gangs of wire-cutters with names like the Blue Devils, the Javelinas, the Land League, and the Owls targeted legal and illegal fences alike, but they were ultimately unable to stop the barbed wire enclosures since the bigger ranchers were able to lobby for greater protection and stiff penalties for captured cutters.

Hundreds of thousands of cows owned by smaller ranchers suffered in the Big Die-Up, which occurred when unseasonable blizzards in the northern Great Plains meant that roaming cattle instinctively shifted south into Texas. The large ranchers there, concerned that the land could not support so many new animals, blocked the newcomers with barbed wire fences to ensure that their own livestock did not die of starvation. Vast herds congregated at the fences and died in droves as the winter weather caught up with them. Smaller ranchers were forced out of business, their remaining animals sold off and assimilated into the bigger herds.

Barbed wire fences also cut off bison migration routes in the Great Plains which, coupled with an enormous growth in hunting—often taking place from the comfort of a railroad carriage—saw the population of the beasts collapse from 35 million in 1840 to near extinction by the turn of the century. The Native Americans, who relied on the bison for their survival, were pushed into reservations granted to them by the federal government, leaving the door open for more settlers to take their ancestral lands.

By the 1890s, two decades after the first barbed wire fence portioned off a part of

The open range allowed cattle ranchers to graze their animals in the west, but it was a way of life whose days were numbered

the west, the age of the cowboy was over. The open range had been contained, with cattle drives limited to trails kept away from agricultural land and herds now belonging to a few rich ranchers and companies.

The forty-niners who rushed to California after gold was discovered there in the middle of the 19th century had to undertake an arduous journey that took weeks, if not months, taking dangerous trails through Native American territory and across the open range. Just fifty years later, migrants who wanted to make a new home on the west coast were able to travel in the comfort and safety of a railway carriage, passing through rapidly growing towns and cities every few hours, seeing pockets of subdivided farming and ranching land out of the window. The speed with which the west was tamed and industrialized came about largely due to two crucial 19th-century inventions: the railroad, which opened up the west to far more migrants, and barbed wire, which enabled them to claim their own small part of it.

## The Last Hurdle

### Why did the Transcontinental Railroad fail to link east and west for three years?

For the first three years of its life, the Transcontinental Railroad was actually a misnomer—it barely reached halfway across the United States. The problem was the Missouri River. The Union Pacific had begun building its line at Omaha on the west side of the river, but the existing east network of track ended on the other side, at Council's Bluff. Up to seven different railroads stopped at the large depot here to transfer to the Union Pacific, but to actually get onto the new line they had to be transported across the Missouri—by ferry in summer, by sleigh in winter when the waters froze. About one mile of river of river separated east from west.

Construction of a bridge over the troubling waters was belatedly begun in 1869, the same year that the golden spike was hammered into the ground to supposedly complete the Transcontinental Railroad. Five hundred workers sunk eleven iron columns into the river until they hit bedrock. On top

they built the track, supported by eleven truss spans to share the load. In 1872, the first train could finally trundle across the bridge in a seamless transfer from the eastern to the western rail networks. The transcontinental railway was finally truly complete.

The first Missouri bridge lasted only fifteen years before it had to be replaced by a new, double-track bridge

# THE HUNT FOR BILLY THE KID

It's the iconic Wild West story and thus, in the 150 years since its making, it has become fraught with embellishment and myth. What was the real history of the hunt that made the legendary lawman Pat Garrett?

Words by Ben Biggs

By the late 19th century, cartographers had mapped much of the world, and the globe, almost as we know it today, was a well-established fact. To the east, the Victorian Empire had peaked despite being ousted from its interests in the New World colonies a century earlier, and the decades that followed Independence Day had seen a fledgling United States simmer with civil war and lawlessness. In the wake of the British, the new American government had made vast territorial gains, picking up the entire Louisiana region—a huge swathe of grasslands over 600,000 square miles—from France's Napoleon Bonaparte for a snip, at just $15 million. Border disputes and infighting followed, but that did not halt the USA's progress from the Great Plains to the coastline of the Golden State.

The boundary of this new nation had spilled westward too rapidly for any population to fill, let alone for the lawmakers of the White House to control. The West was true frontier territory, its people as feral and keen as its unrelenting climate, no place for the fragile. This crucible forged two characters, the outlaw Billy the Kid and sheriff Patrick Floyd Garrett: their independent life stories alone have resonated through generations, but it is Pat's pursuit and the ultimate death of the Kid that has defined them both.

Hollywood has traditionally presented an extremely romanticized notion of this era, so while the stereotypes of sheriff, outlaw, saloon owner, settler, Mexican, cowboy, and their ilk can usually be taken with a mere pinch of salt, the black and White morality of the Silver Screen is laughably far from the truth. There was often little to separate lawman from lawless but a small steel star, so let's rub away the sepia and journey to New Mexico in late 1880, where Pat Garrett has just been appointed the sheriff of Lincoln County.

Garrett was an imposing six feet three inches of lean gunman and a known deadeye shot. Coupled with his imposing figure and reputation, he made a first-class choice for a visiting detective in the employ of the Treasury Department, Azariah Wild, to help track down the source of $30,000 worth of counterfeit greenbacks that were circulating the county. Garrett himself employed another man—Barney Mason—to bait the two suspected of distributing this currency: ranch owner Dan Dedrick and another, W.H. West, who had made himself and their intentions clear in a letter that Mason had intercepted. Those intentions were that they would launder the money by buying cattle in Mexico as fast as they could with an assistant, who would unwittingly take the hit in the event that their ruse was discovered. Mason was to be the fall guy. Now that they had the advantage, Garrett instructed Mason to travel to the White Oaks ranch and play along with their nefarious plans.

In the brisk New Mexico winter, Mason rode out to Dedrick's. There, he ran into three gunslingers on the run from the authorities: Dave Rudabaugh, who had killed a Las Vegas jailer during a break-out; Billy Wilson, another murderer yet to be caught; and the last was none other than Billy the Kid—the unlawful

01

TRUE OR FALSE?

He was famous
throughout
Lincoln county

The shooting of Billy the Kid solidified Garrett's fame as a lawman and gunman

killer who had busted himself out of jail once already, made a living by cattle rustling and gambling, surrounded himself with like-minded outlaws, and whose reputation was on the cusp of snowballing towards near-mythological status. The attitude of the era was such that a lawman and a wanted man could be trading campfire stories one day, then bullets the next. The Kid and Garrett (who ran his own saloon) were once thought to have gambled together, and Mason was also known to these three—he was, in fact, on friendly terms with them. Thus, both parties made their pleasantries then entered a game of high-stakes mind games, whereby the Kid attempted to ferret out the true nature of Mason's visit (suspecting he had come to ascertain his location and then report to the sheriff) while Mason threw the Kid a red herring, stating that he was there to take in some horses. The Kid didn't buy this ruse. Smelling a rat, he met with Dedrick and his

fellow outlaws with the intention of killing Mason, but Dedrick feared the repercussions would ruin his illicit plans, so the Kid relaxed his proverbial itchy trigger finger.

A local posse on the hunt for Billy had been raised and the town of White Oaks was agitated with the news that the outlaw was in the area. The heat was too much for Mason to follow through with his orders without raising suspicion, so he lay low for a few days before returning to report at Garrett's place in Roswell. Shortly after, Garrettt received a letter from Roswell Prison's Captain Lea, detailing the criminal activities of the Kid and his companions in the area. Garrett was commissioned as a United States marshal and given a warrant for the arrest of Henry McCarty, a.k.a. William H. Bonney, a.k.a. Billy the Kid, on the charge of murder. The hunt was on. The Kid's days were numbered and on November 27, 1880, the curtain was lifted on one of history's most famous Wild West dramas.

02
TRUE OR FALSE?
HE SURVIVED THE SHOOTOUT ★ WITH PAT ★ GARRETT

The Kid rode for a time with the gang of cattle rustlers known as the Jesse Evans Gang

The new marshal already had a reputation and might have put the fear of God into the common criminal, but he was no fool. The Kid was by now a true desperado, one who had cut his teeth in the revenge killings of the Lincoln County War, and he was more likely to go out in a blaze of glory than he was to lay down his arms and come quietly. Garrett had raised a posse of about a dozen men from the citizens of Roswell and made his way to Fort Sumner to pick up the outlaws' trail, which would lead them to his suspected hideout at Los Portales. The many miles of desert scrub and overgrown track were neither an easy nor uneventful ride, and saw a Kid associate named Tom Foliard flee the posse in a hail of bullets. When the "hideout" at Los Portales—a hole in a cliff face with a fresh water spring—turned up nothing more than a few head of cattle, the posse fed and watered themselves before returning to Fort Sumner, where Garrett dismissed them. It was not the showdown he had hoped for, but Garrett wasn't the quitting kind.

Over the next few days, Garrett, accompanied by Mason, encountered Sheriff

The Kid is thought to have killed his first victim a few months before his 18th birthday

03
TRUE OR FALSE?
★ HE WAS ★
LEFT-HANDED

"The Kid was by now a true desperado, one who had cut his teeth in the revenge killings of the Lincoln County War, and he was more likely to go out in a blaze of glory than he was to lay down his arms"

## The Wild West in Numbers
Times were hard, but crime was nowhere near as bad as it is in the western United States today

### 3 MURDERS
The highest annual body count for Tombstone, Arizona, happened in 1881, the same year as Wyatt Earp's famous gunfight at the OK Corral

### $5-10 MILLION
The biggest value stagecoach shipments in today's equivalent—usually gold bullion

### 6
The number of bank robberies across 15 states from 1859 to 1900. There weren't many banks and with no cars, it was a lot harder to get away with it back then

### 45
The number of murders from 1870-85 in five Kansas towns, a lower per capita than today

### 28
The number of times the outlaw Black Bart robbed stagecoaches in California, making thousands of dollars a year

# FIREARM SHOWDOWN

For shootouts, showdowns, soldiers, and civilians, these were the guns that won the West. The Kid and Garrett made darned sure their tools of the trade were the best

**04**
**TRUE OR FALSE?**
★ HE KILLED 21 MEN, ONE FOR EACH YEAR OF HIS LIFE ★

## PAT GARRETT'S SHARPS RIFLE

**USA** 1850-81
**Designers:** Christian Sharps
**Manufacturer:** Sharps Rifle Manufacturing Company
**Number produced:** 120,000+
**Effective range:** 460m
**Weight:** 9.4 lb
**Caliber:** .52
**Feed system:** 1 round
**Action:** Falling block, breech loading
**Advantages:** Versatile
**Disadvantages:** Wasteful, expensive
**Popular uses:** Military, hunting, sport

## PAT GARRETT'S FRONTIER COLT

**USA** 1878-1907
**Designers:** William Mason
**Manufacturer:** Colt's Patent Firearms Manufacturing Company
**Number produced:** 51,210
**Muzzle Velocity:** 253 m/s
**Weight:** 2.3 lb
**Caliber:** .44-40 Winchester
**Feed system:** Cylinder magazine
**Action:** Double-action revolver
**Advantages:** Interchangeable ammunition with rifle, good stopping power
**Disadvantages:** Long reloading time
**Popular uses:** Civilian, sheriff

Romero leading a posse of swaggering Mexicans to Puerto de Luna, shot and wounded a known felon named Mariano Leiva, talked his way out of Romero and his posse's misguided attempts to arrest him for this shooting, and then learned of another party—led by an agent for the Panhandle stockmen the Kid had rustled cattle from—who was also hot on the trail of the Kid. Nerves of steel, a steady hand, sharp wit and no short measure of luck had eventually seen Garrett true once again.

Garrett met with Panhandle agent Frank Stewart at Las Vegas, the former Spanish colonial town of New Mexico and not the bright-light city-to-be more than 600 miles to the west. They left on December 14 to catch up with Stewart's party and broke the news to them: some balked at the idea of an encounter with the Kid and his gang, but

Stewart did not reproach any man who had reservations. "Do as you please boys, but there is no time to talk," he told them. "Those who are going with me, get ready at once. I want no man who hesitates." In the end, Stewart, Mason, and Garrett added a further six men to their cause.

Ahead of the party, Garrett had sent a spy, a trustworthy man named Jose Roibal, who rode tirelessly to Fort Sumner to sniff the Kid out. Roibal performed his duty in a suitably subtle fashion and returned to meet Garrett with the news that the outlaw he sought was certainly at Fort Sumner, that he was on the lookout for Garrett and Mason, and that he was prepared to ambush them. The Kid had no idea that Garrett had company with him.

Following this, the posse made their way to an old hospital building on the eastern side of the town to await the return of

the outlaws. The Kid arrived sooner than expected. A light snow carpeted the ground so that, despite the low light of the evening, it was still bright outside. Nevertheless, Garrett and company were able to position themselves around the building to their advantage. Outlaws Foliard and Pickett rode up front and were first to feel the sting of the posse's six-shooters, though whose bullets killed Foliard that day remains unknown. Garrett himself missed Pickett, who wheeled around and made for their ranch retreat along with the Kid, Bowdre, Wilson, and Rudabaugh—the stagecoach robber and a particularly unsavory character who the Kid admitted to being the only man he feared.

The marshal's posse regrouped and made preparations for the chase. There were just five men to track now. Garrett had learned from another reliable local that

## BILLY THE KID'S 1873 WINCHESTER RIFLE

**USA** 1873-1919

**Designers:** Benjamin Tyler Henry and Nelson King
**Manufacturer:** Winchester Repeating Arms Company
**Number produced:** 720,000
**Muzzle Velocity:** 335 m/s
**Weight:** 9.4 lb
**Caliber:** .44-40 Winchester

**Feed system:** 15-round tube magazine
**Action:** Lever-action
**Advantages:** Interchangeable ammunition with pistol, easily transported, accurate
**Disadvantages:** Magazine feeding problems
**Popular uses:** Hunting, civilian

**05 TRUE OR FALSE? WILLIAM H. BONNEY WAS NOT HIS REAL NAME**

## BILLY THE KID'S COLT 1873 SINGLE ACTION ARMY

**USA** 1873-1941

**Designers:** William Mason and Charles Brinkerhoff Richards
**Manufacturer:** Colt's Patent Firearms Manufacturing Company
**Number produced:** 357,859
**Muzzle Velocity:** 253 m/s
**Weight:** 2.3 lb (with barrel)

**Caliber:** .45 Colt
**Feed system:** 6-shot cylinder
**Action:** Single-action revolver
**Advantages:** Well balanced, simple to use, good stopping power
**Disadvantages:** Difficult to fire rapidly
**Popular uses:** Military, civilian model

they had holed up in an abandoned house near Stinking Springs, a piece of parched no-man's land where murky water bubbled up into a pool in a depression. It was a few hours before dawn that they made this short ride, which proved their new information true: horses were tied to the rafters outside the building. The Kid was cornered and furthermore, Garrett's approach had not been detected, so they still had the advantage of surprise. The posse split and spread out along the perimeter to play the waiting game in the darkness.

As day broke, one of the gang left the building via its only exit. In the half-light, he appeared to have the height, build, and most importantly, was wearing the characteristic Stetson of Billy the Kid. Knowing the Kid would not give up easily, Garrett signaled to the posse, who peppered the figure with

bullets. Mortally wounded, Charley Bowdre stumbled back into the house, before the Kid pushed him back out with the words: "They have murdered you Charley, but you can still get revenge. Kill some of the sons of bitches before you die." But if the blood hadn't all leaked out of him by then, the fight certainly had, because Bowdre lurched towards the posse and collapsed before he could even get his hand to his pistol.

The jig was up for Garrett, but the Kid's gang was now down to four and their only exit was covered. Just to tip the scales further in his favor, Garrett shot one of the three horses dead to partially cover the exit and then shot the ropes on the other two, both of which promptly cantered away. The marshal felt he was in a position now, to parley: "How you fixed in there, Kid?"

"Pretty well," came the reply, "but we have no wood to get breakfast."

"Come out and get some. Be a little sociable."

"Can't do it, Pat. Business is too confining. No time to run around."

An idea struck Garrett. Having rode through the pre-dawn and played the waiting game in the bitter cold, his men were likewise famished, so he sent for some provisions from Wilcox's ranch; a few hours later, a fire had been built. The sweet scent of roasting meat further weakened the outlaws' resolve until Rudabaugh dangled a filthy handkerchief out of a window in surrender. An eager foursome exited the house to collect the meal that had just cost them their freedom.

Garrett now had his man, but the Kid was as slippery as an eel. They survived a

**06**

**TRUE OR FALSE?**

HE SPOKE
FLUENT
SPANISH

Pat Garrett (left) with
fellow Lincoln County
sheriffs James Brent
and John W. Poe

# EXPERT Q&A

**Robert Stahl**

Robert was a historian,
professor emeritus at
Arizona State University, and
member of the Billy The Kid
Outlaw Gang (BTKOG)—a
non-profit organization with
aim of preserving the truth and promoting
education in the history of Billy the Kid.

**Several theories counter the reports of the
Kid's death with tales of his survival. Why do
you think these tales persist today?**
Number one is that a great many people
who accept the "survival" tale have not
read the histories of the Kid's death by
serious historians, so they are susceptible to
entertaining stories about the Kid not being
killed. Number two is the fact that many people
cannot accept that it was mere coincidence
that Garrett and the Kid were in Pete Maxwell's
bedroom at the same time while believing
the Kid was too smart or too fast on the draw
to allow himself to be killed in the dark as
he was. Number three is the fact that many
documentaries—even those that include
professional historians—bring up the rumors
that the Kid was not killed as though these
rumors have a touch of credibility.

**Is it possible that Garrett could have shot the
wrong man in that darkened room?**
The whole hamlet of more than fifty people
saw the Kid's body once or more during the
morning of his death, as his body was washed
and clothed by local women and was on display
in the saloon for part of the morning. It was
also taken back to Pete Maxwell's bedroom

and placed at or near the spot where the Kid
fell. Not one of the individuals who were there
ever said it was not the Kid. Indeed all went
to their graves, some over fifty years after
the Kid's death, insisting they saw the Kid
dead. Furthermore, six men who knew the
Kid well both in person and on sight served
on the coroner's jury, and all swore it was the
Kid. So there is ample eyewitness support by
numerous credible persons that Garrett did not
kill the wrong man in that darkened room.

**You've been pursuing a death certificate from
the New Mexico Supreme Court for the man
known as "Billy the Kid," for July 15, 1881.
Why wasn't that originally issued? What
would the reason be for the court not to
create the certificate today?**
My colleagues, Dr. Nancy N. Stahl and Marilyn
Stahl Fischer, and I pursued a death certificate
for the Kid because one was never created—
and as part of that certificate we have been
adamant about the fact that it should include
the Kid's actual death date of July 15, 1881 as
opposed to the traditional date of July 14. The
coroner's jury report never stated a time or
date of death, which was typical of the era in
rural areas of the Old West. Furthermore, I
have yet to find a violent death in New Mexico
in the 1800s that was followed by a death

William Henry Roberts claimed to be Billy
the Kid after his death

certificate being created. The Supreme Court
cannot "create" a death certificate, but can
order the state office that can to do its duty
and create one. We went to the Supreme Court
after months of trying to get the Office of the
Medical Investigator to act. They refused to do
their statutory duties and then refused to get
back to us. We had no other legal recourse in
New Mexico other than to go to the Supreme
Court. We supplied credible and substantial
documentary evidence to the Supreme Court
for them to act in our favor, but they have
not issued the court order to the New Mexico
Office of the Medical Investigator for them to
act. We believe that the Supreme Court and the
New Mexico Office of the Medical Investigator
consider our efforts to be publicity stunts
rather than a good faith request by three
historians to correct the historical record.

**The BTKOG seeks to preserve and promote
the truth about the Kid. Is there much in the
way of rumor surrounding the legend you'd
like to quash?**
I do believe that important events in the
current accepted stories of his escape from
the Lincoln County Jail on April 28 need to be
"squashed," such as the notion that he picked
up a gun in the bathroom when he went to
relieve himself and that he intended all along
to kill Bob Olinger. Another that needs to
end immediately is the rumor that there was
widespread belief that Garrett did not kill the
"real" Billy the Kid. Quite the contrary, for more
than three decades after 1881 there were no
stories—not even a hint of a rumor—printed
in even one New Mexico newspaper that
suggested the Kid was still alive. Indeed, at
the time of his death in 1908, Garrett was well
recognized throughout New Mexico and the
nation as the man who killed Billy the Kid. Had
there been any doubt, he would not have been
acclaimed by everyone as the killer of the Kid.

# How the Kid Met his Maker

## A blow-by-blow account of how Pat Garrett sent Billy the Kid to his grave

**07**
**TRUE OR FALSE?**
★ THE KID AND GARRETT WERE FRIENDS ★

**11:55 p.m., 14 July 1881**
The Kid is in one of the run-down houses on Peter Maxwell's property when he decides he's hungry, grabs a knife and makes his way over to Maxwell's house to cut himself some beef.

**Midnight, July 15, 1881**
Garrett has already entered the house himself and goes to the bedroom to speak to Maxwell to glean information on the whereabouts of the Kid. He sits on a chair near his pillow.

**12:04 a.m.**
Garrett's companions are outside when the Kid passes them, but they have no idea what he looks like and this person speaks fluent Spanish to some nearby Mexicans, so they don't identify him.

**12:05 a.m.**
The Kid enters the house. He is barefoot and not wearing his trademark hat. It's dark, so Garrett doesn't recognize him. Garrett stiffens as Maxwell whispers the identity of the man.

**12:05 a.m.**
As the Kid approaches Maxwell, he makes out a second figure in the chair. Garrett pulls his gun and, almost simultaneously, the Kid goes for his own revolver, asking: "Quien es? Quien es?"

**12:05 a.m.**
A heartbeat later, Garret has pulled the trigger and thrown himself to the floor for another shot, but his aim was true. The Kid falls to the floor and barely has time to exhale before he is dead.

lynch mob at Las Vegas before the Kid was tried at Mesilla for the murder of Andrew "Buckshot" Roberts. He was acquitted in March 1881, but was then found guilty of the murder of Sheriff William Brady and sentenced to be hung five weeks later on May 13. Because there was no jail in Lincoln county, he was held in a two-story repurposed warehouse watched by Deputy Sheriff Bell and Deputy Marshal Olinger, where the Kid made the most of a window of opportunity afforded to him by his lackadaisical wardens to steal a gun, kill his guards, and make a spectacular escape from his prison.

Garrett was smarting when he realized his inadequate provision for the incarceration of the Kid and returned to Fort Sumner, where the Kid was believed to have fled, but the trail had once again gone cold. For the next two and a half months, Garrett would be kicking over stones well into the sweltering New Mexico summer before his final encounter with the fugitive.

In early July and in the company of Frank Stewart's replacement, John W. Poe and Thomas K. McKinney, who had been deputized, Garrett could be found a few

miles north of Fort Sumner, adjusting his course according to hearsay and instinct. This took them to the home of Peter Maxwell where, near a row of dilapidated buildings, a slim man in a broad-rimmed hat could be heard talking in Spanish to some Mexicans. They had found their man—but none of the trio recognized him from a distance. As it turned out, the Kid hadn't recognized them either. He slipped off the wall he was perched on and walked casually away to Maxwell's house.

After the stand-off at Stinking Springs and the Kid's dramatic escape from jail, his death seems anticlimactic: just after midnight on July 15, Billy the Kid entered Peter Maxwell's house to pick up some beef for his supper. Garrett was in Pete's darkened bedroom quizzing him on the whereabouts of the Kid when the very man he was hunting stepped through the door. Pete whispered

to Garrett his identity and, leaving nothing to chance, Garrett took two shots, struck the Kid in his left breast, and killed him. In the memoirs he wrote shortly after the inquest that had discharged the marshal of his duty and deemed the homicide justifiable, Garrett dedicates no more than a short paragraph to the unfolding scene in the dark room. There was no classic showdown; the men weren't even aware of each other's presence until those final mortal seconds, and with his last words, it seems Billy the Kid didn't even know who had sent him to meet his maker.

In as much that the Kid's infamy began to spread during the long nothing periods of Garrett's hunt, when rumor of this rebellious young gunslinger and his long-legged lawman nemesis gestated into legend, his ignominious demise has, perhaps fittingly, been made much of by countless authors and Hollywood film makers since.

## The Answer

**01. False**
He was just another nobody outlaw until his escape from Lincoln jail in April 1881 and it wasn't until the 1926 book *The Saga Of Billy The Kid* that the legend really took off.

**02. False**
Several witnesses, including Garrett himself, testified to the death of the Kid that day.

**03. False**
The only authenticated photograph of him had been flipped, so his rifle was shown on the wrong side.

**04. False**
The Kid is thought to have killed nine, five of those in shootouts.

**05. True**
Billy the Kid was actually born as Henry McCarty and Bonney was just another alias.

**06. True**
In the years following former colonial Mexico, Spanish was as common as English.

**07. False**
Although they did know of each other prior to Garrett's deputization and bore each other no ill will.

# WYATT EARP'S WILD WEST

With his own and his family's lives threatened by a murderous band of outlaws, Wyatt Earp took the law into his own hands and formed a posse to track them down, becoming a hunted outlaw himself

Words by Robert Jones

Four gunshots splintered another dry and dusty night in Tombstone, Arizona. A man, wandering from the town's central Crystal Palace Saloon back to the Cosmopolitan Hotel, suddenly felt time slow to a crawl as his back and arm were lit up in a blaze of agonizing pain. The contact of three loads of double-barreled buckshots slammed into him like a runaway freight train. The force of the impact sent him crashing back into the side of the Crystal Palace, with excess shots peppering the saloon's walls and smashing through its windows. In excruciating pain, the fallen man stumbled toward the Cosmopolitan, his blood dripping onto the baked earth. Drawing upon his last reserves of energy, he managed to reach the hotel's entrance and fall through its door—a moment later, everything was black. Across the street on the upper floor of an unfinished building, the assassins slipped away into the night.

The morning after, on December 29, 1881 Tombstone's Deputy Town Marshal Wyatt Earp sent a telegram that read: "Virgil Earp was shot by concealed assassins last night. His wounds are fatal. Telegraph me appointment with power to appoint deputies. Local authorities are doing nothing. The lives of other citizens are threatened. Wyatt Earp."

For weeks, Wyatt, his brothers, and their friends had been receiving death threats for their role in the shootout at the OK Corral, a gunfight that had seen a number of infamous outlaws taken out. The critical condition of his brother Virgil convinced Wyatt that everyone he knew and loved had been marked for death. Unfortunately, while the lawman knew those responsible, he was powerless to act, with the sheriff of Tombstone, Johnny Behan, openly hostile to the Earps. Behan was close friends with William "Curly Bill" Brocius whom Earp believed had his brother's blood on his hands.

The tall, pale, and serious-looking Wyatt, with his rough and gravelly voice, was going over the head of Behan to US Marshal Crawley P. Dake, a man who had the authority to grant Wyatt deputizing powers to assemble a posse capable of bringing the assassins to justice. The question was whether or not Dake would free his hands and if so, how quickly his confirmation would reach Tombstone. With the assassins still at large, the danger to all of the Earps and their friends was at a critical level. Luckily for Wyatt, he soon received a return telegram. In it, Dake officially bestowed deputizing powers on Wyatt and issued a mandate that he was free to pursue the assassins at his discretion.

Back at the Cosmopolitan, local doctor George E. Goodfellow amazingly announced that Virgil would live, although his left arm would be permanently crippled. Upon finally waking from his coma and being told about his crippled arm, Virgil showed the characteristic Earp grit by telling his wife Allie: "Never mind, I've got one arm left to hug you with."

While relieved that his brother had survived, hatred for the assassins had begun to take hold of Wyatt, with him thinking of little other than revenge. He also knew who could help him get it. His old ally Doc Holliday would ride with him, as would his other brother Warren Earp, but for a job like this he needed ruthless professionals. As such, Sherman McMaster and Jack "Turkey Creek" Johnson were first on his list; tough men who had what it takes to kill a man. Joining McMaster and Johnson would be Charles "Hairlip Charlie" Smith and John "Texas Jack" Vermillion—men who had a checkered past but experience of battle.

Three months passed after Virgil's shooting with no major activity. One of the Wild West's greatest lawmen hadn't been idle, though, as by March 18, 1882, he had his posse gathered in Tombstone while his brother Virgil was making his first tentative steps out of his sickbed. It seemed things were falling into place for Wyatt. He just needed to ensure his brother's safe passage out of Arizona and the vendetta ride could begin. However, his plans were shaken to their foundations as the very night Virgil started walking again, his younger brother Morgan was set upon at Tombstone's Campbell & Hatch Billiard Parlor. He was shot through the establishment's window, the bullet shattering his spine and sending him shuddering back into a billiard table. Wyatt rushed to the parlor where he was forced to listen as his brother slowly bled to death. The outlaws had gone after two of his

The vendetta ride posse, June 1883. From left to right: W.H. Harris, Luke Short, Bat Masterson, and seated, Charlie Bassett, Wyatt Earp, Frank McLain and Neal Brown

> "Drawing his .44 Schofield Smith & Wesson revolver from his holster, Wyatt carefully aimed for Stilwell's head and fired a single round"

## Earp's Vendetta Posse
### The gang of men that strutted around the Wild West

### JOHN "DOC" HOLLIDAY
**1851-1887**
A trained dentist, professional gambler, and sharp-shooting gunfighter, Doc Holliday was one of Wyatt Earp's best and oldest friends, famously fighting with him at the shootout at the OK Corral. By the time of his death five years after the vendetta ride, Holliday had survived a total of eight gunfights, killed six men, and wounded countless others.

### JOHN "TEXAS JACK" VERMILLION
**1842-1911**
A close friend of Doc Holliday, Texas Jack was renowned throughout the Old West for his gunfighting abilities and ice cold demeanor when under fire. He played a key role in the closing Iron Springs gunfight of the vendetta ride, fighting fiercely and fearlessly even when his horse was shot dead from under him during the confrontation.

### DAN "TIP" TIPTON
**1844-1898**
An experienced sailor and gambler, Dan Tipton was one of the people present when Wyatt Earp's brother Morgan was assassinated at the Campbell & Hatch Billiard Parlor in Tombstone, Arizona. He rode with Earp for the first part of the vendetta ride, witnessing the gunning down of outlaw Florentino Cruz at Pete Spence's woodcamp.

brothers, injuring one and killing the other. Wyatt swore that those responsible would be brought to justice and that he would be the one to deliver it.

The following day he decided that, regardless of Virgil's still-weak state, he had to get him out of Arizona now or he would be the next to be taken out. At the same time the coroner Dr. D.M. Mather held an inquest into Morgan's death and discovered that Marietta Duarte, the wife of well-known outlaw Pete Spence knew something and was ready to talk, as she had been habitually abused by Spence. Duarte told Matthew that the day before Morgan's assassination she had overheard her husband talking with Florentino "Indian Charlie" Cruz. Apparently, Morgan had walked by and she had heard Spence say to Charlie, "That's him, that's him."

Duarte also said that this same night, Indian Charlie and Frank C. Stilwell came to Spence's house, armed with pistols and carbine rifles, and that they all talked outside for a while in hushed tones. The following morning, when Marietta confronted Spence about the night's activities, she recounted that Spence hit her and threatened to shoot her if she spoke to anyone about what she had heard. Spence, Stilwell, and Cruz were now the prime suspects in Morgan Earp's murder. Duarte was called to testify this in court and did so, Wyatt looking on from the rear of the courthouse. However, thanks to the then-antiquated legal system, Duarte's testimony was dismissed because a spouse could not testify against her husband. Learning of the judge's decision to free the men, Wyatt knew the law could not be relied on to bring the outlaws to justice and realized the only way to put an end to his family's bloodshed would be to kill them all himself.

Before he became a man of the law, Wyatt Earp had several very different jobs, such as a buffalo hunter and saloonkeeper

In the Wild West, saloon bars were often where vendettas were settled

# SHOOTOUT AT THE OK CORRAL

## 01 A THREAT TOO FAR

In the preceding days and weeks running up to the gunfight, dangerous outlaw Ike Clanton had repeatedly threatened the Earp family and their close friend Doc Holliday. Tired of threats, the Earps moved to bring the cowboy and his gang in to jail.

## 06 TOM AND BILLY BLEED OUT

By the time the shooting stopped, Ike Clanton had fled the scene, Frank McLaury lay dead, and Tom McLaury and Billy Clanton were wounded. Despite being moved to a nearby house, both Tom and Billy would bleed out from their wounds.

**When and where did it take place?**
Wednesday, October 26, 1881 in Tombstone, Arizona.

**Who was involved?**
On one side were the Earp brothers Virgil, Morgan, and Wyatt and Doc Holliday. They went up against Billy Claiborne, Ike and Billy Clanton, as well as Tom and Frank McLaury.

**Who died?**
Billy Clanton along with both Tom and Frank McLaury.

**What happened next?**
The fight led to a bitter feud that set in motion the events which would end with Wyatt Earp's vendetta ride.

Tombstone, Arizona, 1881

Arrangements were made to escort Virgil and his wife to the train station in Contention City, which they were to board on March 20 and leave the state. Upon arriving, news was received that Frank C. Stilwell and others were hunting Virgil and waiting in Tucson—the next stop on Virgil's intended trip to California—to murder him. As such, Wyatt and his men remained with Virgil up to Tucson.

After spending a night in a nearby hotel before escorting Virgil and his wife to the train the next morning, Wyatt spotted two figures lying in wait on a nearby flat-car; Frank Stilwell and accomplice Ike Clanton. Years of experience as a lawman mixed in with the culminate rage of months of death, threats, and living in fear and Wyatt Earp ran full speed, shotgun in hand, at the men. Seeing Wyatt and Doc Holliday approaching, Stilwell and Clanton turned to run, but Stilwell tripped and fell. Scrambling around in the dust of the train yard, Stilwell attempted to regain his footing but it was too late; Wyatt was on him. A double-barreled shotgun pointing directly at his chest at point-blank range, Stilwell caught a glimpse of the burning hatred within Wyatt's eyes before both barrels were unloaded into his torso.

## 04 A DOUBLE-BARRELED DEATH

After two opening revolver shots, one from Billy Clanton one from Virgil, the latter hitting Frank McLaury in the stomach, Doc Holliday moved around Tom McLaury's horse and surprised him with a double-barreled shotgun blast. Tom tried to escape down the street but collapsed.

## 03 FAST ON THE DRAW

Upon discovering the cowboys, Virgil Earp shouted, "Throw up your hands, I want your guns!" Frank McLaury and Billy Clanton moved to draw and cock their six-shooters. Virgil yelled, "Hold! I don't mean that!" but it was too late and the shooting began.

## 02 NOT OK

The location of the shootout at the OK Corral was actually not directly at the building, but in a narrow lot six doors west of its rear entrance. When the Earps and the Clanton gang faced off, they were only about six feet from each other.

## 05 MCLAURY GUNNED DOWN

A chaotic exchange of gunfire then occurred, with Billy Clanton shooting Morgan Earp across the back, wounding his shoulder and he himself being hit in the wrist. Frank McLaury exchanged some shots with Doc Holliday but was then shot through the head and killed instantly.

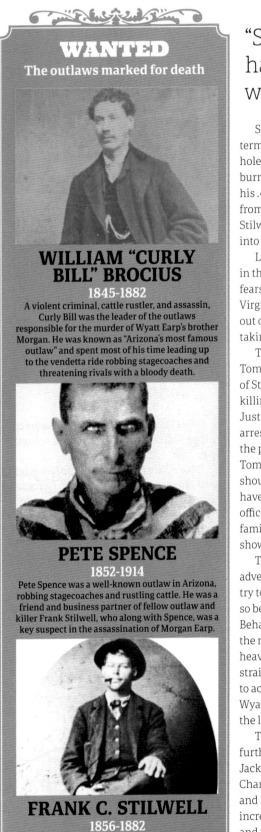

## WILLIAM "CURLY BILL" BROCIUS
### 1845-1882

A violent criminal, cattle rustler, and assassin, Curly Bill was the leader of the outlaws responsible for the murder of Wyatt Earp's brother Morgan. He was known as "Arizona's most famous outlaw" and spent most of his time leading up to the vendetta ride robbing stagecoaches and threatening rivals with a bloody death.

## PETE SPENCE
### 1852-1914

Pete Spence was a well-known outlaw in Arizona, robbing stagecoaches and rustling cattle. He was a friend and business partner of fellow outlaw and killer Frank Stilwell, who along with Spence, was a key suspect in the assassination of Morgan Earp.

## FRANK C. STILWELL
### 1856-1882

A miner and livery stable owner who was known to partake in illegal activities, Stilwell was famously identified as one of the outlaws who had ambushed and murdered Morgan Earp. Lack of evidence saw Stilwell walk free of any punishment, placing him high up on Wyatt Earp's vendetta kill list.

# "Stilwell caught a glimpse of the burning hatred within Wyatt's eyes before both barrels were unloaded into his torso."

Stilwell's short scream was immediately terminated with the blast, with six buckshot holes blown through his body and powder-burnt holes on the back of his coat. Drawing his .44 Schofield Smith & Wesson revolver from his holster, Wyatt carefully aimed for Stilwell's head and then fired a single round into his skull.

Leaving Stilwell's corpse to grow cold in the early morning sun, Wyatt and his fearsome posse watched as the train with Virgil and his wife onboard slowly pulled out of the station, bound for California and taking them to safety.

The gang made their way back to Tombstone but back in Tucson the remains of Stilwell had been discovered and his killing linked to the Earp posse. Tucson Justice of the Peace Charles Meyer issued arrest warrants for all five members of the posse and sent a telegram back to Tombstone, stating that Sheriff Behan should arrest them. What Meyer couldn't have known, however, was that the telegraph office manager was a friend to the Earp family and upon receiving the telegram showed it to Wyatt when he rode into town.

The gunslinger knew that if his old adversary Behan saw the telegram he would try to stop the vendetta posse in its tracks, so began preparing a quick exit. However, Behan had rushed to the hotel and found the men he was looking for in the lobby, heavily armed and about to leave. Walking straight up to Wyatt he told him that he was to accompany him back to the sheriff's office. Wyatt ignored him before walking through the lobby and outside.

They were met outside the hotel by further members of the posse, John "Texas Jack" Vermillion and Dan "Tip" Tipton, Charlie Smith, Fred Dodge, Johnny Green, and Lou Cooley. Continuing to ignore an increasingly irate Behan, they saddled up and rode out of Tombstone.

The following morning, on March 22, Wyatt rode into Spence's woodcamp in the South Pass of the Dragoon Mountains. A quick inspection of the area revealed that Spence wasn't there—in fact, he had become so paranoid that Wyatt was going to kill him that he had handed himself in to Sheriff Behan's custody for protection. Wyatt was unaware of this and so decided to make one final search of the premises to make sure Spence wasn't hiding like the coward he knew he was. He suddenly saw movement, a figure running out to the rear and diving into the scrub. It wasn't Spence though, it was Florentino "Indian Charlie" Cruz, Spence's right-hand man.

Wyatt drew his pistol but couldn't get a clear shot, so he called for his men. Holliday, McMaster, and Johnson were the fastest, drawing and firing from multiple positions at the fleeing Cruz, who was hit simultaneously in the arm, thigh, and pelvis, bringing him crashing into the dust. Cruz's cries of anguish echoed throughout the pass as he started to bleed out, all the time attempting to crawl into cover. Wyatt was on him, quick as a flash though and Cruz started begging for his life. When questioned about the assassination of Morgan, he confessed that he had been the lookout. As Wyatt pressed down on Cruz's wound with his spurred boot, a scream curdled out of Cruz into the pass and he shouted the names of the killers. William "Curly Bill" Brocius. Frank Stilwell. Hank Swilling. Johnny Ringo. As he said each name, a death sentence was passed on them.

Cruz started shouting that Wyatt had got what he wanted and he should leave him alive and send him back to Tombstone. Drawing his pistol, Wyatt placed it to the side of the assassin's head and, punctuated only by a final scream from Cruz, pulled the trigger. A single trail of gunsmoke from his pistol rose slowly into the air. One down, three to go.

So, it had been Brocius who had orchestrated the murder. He should have known that his old enemy from the OK Corral was the mastermind behind his family's enduring misery. Wyatt and his posse saddled up their mounts and headed straight for Brocius' old prowling ground, the Whetstone Mountains.

OK Corral casualties—Tom and Frank McLaury and Billy Clanton in their coffin after being killed at the famous gunfight

# Law and Order-Wild West Style

### Was there any system of justice in the Wild West?

A key player not just in Wyatt Earp's vendetta ride but also the famous shootout at the OK Corral, Johnny Behan was the sheriff of Cochise County in Arizona Territory during both. After the climactic gunfight at the Corral, Behan famously testified against the Earp family, saying they precipitated the shootout and therefore murdered three outlaw cowboys in the encounter. The Earps were later exonerated, however, and so started a bitter feud between them and Behan.

While he was known to think himself a model of law and order, Behan in fact had a checkered life, with his wife leaving him in June 1875 for taking a mistress and sleeping with prostitutes. He was also particularly violent toward women, threatening them consistently, both verbally and physically. Behan also liked to associate and deal with

Behan was stripped of his rank soon after the Wyatt's vendetta ride

known outlaws while off official business, dealing with cowboys such as Ike Clanton, Johnny Ringo, and William Brocius, all three of whom were instrumental in the maiming of Virgil Earp and the murder of Morgan Earp.

Following Behan's famous confrontation with Wyatt Earp in the Cosmopolitan Hotel, Tombstone, and then failed pursuit of Wyatt and his vendetta posse, Behan fell into another feud with his own deputy Billy Breakenridge. Breakenridge accused Behan of misappropriation of illegal monies and after an investigation Behan was shown to have set aside $5,000 from unknown sources while sheriff. While Behan escaped jail, he failed to be renominated as sheriff of Cochise County and was stripped of his rank and authority months after Wyatt left the state.

The posse searched the surrounding area for the next two days, to no avail, eventually arriving at Iron Springs in the Whetstone Mountains. The area looked to be empty when the posse stumbled onto a group of cowboys cooking dinner alongside the spring. It took only a split-second for Wyatt to identify Brocius and, in a heartbeat, he dismounted from his horse, grabbed his double-barreled shotgun, and burst around a ridge and down into the men's camp with Texas Jack, Doc Holliday, and McMaster hot on his heels. Wyatt walked toward Brocius purposefully, trench coat flapping behind him in the wind.

Panic broke loose in the camp, with the outlaws all scrambling for their weapons. Like a rattlesnake, Brocius weaved to his own shotgun and turned and fired at the advancing Wyatt, but missed the avenging town marshal. Texas Jack, who was sticking closely to Wyatt, drew his dual pistols and

Before he became a lawman, Wyatt Earp was one of the co-owners of the Oriental Saloon

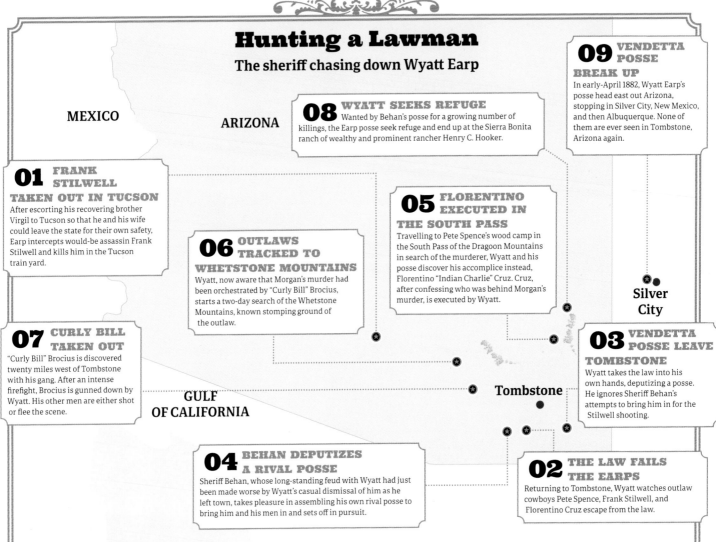

# Hunting a Lawman
## The sheriff chasing down Wyatt Earp

MEXICO

ARIZONA

**09 VENDETTA POSSE BREAK UP**
In early-April 1882, Wyatt Earp's posse head east out Arizona, stopping in Silver City, New Mexico, and then Albuquerque. None of them are ever seen in Tombstone, Arizona again.

**08 WYATT SEEKS REFUGE**
Wanted by Behan's posse for a growing number of killings, the Earp posse seek refuge and end up at the Sierra Bonita ranch of wealthy and prominent rancher Henry C. Hooker.

**01 FRANK STILWELL TAKEN OUT IN TUCSON**
After escorting his recovering brother Virgil to Tucson so that he and his wife could leave the state for their own safety, Earp intercepts would-be assassin Frank Stilwell and kills him in the Tucson train yard.

**06 OUTLAWS TRACKED TO WHETSTONE MOUNTAINS**
Wyatt, now aware that Morgan's murder had been orchestrated by "Curly Bill" Brocius, starts a two-day search of the Whetstone Mountains, known stomping ground of the outlaw.

**05 FLORENTINO EXECUTED IN THE SOUTH PASS**
Travelling to Pete Spence's wood camp in the South Pass of the Dragoon Mountains in search of the murderer, Wyatt and his posse discover his accomplice instead, Florentino "Indian Charlie" Cruz. Cruz, after confessing who was behind Morgan's murder, is executed by Wyatt.

Silver City

**07 CURLY BILL TAKEN OUT**
"Curly Bill" Brocius is discovered twenty miles west of Tombstone with his gang. After an intense firefight, Brocius is gunned down by Wyatt. His other men are either shot or flee the scene.

GULF OF CALIFORNIA

Tombstone

**03 VENDETTA POSSE LEAVE TOMBSTONE**
Wyatt takes the law into his own hands, deputizing a posse. He ignores Sheriff Behan's attempts to bring him in for the Stilwell shooting.

**04 BEHAN DEPUTIZES A RIVAL POSSE**
Sheriff Behan, whose long-standing feud with Wyatt had just been made worse by Wyatt's casual dismissal of him as he left town, takes pleasure in assembling his own rival posse to bring him and his men in and sets off in pursuit.

**02 THE LAW FAILS THE EARPS**
Returning to Tombstone, Wyatt watches outlaw cowboys Pete Spence, Frank Stilwell, and Florentino Cruz escape from the law.

An illustration of Wyatt Earp winning a duel in Dodge City

# "Drawing his pistol, he placed it to the side of the assassin's head and, punctuated only by a final scream, pulled the trigger"

began firing at the outlaws. Brocius' men began firing back, rounds hitting Wyatt's coat and even Texas Jack's horse, which was killed instantly. Doc Holliday, McMaster and Johnson moved to cover and started shooting; while Texas Jack, after exhausting all the rounds in his pistols, dashed to his fallen horse in an attempt to retrieve his rifle.

During the chaos, Wyatt Earp had never taken his eyes off Brocius and calmly advanced on the killer. Time slowed and, with an unshakable purpose, Wyatt raised his shotgun, aimed directly at Brocius at point-blank range, and watched as his brother's killer was blown in two. Seeing their leader dead, the rest of Brocius' party fled for their lives, but not before Wyatt had continued his vengeful rampage by killing Johnny Barnes with a gunshot round to the chest and wounding Milt Hicks with another shot.

The rest of Wyatt Earp's vendetta ride ran its course in the only way it could. Wanted by the law, Wyatt and his posse could not return to Tombstone. As such, after making a couple of stops at safe houses, most of his posse headed east out of Arizona, riding out of the state. Behan never did catch them and after arriving in Albuquerque, New Mexico, they went their separate ways. Vengeance had been delivered with a efficiency and brutality that would permanently affect the lives of all the men involved and cement their reputation as legendary figures. Justice—Wild West Style—had been served.

# 10 DEADLIEST GUNSLINGERS IN THE WEST

## JAMES "WILD BILL" HICKOK
### 1837-1876

Wild Bill Hickok—real name James Butler Hickok—was the best sharpshooter and gunfighter of his day. Famously, Hickok was involved in the first-ever recorded quick-draw duel, with him gunning down a gambler called Davis Tutt Jr. in the town square of Springfield, Missouri. Hickok is also recorded as shooting an outlaw called David McCanles with a single bullet from 225 feet away—a remarkable achievement with pistols of that time.

### KILLS: 36
**Did he ride off into the sunset?** Hickok was shot through the back of the head by gambler Jack McCall while playing five-card draw at Nuttal & Mann's Saloon in Deadwood, Dakota Territory.

## BILLY THE KID
### 1859-1881

The gunslinger—real name William H. Bonney—killed many men during his short lifetime, with many saying it was twenty-one, one kill for each year of his life. Often depicted as a bloodthirsty raving killer of a man, surviving testimony from people who knew him said in reality he just repeatedly ended up on the wrong side of the tracks, killing other men who were worse than himself. Regardless, due to his excellent marksmanship and wily nature, Billy became infamous across the USA, something only exacerbated by a daring escape from jail and years spent on the run.

### KILLS: 15-26
**Did he ride off into the sunset?** Bonney was shot dead by Sheriff Pat Garrett on July 14, 1881.

## JOHN WESLEY HARDIN
### 1853-1895

Hardin had his first kill registered at the tender age of fifteen and his life consisted of a series of run-ins with outlaws and lawmen alike. While Hardin was known as a good shot, it was his cunning in combat that earned him a deadly reputation, often killing men after confrontations in cold-blooded, unseen ways. His most famous kill was Sheriff John Helms on August 1, 1873. Hardin was eventually captured and spent seventeen years in Huntsville Prison before being released on February 17, 1894.

### KILLS: 27-42
**Did he ride off into the sunset?** Hardin was shot through the back of the head in the Acme Saloon, Texas, by lawman John Selman Sr. on August 19, 1895.

"Within one year, Stoudenmire had killed six men in shootouts and executed a would-be assassin"

## KING FISHER
### 1854-1884

Fisher was a celebrated gunslinger, racking up double-digit kills by the age of thirty. He was known to carry twin ivory-handled pistols and to dress in bright-colored clothes. His most memorable trait, though, was his brutality in combat. The most famous example of this was in his fight with a rival bunch of Mexican cowboys, clubbing one to death with a branding iron, outdrawing and shooting another and then executing the remaining two.

### KILLS: 14
**Did he ride off into the sunset?** Fisher was shot thirteen times in an ambush at the Vaudeville Variety Theater by Jacob Coy and Joe Foster.

## TOM HORN
### 1860-1903

Horn was at one time a lawman, scout, soldier, hired gunman, assassin, and outlaw, fluidly shifting from one side of the law to the other. During his eventful life, Horn reportedly garnered fame for his tracking abilities, bringing many outlaws to justice and then, once his appetite for blood became too problematic—he was linked to the unlawful murder of seventeen people—he had to turn to mercenary work, fulfilling contract killings with brutal efficiency. His legacy of murder only came to a close when he was captured after his killing of a 14-year-old boy in 1901.

### KILLS: 35-50

**Did he ride off into the sunset?** Horn was captured, tried, and hanged in Cheyenne, Wyoming, on November 20, 1903.

## CHEROKEE BILL
### 1876-1896

The outlaw actually called Crawford Goldsby was known for his fast and itchy trigger finger. In a period of two years from the age of eighteen, Bill along with his gang robbed, pillaged, maimed, and killed anyone who stood in their way, with Goldsby earning the reputation of one of the meanest outlaws of the Old West. Goldsby even shot and killed his own brother-in-law Mose Brown in an argument over a simple bunch of hogs. Despite the terror he inflicted, two years later he was caught and imprisoned, later going on to hang for his various crimes.

### KILLS: 7

**Did he ride off into the sunset?** At the age of just twenty, Goldsby was hanged as a convicted murderer at Fort Smith, Arkansas.

## JESSE JAMES
### 1847-1882

Along with his brother Frank, Jesse led a gang that robbed banks, trains, and stagecoaches. Before turning to crime, Jesse had been a guerilla fighter in the Confederate Army, but when the Union triumphed in the American Civil War, he was left disenchanted. James famously shot a clerk while holding up the Daviess County Savings Association bank in Gallatin, Missouri, living permanently on the run along with his gang from the event until his death. After James' death, rumors spread that he had survived, but there is no evidence to suggest this was true. Frank James, on the other hand, slipped the noose, living to the age of seventy-two and dying years later in 1915.

### KILLS: 1-5

**Did he ride off into the sunset?** James was shot through the back of the head by fellow outlaw Robert Ford—who hoped to cash in on his bounty—on April 3, 1882.

## JIM "KILLER" MILLER
### 1866-1909

Legend has it that Miller survived more duels than any other person. The most famous duel was with Pecos Sheriff George A. "Bud" Frazer, where Miller was set on by Frazer and shot four times in the chest. He gang rushed him to a doctor where it was revealed he had been wearing a steel plate under his clothes across his chest, which saved his life. Two years later, he tracked Frazer down and executed him with a shotgun.

### KILLS: 14

**Did he ride off into the sunset?** Miller was dragged from prison and hanged by a lynch mob on April 19, 1909.

## DALLAS STOUDENMIRE
### 1845-1882

Stoudenmire was one of the most feared gunslingers of his day, with him ruling the rough and violent city of El Paso, Texas, with an iron fist. Shortly after arriving in El Paso, Stoudenmire would be involved in one of the most famous gunfights of the American Old West—the Four Dead in Five Seconds shootout. Within one year, Stoudenmire had killed six men in shootouts and executed a would-be assassin—the latter sent to his death with eight gunshot wounds.

### KILLS: 10

**Did he ride off into the sunset?** His luck ran out in 1882 when he was killed in a shootout.

## ROBERT CLAY ALLISON
### 1840-1887

While Allison did not rack up the largest body count in the Old West, the way in which he killed was brutal. Allison cut the head off a man and displayed it on a pole outside a saloon, hung another publicly after gunning him down over a minor disagreement and executed many others with point-blank headshots. On January 7, 1874,, Allison accepted an invitation to eat with a known gunman called Chunk Colbert, despite knowing that Colbert was trying to kill him. While eating the meal, Colbert tried to draw on Allison, however, he was too slow and shot through the head by Clay.

### KILLS: 6

**Did he ride off into the sunset?** Allison fell from a wagon and broke his neck on July 3, 1887.

# THE CLOSING OF THE AMERICAN FRONTIER

When the director of the US Census Bureau announced the "closing of the frontier" in 1890, the Wild West lost its wildness

Words by Dominic Green

When the thirteen colonies of British-Americans declared their independence in 1776, the territory of the new American nation lay entirely between the Atlantic coast and the Appalachian foothills. The adventurous and the heavily armed might enter the Ohio Valley, a wild terrain of forests and Native tribes, but the vast tracts of the Great Plains and the Far West were pretty much obscure to European settlers, and avoided as the "Great American Desert."

Nor was the new American government the only government on the North American continent. The British ruled in Canada. The French ruled the southern territories around the Mississippi Delta. The Spanish ruled in Florida and, through their empire in Mexico, in the future states of California and Texas.

The "pioneer spirit" is a legend, grounded in two distinct facts. The United States of America were created by the settlement of immigrants from Europe and emigrants from the cities of the eastern seaboard. Their "frontier" was the furthest limit of settlement, the last farm in a chain of settlement reaching hundreds of miles back to the first settlements of Jamestown, Virginia

and Plymouth, Massachusetts. The United States were also created as a political ideal, sprung from a written constitution. For the government, the "frontier" was a legal and political boundary.

These two "frontiers" did not align until 1890. In the December of that year, the US Census Bureau announced that the frontier line, which had been inching west ever since the first European settlement, had disappeared. The frontier had dissolved into the Pacific Ocean, or met up with the extant borders of California, Oregon, and Washington. The Census Bureau also noted that no further tracts of land remained beyond the authority of the government in Washington, D.C., and that the population density of the United States now stood at two people per square mile.

The frontier was closed. This was a watershed in American history, and in Americans' understanding of themselves. The previous three centuries had seen the gradual expansion of European settlement from the Atlantic coast, over the Appalachian Hills, into the Old Northwest and the Mississippi Valley, and on to the Plains, the Old Southwest, and the Far West. Americans

had built their ideal selves in the image of these facts. The values of the pioneer were individualism, toughness, and self-sufficiency, a rough democracy that defined itself by opposition to European manners.

The United States changed dramatically in the half-century between the War of 1812 and the outbreak of the Civil War in 1861. As the populations of the eastern states rose through immigration from Europe, waves of emigrants set off west in search of arable land. The government in Washington, D.C. laid the ground for settlement in advance, by negotiating the expansion of the frontier for cash.

In the Louisiana Purchase of 1803, the US government paid $15 million for more than 800,000 square miles of French-held territory; at present value, a bargain at around a $250 billion. In 1818, Britain and the US agreed to a "joint occupation" of the Oregon territory, in the Pacific Northwest. In the Transcontinental Treaty of 1819, the Spanish ceded Florida and their claim to Texas. In the 1820s, Russia acknowledged that its claim to Alaska stopped at Alaska's current southern boundary.

Between 1865 and 1890, more than half a million Black "freedmen" and their families moved to the frontier territories

A prairie schooner on the Blue Mountain Crossing of the Oregon Trail, now part of a National Park

The economic depression of 1837 sent a sudden wave of emigrants west with "Oregon Fever." The 2,759-mile Overland Trail began at Independence, Missouri, crossed the Great Plains to the Continental Divide, and entered the Far West via the South Pass of the Rocky Mountains. From there, the wagon trains of "prairie schooners" headed north to Oregon or south to California. Some 300,000 people made the six-month journey in the decades before the Civil War. Most were young families, but young men, hoping to find a fortune in the gold fields, were disproportionately represented.

By the 1840s, there were ten American settlers in the Oregon Territory for every British settler, and the government in Washington, D.C. was asking the British to renegotiate the "joint occupation." Meanwhile, the populism and agricultural economy that had underpinned "'Jacksonian democracy," named after President Andrew Jackson, became an industrial economy split by debates over slavery and the emancipation of women. This optimistic "Age of Reform" ensured that America's democratic experiment had not only survived, but was prospering. America's resources, including the vast expanses of land in the west and the constant flow of immigrants from Europe, would continue to allow its further development from a peripheral state into a world super power.

The "Expansionists" realized that the settlement of the west was absolutely essential for the fulfilment of this vision. They also viewed it as the continuation of America's original vision, which was the expansion across the continent of self-government and democratic institutions. This universal vision would frequently draw upon convictions of religious and racial superiority. The language of Expansionism identified America's destiny with the Protestantism and Anglo-Saxon origins of the early settlers. In the settling of the west, God's will was made manifest.

In 1845, John L O'Sullivan, the editor of the *United States Magazine and Democratic Review*, pinpointed this particular brew of ambition, hope and bigotry. It was, O'Sullivan wrote, "the fulfilment of our manifest destiny to overspread the continent allotted

Between 1866 and 1888, cowboys herded more than forty million longhorn cattle from the ranges to the railheads

Last of the cowboys: Austin, Texas, 1915

## "This optimistic "Age of Reform" ensured that America's democratic experiment had not only survived, but was prospering"

by Providence for the free development of our yearly multiplying millions."

Manifest Destiny was not a prescription for government policy, so much as a description of what was already taking place. By the early 1840s, the final lineaments of the American frontier territories were key electoral issues, capable of making a president or breaking a party. In 1840, when President John Tyler announced his support for annexing the self-declared Republic of Texas, where thousands of Americans had now settled, Tyler's Whig party supporters deserted him.

When big ranchers fenced off grazing lands, small farmers fought back in the Fence Cutters' War of 1883-84

The presidential election of 1844 turned on the annexation of Texas, and the status of the Oregon Territory. The Democratic Party's nomination contest between former president Martin Van Buren, who opposed annexing Texas, and Tennessee senator James Polk, who advocated for pushing America's borders southwest towards the Rio Grande, ended in a victory for Polk and Manifest Destiny.

In December 1844, one of outgoing President Tyler's last acts in office was to engineer a pro-annexation resolution from both houses of Congress. In March

1845, one of incoming President Polk's first acts in office was to order American troops southwest to the Nueces River. In May 1846, Polk declared war on Mexico.

The Whigs divided yet again over "Mr. Polk's War." Abolitionists in the Northeast were appalled that Polk was willing to incorporate the slaveholders of Texas into the Union without requiring them to free their slaves. Since the Missouri Compromise of 1820, abolitionist states and slaveholding states had agreed to disagree, but Polk now proposed to tip the balance in favor of the slaveholders, as the price of pushing the frontier west.

In Concord, Massachusetts, Henry David Thoreau, the author of "Civil Disobedience," refused to pay his poll tax, and deliberately sought to spend a night in the town jail; a model of nonviolent resistance that would inspire subsequent pacifists like Tolstoy, Gandhi, and Martin Luther King. The general public, however, approved of Mr. Polk's War.

'The United States will conquer Mexico," Thoreau's mentor Ralph Waldo Emerson warned, "but it will be as the man swallows the arsenic, which brings him down in turn." The Treaty of Guadalupe-Hidalgo, imposed upon a defeated Mexico in February 1848, was a

Horace Greeley, the newspaperman who may have coined the phrase, "Go West, young man"

## Fifty-Four Degrees, Forty Minutes, or Fight!

### How the British and the Americans nearly came to blows over territory

The Americans and the British fought two wars, the War of Independence (1776-1783) and the War of 1812. In the 1840s, they nearly came to blows for a third time over the Oregon Territory.

Under the "joint occupation" agreement of 1818, the border between British-ruled Canada and the United States was fixed at the 49th Parallel from the Lake of the Woods in the Minnesota Territory to the Rocky Mountains. The British had wanted the rest of the border to follow the Columbia River west to the Pacific, but the Americans had wanted the border to follow the 49th Parallel. Unable to agree, the negotiators had agreed to wait ten years. In 1827, they agreed to disagree again, permanently postponing the issue.

In the early 1840s, American immigration into the Oregon Territory caused a crisis. In Congress, there were calls for war, and pushing the border north: "Fifty-four degrees, forty minutes, or fight!" In 1846, President Polk proposed the 49th Parallel as the border, and the British accepted, with minor modifications, including the passing of Vancouver Island to Canada.

A subsequent dispute over the Juan de Fuca Strait, where the Salish Sea reaches the Pacific Ocean, was resolved by international arbitration. The current Canadian-American frontier runs down the middle of the 94-mile-long strait. The Canadians dislike the results of the arbitration, but are wary of reopening another border dispute, far to the east in the Gulf of Maine.

James Polk, 11th president and resolver of the Oregon Territory border dispute

victory for Manifest Destiny, but one with extensive consequences.

The Whigs never truly recovered from their split over Texas, and rapidly dissolved into the Republican and Democratic parties. The entry into the Union of the slaveholders of Texas pushed the country further towards civil war. And with settlers already rushing west to the California Gold Rush, the Treaty of Guadalupe-Hidalgo opened the ultimate prize—California—to the United States' government.

The population boom that followed the Gold Rush led to California joining the Union in 1850. The discovery of gold at Pike's Peak, Colorado in 1858 drew another 100,000 would-be miners to Colorado. Though few made their fortune and many died in the attempt, the miners were to accelerate Colorado's entry into the Union in 1876. Miners also flocked to extract silver from the "blue earth" of Nevada, which entered the Union in 1864.

The Civil War shaped the future of American politics. The future of the American frontier was shaped in the midst of the Civil War, when Abraham Lincoln's administration passed the Homestead Act of 1862. This guaranteed up to 160 acres of land in the Great Plains to any farmer who staked a claim. After six months on the land, the farmer would have the right to buy his land

Utah became a state in 1896, after the Mormons had agreed to abandon polygamy

The golden spike: completing the Transcontinental Railroad at Promotory, Utah, 1869

# The American Dream—or Dreams?

The world knows the American Dream when it sees it, but in truth there have been several American Dreams. The phrase derives from the 1950s, and the affluence of the postwar Eisenhower era. The content, however, might describe any era of American history, from the first settlement to the present day.

The first Europeans in America dreamed of wealth, the profits of trading in silver, gold, and furs. So did the indentured laborers who contracted themselves to commercial ventures for ten or twenty years. The Puritans who arrived on the Mayflower in 1620, however, dreamed of religious freedom, and the opportunity to build an ideal community. These are the two contrasting ideals at the very heart of the American Dream.

The Constitution of the United States manages to neatly combine both ideals, by promising "life, liberty, and the pursuit of happiness." The precursor to this phrase comes from the English philosopher John Locke, who thought that the government should ensure the "life, liberty, and property" of its subjects, but not much more. The belief that owning property might make you happier remains strong in Anglo-Saxon and Protestant countries. Almost all Americans own their own homes, and home ownership is much more common in Britain and Scandinavia than in southern Europe.

Dream imagery recurs in modern American politics, too. "I have a dream," Martin Luther King said, as he campaigned for racial equality. When Ronald Reagan campaigned for the presidency in 1980 on a promise of economic revival, he revived a Puritan image of America as "a shining city on a hill." More recently, when Barack Obama tried to legalize the status of the children of undocumented immigrants, he called his proposal the Development, Relief, and Education for Alien Minors Act: the DREAM Act.

A 1956 Cadillac Coupe de Ville symbolizes the American Dream—and American restlessness

Big Foot's camp after the massacre at Wounded Knee in 1890, the year that the frontier closed

---

from the government at $1.25 per acre. If the farmer lived on it for five years, he received the title for free.

The Homestead Act sparked a wave of westward emigration from easterners seeking to escape the Civil War. The end of the Civil War saw a further wave, this time of "freedmen;" Southern Blacks who had been freed from slavery.

When the war ended, Horace Greeley, editor of the *New-York Tribune*, issued orders to the next waves of emigrants: "Go West, young man."

The frontier territory, already contracting through settlement and the creation of new states, was further condensed by a second initiative of 1862. At the time, the railroad network ran from the eastern cities to the eastern bank of the Missouri River. From there, settlers crossed the Great American Desert, the Great Plains, by wagon. Lincoln's government recognized that none of America's railroad companies could afford to lay a railroad across the Great American Desert, so it hired two companies to complete the Transcontinental Railroad.

The Union Pacific company was engaged to lay 1,085 miles of track west from the Missouri River, across the Great Plains, and over the Rockies. The Central Pacific company was engaged to lay 688 miles of track running east from Sacramento in California, up to the Sierra Nevada Mountains. On May 10, 1869, Leland Stanford, governor of California, conducted the "wedding of the rails" at Promontory, Utah, and completed the railway by nailing a golden spike.

Soon, further railroads were built, crisscrossing the country. The railroads shaped the final development of the frontier. Farms and towns popped up along the lines. The mining industry grew, as the trains ferried ore back to the east for processing. The government's reach extended, because communications had accelerated—the telegraph cable soon snaked alongside the railroad lines—and because troops could be moved quickly across the country.

The railroad companies had extracted favorable terms from a government caught in a civil war. For each mile of track it laid on level ground, each company received $16,000 and a further 6,400 acres of federal land. In the following decades, the "robber barons" of the railroads profited further by selling their land to settlers, or fencing off huge areas for sheep and cattle ranching. The "open range" was closing. In 1873, Joseph Glidden invented a cheap way of fencing off the huge ranches that grew up after the railroad—barbed wire.

The railroad made and unmade the cowboy. Cattle had to be herded from their ranges in Texas and the Plains to the giant stockyards which sprung up at the new railheads. From there, the cattle were shipped east in railroad cars. After the Civil War, some 40,000 ex-soldiers found new work as cowboys, driving herds of as many as 10,000 cattle to the stockyards. The Chisholm

Frederick Jackson Turner, historian of the closing of the frontier

The railroad companies tripled their profits to $48,000 per mile in mountainous areas

Interior of a shack built in Kansas after the Homestead Act of 1862

Nevada is known as "The Silver State" because of the silver and gold discovered there in 1856

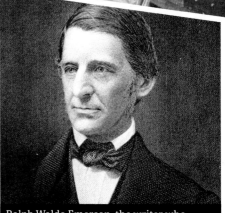

Ralph Waldo Emerson, the writer who warned that extending the frontier into Texas would cause civil war

Trail ran 500 miles, from central Texas to Abilene, Kansas. The Western Trail to Dodge City was shorter, but the Goodnight-Loving Trail, from Central Texas to New Mexico to Cheyenne, Wyoming, was a whopping 700 miles.

As the railroad network grew, the trails got shorter. After the invention of the refrigerated railroad car in the 1870s, cattle were slaughtered at the closest railhead, or at Kansas City and Chicago. The cowboy, that hero of the frontier, was heading for the sunset. So was another fixture of frontier mythology; the Pony Express courier. And while the railroad gave a last burst of glory to the cowboys, it was simply fatal for the Natives.

The Native Americans had already been pushed west with each stage of White emigration. The US government, always susceptible to pressure from public opinion back east, and often so weak in the frontier territories that it was not able to fulfil its good intentions, was complicit with the violent extirpation of the Native Americans from their ancestral lands. The survivors were corralled into reservations. These were reserved because White settlers could not

Union Pacific laborers were mostly Irish immigrants and ex-soldiers. Central Pacific laborers were mostly Chinese immigrants

find a use for the land. In cases where the settlers did find a use—a gold rush in South Dakota, for instance—the Natives were forced to move again.

The Oklahoma Land Rush of 1899 was the last wave of emigration before the frontier officially closed. At noon on April 22, 1889, more than 50,000 men, women, and children stampeded on wagons and horseback into two million acres of former Native Territory in central Oklahoma. In the same year, South Dakota, North Dakota, Montana, and Washington entered the Union. Idaho and Wyoming followed in 1890.

When Frederick Jackson Turner, a young historian at the University of Wisconsin, heard that the Census Bureau now considered the frontier closed, he realized that a chapter of American history had closed too. In 1893, Jackson Turner read a paper to the American Historical Association, entitled "The Significance of the Frontier in American History."

The idea of the frontier, as a lived fact and a legal fact, had shaped not just America's internal and external borders. It had shaped the experiences of those Americans who had "gone West" to seek their fortune or to

seek a living diet from the soil. It had also shaped the experiences of those who had remained "back east," for distance did not weaken their zeal for expansion. The frontier, Turner believed, had been the zone in which the ideal of the American character had been shaped and tested.

Frontier life encouraged democracy, practicality, and what Emerson called "self-reliance." For the same reasons, the frontier also encouraged contempt for high culture, and a dependency on violence. American democracy, Turner argued, was "born of no theorist's dream." It came "out of the American forest."

American democracy retained the ideal of the frontier, even as the United States became the world power of the 20th century. The internal empire of the Plains, the Southwest, and the Far West had been conquered. New frontiers would be found outside America's borders in the imperial conquest of Cuba in 1898, and in President Kennedy's exhortation that the United States beat the Soviet Union in the "space race" of the 1960s. As the voiceover of a popular television series said, space could be America's final frontier, an end to the restless expansion that had defined its history.

128

132

128

# LEGACY OF THE FRONTIER

# DEALING WITH THE NATIVE PROBLEM

The American frontier had a problem—Native Americans. But Richard Henry Pratt had a plan; turn them into White Americans. The school he created to do it attracted praise, disdain, and widespread controversy

Words by Frances White

Ever since White Europeans arrived in North America, their relationship with Native Americans has been complex, unstable, and plagued with broken promises. While initially Europeans worked alongside Native Americans, trading fur and other goods, and also filling the ranks of their armies with Natives, over time the relationship grew into one that was contemptuous and fractured. Europe promised to honor the tribe's traditional lands and independence in return for their help, but European governments gradually secured control of more and more territories from Native Americans. This dramatically changed the lives of the Native Americans within these lands, completely disrupting ways of lives that had lasted centuries.

The United States followed the European precedent, teaming up with the Native Americans when it benefitted them, but immediately abandoning their good relations when they needed to absorb their lands. This was especially the case as the American frontier moved west. To put it simply, the Native Americans were in the way of expansion, so their needs, traditions, and ways of life were deemed unimportant. Promises were forgotten and American expansion became the paramount consideration. Once the Native Americans had served their purpose, the wooing period was over, and they became an obstacle to the all-important, ever-expanding frontier.

George Washington was the first to come up with a policy to "civilize" the Native Americans, and in 1830 the Indian Removal Act relocated tribes east of the Mississippi river to the west. While this was supposed to be voluntary, the system was abused by government officials, forcing entire tribes to relocate outside their ancestral lands against their will. When the Cherokee tribe was forced to relocate in 1838, 4,000 Cherokees died in the resulting protests and march, now known as the Trail of Tears. Tensions and relations between White and Native Americans were beyond stretched. Many Americans began to believe the Native Americans were a different breed of human, who had no place or purpose in White American society, unable to break free of their "savage" roots. But not all agreed.

Richard Henry Pratt was one of these people. He was a man with a mission. He wanted to prove

Some regard the forced cultural assimilation of Pratt's school as a form of cultural genocide

Pratt is credited with the first recorded use of the word 'racism'

## "The idea of using education to assimilate Natives into White culture was, at the time, seen as 'saving' the suffering race"

that Native Americans were equal to Whites. A revolutionary attitude for his time, he believed that all humans, Native American or otherwise, were born a blank slate, of which any number of morals or skills could be imprinted. "Transfer the savage-born infant to the surroundings of a civilization and he will grow to possess a civilized language and habit." In laymen's terms, Pratt believed that the Natives had it in them to abandon their "savage" roots and reach the dizzying heights of European society and culture.

Pratt did not just believe the words he said, he set about proving them. At Fort Marion he gathered Native American prisoners and began teaching them English language, art, guard duty, and craftmanship. When the lessons actually proved successful, the government was stunned—Natives could learn the skills used by White men. It is easy to see how lowly the government regarded the Natives, as well-known and distinguished men from around the country actually began to visit the makeshift school to marvel at the wonder of being able to transform a "savage" into a contributing member of society. With the

US commissioner of education impressed with his work, Pratt became convinced that "distant education" was the best way to educate the Natives, and he lobbied Congress to allow him to prove it on a greater scale. "Give me 300 young Indians," he said, "and let me prove it." Congress didn't quite give him 300 but 147 was enough, and the Carlisle Indian Industrial School was born.

Founded at the old barracks in Carlisle, Pennsylvania, the Carlisle school took in a huge variety of pupils, although obviously all Native American. Their ages varied from just six years old to twenty-five, and the vast majority were the children of Plains Indian tribal leaders from Lakota, Cheyenne, Kiowa, Pawnee, and Apache. The aim of the school aligned with Pratt's own beliefs—he wanted to immerse the Native children completely in White culture. They would be taught English, not only in language, but also in skills and customs to enable them to survive in the White European world that was developing and progressing around them.

Looking at this today, this attitude seems drastic and bordering on racist, but it is important to consider the situation at the

time. Native American tribes, especially the Lakota, were suffering greatly after their defeat in the Great Sioux War in 1877. Their land had been taken, the people were confined to reservations, living an impoverished life. There was real fear that the entire race of people would be completely gone in a matter of decades, dubbing them a "vanishing race." The US government could not contemplate or see a way that Native Americans could live in White America and still keep their cultural identities. The only hope, many believed, was cultural transformation, and this had to happen quickly. The idea of using education to assimilate Natives into White culture was, at the time, seen as "saving" the suffering race, and Pratt likely thought the Carlisle school was their savior. The school, Pratt, and the idea of "assimilation" was more complicated than one man who was racist; Pratt was a person who thoroughly believed in equality—who preached it and worked for it and rallied for it—but his mind was moulded by an era where to be equal meant all races had the chance to be White Europeans. Pratt wanted to give the Natives a place in White America and the school was his answer.

This attitude can explain, though not excuse, some of the drastic and, by todays standards, extreme measures taken by the school to transform these Native American

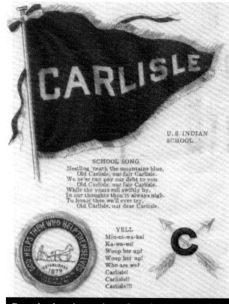

Carlisle became the model for 26 similar schools across 15 states, as well as hundreds of private schools

Pratt had no intention of students returning to their tribes, instead treating the school as a method to "Kill the Indian; save the man"

Many Carlisle students went on to become professional athletes and coaches

children into "civilized" White men and women. Every student was expected to learn and speak English and their transformation began with them taking on a new English name. While some were assigned names, other students were able to choose their new name. This led to children who had no idea of how to speak or read English faced with a wall of names they could not understand. Native children would randomly pick at symbols they could not read, unknowingly naming themselves something entirely new. The Indian names were gone, and the White names were taken.

## The Ghost Dance
### How a dance prompted a war

Not all Native Americans were so comfortable with the idea of "turning white" to be accepted in modern society and the 1890s saw a resurgence of the traditional Ghost Dance.

The idea behind this ceremony was that if conducted correctly, it would reunite the spirits of the dead with those of the living. A prophet figure called Jack Wilson, or Wovoka, said he had a vision where God ordered him to take the dance back to the people. By performing it, Wovoka said God promised to cleanse all evil in the world, make the White colonists leave, and bring peace, prosperity and unity to all Native American peoples. Many tribe leaders believed Wovoka's message and took it back to their people, and the popularity of the Ghost Dance rapidly spread. Such was the people's belief than many would wear ghost shirts, which they believed could protect the wearer from bullets. The ritual scared many White government figures, who believed it was a prelude to war and American troops were deployed in the Great Sioux reservation of South Dakota. The tension and heightened panic resulted in multiple deaths on both sides. Further massacre occurred infamously at Wounded Knee, where 153 Lakota were killed. After the massacre, interest in the Ghost Dance faded rapidly, with many Native Americans fearful they would be killed if they continued to practice the ritual.

Controversially, twenty US troops were awarded the Medal of Honor for their role in the Wounded Knee Massacre

# "[A] method for recruiting reluctant tribe leaders was to send 'successful' students to demonstrate the skills they had learned"

It was the beginning of a transformation of their entire lives.

It wasn't just Natives' names that were out, their Native clothes were given up, moccasins and blankets swapped for suits and school uniforms, and the boys' long hair was cut short, as if the long locks stood in the way of their enlightenment. Those students who could speak English were used by the facility as translators but also, abusing the very Native American idea of respect and devotion to elders, as spies on their fellow pupils. Discipline was tough in the school, and stepping out of line could see students facing "court marshals." Carlisle was clever in the way it subliminally appealed to Indian values, while dressing them up like White boys and girls. For example, the boys were organized into squads and companies, which appealed to their warrior traditions. The young men were eager to get "promoted" and receive officers' ranks and privileges, so Carlisle abused this eagerness to make them compliant. Perhaps not surprisingly though,

not all students were able to cope at Carlisle, and many were returned to their families, and some even ran away from the school.

The government, however, must have been impressed with the early results from the school as in November 1878, it ordered Pratt to recruit more students. However, this time there was a game plan. Pratt was told to take students from the Lakota, Dakota, and Nakota tribes specifically. The reason was obvious—these were the tribes that had shown the most resistance towards the United States in the past. Pratt, however, didn't like this idea. He didn't want to take hostile students into his school, and was unfamiliar with most of these tribes. Congress, on the other hand, didn't really care about Pratt's misgivings and argued that if Pratt was able to claim their children from them, then they could act as hostages to encourage the good behavior of the rest of their tribe.

Still with misgivings, Pratt went ahead with the plan anyway, and appealed directly

to chiefs Red Cloud and Spotted Tail. These chiefs were hostile and resistant to the idea of handing over their children, but Pratt was incredibly persuasive. He argued that it was due to the chief's inability to write that the government was able to trick his people and place them in reservations. He said that if the chief could have read what he was signing he would have said no, and avoided the awful mess the Natives had found themselves in. If they educate their children, Pratt argued, then they would be able to meet the White man on level ground, and he promised that, if the children were sent to his school, they would return to the tribes able to help the chiefs. It was a compelling argument, and not entirely untrue, and Lakota chiefs were convinced enough to enroll their children in the school.

Another method for recruiting reluctant tribe leaders was to send "successful" students to demonstrate the skills they had learned. For example, Luther Standing Bear, a student of the school, made frequent visits to reservations to persuade leaders that sending their children was worthwhile. This was no easy task; many children who went to boarding schools like Carlisle had died from infectious diseases,

## The Killing of the Buffalo
### The fate of the buffalo and the Natives were intrinsically linked

Bison hunting was fundamental to the Native Americans, not only to their society, but also their economy. Huge numbers of tribesmen would cross the plains in traditional tribal hunts steeped in religion. Bison-rich areas were hotly contested between different tribes, even leading to tribal warfare and villages set ablaze. However, bison numbers remained fairly consistent, with twenty-five to thirty million in the 16th century, but this was all soon to change.

In the 19th century the bison were hunted to near extinction, with less than 100 remaining in the wild in the 1880s. The reasons for this dramatic decline are complicated, but almost certainly map the trends of White development and colonization of the Americas. Settlers were known to hunt bison to increase their own economic stake. Leather, tongues and fur were all sold and traded excessively, and many Native Americans also took part in this trade and began to hunt bison like the White settlers— on horses. The US Army actively encouraged the slaughter of entire herds of bison in order to weaken the Native American population. Bison was their main food source and with the numbers diminished, the people had little choice but to move to the reservations or starve to death. The land delegated to the indigenous tribes was far from bison herds, and

this huge loss of food also made the Natives more reliant on the US government, leading to a loss of autonomy. A high-ranking US military officer was quoted as saying, "If we kill the buffalo we conquer the Indian." The destruction of the buffalo was the final, brutal act in the American Indian Wars, delivering a crippling blow and turning a bountiful green land into a graveyard.

This gigantic pile of Bison skulls was gathered to be ground for fertilizer

with the parents not notified until after the children were dead and buried. Despite this very real threat, Pratt and his team of recruiters managed to gain a considerable amount of support from the Natives. Lakota chief, Standing Horse, was a great supporter of the school, realistically believing that his children would have to face White men sooner or later, and being prepared could never be a bad thing. The fact that many Natives on the plantation were literally starving and freezing to death was no small factor in encouraging enrolment, too. Eventually it became the chiefs writing to Pratt, begging him to take their children, rather than the other way around, and Carlisle grew and grew. Being White, it was decided, was better than being dead.

For all its bravado, Carlisle school was producing results. Between 1899 and 1904 the school issued forty-five degrees, and a host of students had entered government service. The school's football team received national acclaim and the school band was widely praised as one of the best in the country. If Pratt wished to prove that the Native American could be integrated into the White man's world he was doing a spectacular job, however, this came at a cost. One of the

programs at the school placed the students in homes as domestic servants or on farms through the summer. This went down well with the administrators and reformers, who saw it as proof that the children could be assimilated. However, some Natives were not so convinced. Zitkála-Ša taught music to the school and was sent by Pratt to recruit new students. Unfortunately when she went home, she discovered her mother's house was in disrepair, and her family in poverty. White settlers were invading and occupying the land promised to her people. For as much as she had enjoyed her time teaching, she was yet to see any actual benefits to her people. She told Pratt that the curriculum was designed to keep Native American children in lives of menial labor. She was later dismissed for her outspoken views.

Although Carlisle school may feel like a small part of what was happening to Native Americans, in fact the school and the values it was trying to push were hugely demonstrative of the war waging outside the school gates. Pratt and his fellow reformists were trying to change the image of Native Americans across the United States. They were attempting to oppose the theatrical, somewhat over the top, portrayal

of Native Americans in popular Wild West shows of the era—maintaining that such shows presented the Natives as savages. However, opinions differed. Another famous progressive of the era, "Buffalo Bill" Cody, believed that what Pratt was trying to do was damaging Native American culture, and that it was better to allow Indians to be Indians. He said it was preferable for the Natives to adjust and change at their own pace, rather than have change forced upon them. Both men offered a chance for the Natives to save themselves from vanishing, but their outlooks and methods differed.

During the 19th and early 20th century there was a huge increase in public interest towards Native Americans. The belief that they were becoming a vanishing race promoted a host of people including journalists, historians, and artists to study Native American culture to preserve it for future generations. However, while the people were enthralled, the government was doing everything it could to hurry the vanishing along. Government policy was taking Indian lands, restricting their cultural practices, and sending more and more children to boarding schools to eliminate the last threads of their culture within them. Pratt's impressive results easily convinced the politicians that his work and that of his school was vital. The public did not agree. At the inaugural parade of President Roosevelt in 1905, Wild Westerners appeared alongside the marching band from Carlisle. The powerful imagery of six Native American chiefs in full traditional dress on horseback delighted the nation and were said to have "created a sensation." The intention had been for the band to demonstrate the success of the school, but they were eclipsed by the sensational image of the chiefs, and barely received a passing mention in the newspapers.

It is easy to criticize the show and the idea of Wild West shows, as both seemed to be exploiting the Native American culture in different ways. However, it is also important to understand the dire situation the Natives found themselves in. They were impoverished, harassed, struggling to survive in the world being created around them. Both the school and the shows offered the Natives portals to education and opportunity. Even the Wild Westers understood the benefits of the school, and enrolled their own children in it. Some children attended the school and also took

The school band performed at every president's inaugural celebration until the school closed in 1915

part in Wild West shows, where they would receive good money for their time. The Natives did not have a lot of options due to their dire circumstance, but it would be incorrect to say they were all forced, or loathed their role in the Wild West shows or time at the school. For many they both presented opportunities that would otherwise be impossible. It was a brutal era for Natives, where the choice was assimilation or death, and people like Pratt and Cody offered a sliver of hope in a world designed for their destruction.

It is important to remember this only because it helps us understand why Pratt was so convinced he was doing the right thing, despite some actions that today we would condemn immediately. Pratt clashed with the government repeatedly over his extreme views about the need for Native Americans to assimilate. His outspoken views regarding the Indian Bureau and the reservation system forced him into early retirement. He continued to campaign and remain outspoken about Native American rights until his death. This was not a flash in the pan for Pratt, but a lifelong dedication that he seemed to care greatly about.

Despite Pratt's obvious dedication to the betterment of the Native American's situation at the time, his goal was extreme— total immersion into the White man's world. Pratt's personal slogan was "to civilize the Indian, get him into civilization. To keep him civilized, let him stay." It was a harsh and extreme reaction to the "popular" goal of the time, basic extermination of the entire race. Many Native Americans, however, did not look fondly upon Pratt's interference in their lives. One of the hot points of contention was around the school's unspoken policy for Native Americans to marry interracially. Natives claimed that the school was trying to take the Indian out of the man, pushing them towards interracial marriage to breed the Indian genes out of the pool in a very literal interpretation of assimilation.

It wasn't just through the genes the school attempted to strip children of their

A COMPANY OF WILD WEST COWBOYS.

Native American performers were a major draw and huge attraction in Wild West shows

> "Pratt's personal slogan was 'to civilize the Indian, get him into civilization. To keep him civilized, let him stay'"

heritage. It was in the shame around their traditional dress, forcing them to abandon their clothes and hair for more acceptable White alterNatives. They were forced on new diets, given new names, and encouraged to completely change their way of thinking. One of the most extreme changes that Native American girls in particular had trouble with was the new gender norms imposed upon them. Traditionally, Native women held powerful posts in their gender-equal societies. Native women were commonly warriors, doctors, leaders of religions, and some even achieved the rank of chief. At Carlisle, the girls would be told to aspire to the dizzy heights of wife, housekeeper, and seamstress. For many girls this robbed them not only of their cultural identity, but of their sense of importance and role in their own futures. Such a drastic change in their outlook caused confusion, alienation, and resentment against the school. There are multiple examples of girls especially rebelling against their new lives and reality at Carlisle.

The Carlisle school's method for forcing the children to speak English was also frowned upon. Members of different tribes were placed together in dorms, with only English as their common language. Any student discovered speaking another language would be harshly disciplined. One idea was to place some of the Native children with White boys, with the belief that this would encourage the Natives even further to speak English. Sixty White children were mixed with sixty Native boys. In an ironic twist of fate, however, the White boys instead starting speaking the Sioux language and the program came to a screeching halt.

There were even more problems for those returning to their homes and reservations after attending the school. Luther Standing Bear, one of the most famous and accomplished Carlisle graduates, returned to mixed reactions, with some of the tribe proud of all that he had achieved, and other members refusing to shake his hand, branding him a traitor. It had been instilled within Carlisle students to hate what they came from, and to want to be White above all other desires. Some would return refusing to speak their Native tongue with their families, having been forced to be ashamed of their own cultures. This created a fracture for the students, who ended up with one foot in both cultures but belonging in neither. Some decided to abandon what they had learned at the school and return to their Native ways, thereby rejecting everything the school had set out to do. Others decided to completely reject their culture and immerse themselves in White society. Some were able to do both, but it was not without difficulty.

By the 1900s the Carlisle school came to be less and less relevant. Reservation schools and private schools were springing up around the country, which were far more convenient than traveling all the way to Pennsylvania. Heated debate among the faculty and pressures from the US Army and Indian Commission lowered not only the morale of the school, but also the attendance. By the time World War I broke out, Carlisle's place in the world was all but lost. The school was transformed into a rehabilitation hospital for soldiers and students sent home or to off-reservation boarding schools. The doors of the school shut, but the impact and legacy among the students who attended would not be so easy to walk away from.

Luther Standing Bear went on to become an author, educator, philosopher, and actor

## Dawes Act 1887

### How the US government fractured the Native's lives, land, and communities

For quite some time, White Americans had come into conflict with the Natives regarding tribal lands in the west and believed the only way for the Natives to survive was by assimilation. The Dawes Act of 1887 was the political consensus of these ideas and officially allowed the United States president to confiscate and redistribute tribal lands in the west. One-hundred-and-sixty-acre homesteads were made into individual plots that were allocated to Native American families. Only those who accepted these plots would be granted US citizenship. Any land that remained was sold to White settlers. This dividing up of land meant Plains Indians lost over half their lands to White Americans. But more than that, it broke up the power of the united tribes. The separation of land meant individual families were encouraged to farm for themselves and reject the structure of the tribe that had sustained Native Americans for generations. Although the government saw it as a huge success, for Natives, the Dawes Act made life much harder; most found it impossible to make a living farming the lands they had been given and had to sell them on to Whites in the end. Ultimately the act fractured entire communities of Native Americans, leaving families landless and destitute.

Ninety million acres of former Native-owned lands were sold to non-Natives

# WAS THE WEST SO WILD?

Over the past 150 years, the Wild West has been depicted as a lawless, violent place—but why, and was it really so bad?

Words by Nell Darby

Today, the Wild West is remembered and promoted through the opening of old mining towns as tourist attractions. In California, for example, Bodie and Calico have become popular destinations—in the former, gun fights featuring actors take place and you can sip a Sarsaparilla in a saloon. But where does such imagery come from, and does it accurately reflect America's past?

In fact, this perception of the Wild West as a lawless place had already become ingrained in both American and British culture by the end of the 19th century, when the press was referring to the "lawless times in the wild West of America thirty or forty years ago." The America of the mid-nineteenth century was mythologized as a place where local newspaper editors had "one eye on their manuscript and the other on the door," with their knives and guns close by, as they knew that arguments were settled through violence rather than through the courts. The perception was that in order to win a fight, a man simply had to demonstrate that he was a fraction faster with his hand and his gun than his opponent. In fact, a popular comment was that whoever could fight or flee the quickest would be the one who would live the longest.

These depictions of the American West as a wild place were based on stories about it that emerged in the late 1840s, when the American Gold Rush took place. Prospectors from across America and beyond moved west in search of their fortunes, taking land and establishing towns to serve and home these gold hunters. They also had to be hardy individuals to survive in a cutthroat and rather primitive environment: to search for gold involved good physical fitness, shifting rocks, sifting through material while standing in cold streams, eating poor food, and suffering from various illnesses. They were also competing with an ever-growing number of people as word spread about the gold, making resources scarcer. In such a harsh world, these gold hunters became seen as tough people who would resort to violence in order to survive themselves. In addition, because many fortune hunters were originally based in basic, temporary camps, they were seen as living a life away from the order of conventional society in the established towns and cities. Instead, they were considered as being drinkers, irreligious, and lawless, even though more recent research has suggested that they were far more lawful—and owned far fewer weapons—than the myth suggests.

Yet this was not the only reason that the West was seen as wild. Violence on the American frontier really came from attitudes towards the Native Americans living on the plains. It was their historic lands that were sold off to settlers, but prior to the American Civil War, settlers often negotiated with Native Americans and relationships could be established between the two groups without violence necessarily being involved. However, following the end of the Civil War in 1865, the US Army became established in the West, and helped settlers to take Native-held lands through violence. The involvement of the army, some have argued, helped replace the traditional negotiations with violent raids. In 1871, Congress decided to stop trying to negotiate with the Native Americans in the west, refusing to ratify any treaties with them. Although new proposals to "enslave" the Native American

Film depictions of the Wild West have tended to focus on gun violence and vast, bleak landscapes

The frontier town of Tonopah, Nevada, at the turn of the twentieth century

communities in order to force them to help construct new railroads were rejected by the US government, they were increasingly seen as obstructions to the modernity sought by the settlers, and racially inferior. Violence and deaths increased post-war, and the desire by some settlers to gain land and build at whatever cost to the Native American communities helped construct an image of a lawless Wild West.

In the 1880s, Buffalo Bill's Wild West show caught the public's imagination not just in America, but also across the Atlantic in Britain. The exhibition demonstrated "typical" American pursuits, primarily horsemanship, marksmanship, and archery, conjuring up an image of wildness and an uncivilized expanse of land where men needed to be strong and skilled in order to tame both the landscape and its animals. Buffalo Bill— born William Frederick

It was only after Wyatt Earp's death in 1929 that his involvement in the gunfight at the OK Corral forty years earlier became well known

Cody in Iowa Territory in 1846—was a key part of the mythologization of the Wild West. A Pony Express rider at fourteen, and a Unionist soldier in the Civil War of the 1860s, he had been performing in cowboy-style shows since his early twenties. He claimed to have killed his first man—a Native American—in his early teens, a story that later made its way into his own memoirs. He used the history of the American frontier and its people in these shows, and in 1883 started his Buffalo Bill's Wild West show, or exhibition, which toured America and then, from 1887, Britain and the rest of Europe. By the 1890s, the show was featuring horseriders and performers from around the world, but it is the cowboys and Indians that it is best remembered for. Bill included many historical figures, including Sitting Bull, and also employed sharpshooters such as the infamous Annie Oakley.

Bill was friends with another key figure, Wild Bill Hickok—the two had first met in Kansas in 1866. "Wild Bill" was James Butler Hickok, born in Illinois in 1837, and was a

notorious figure of his day, partly due to the tall tales Hickok told about his life. These fictional exploits help create a folk hero—a shooter, a gambler, a spy, and a bandit. The fact that Hickok was shot and killed while he was playing poker in a Dakota saloon in 1876 further added to his mystique and position within frontier history. In reality, however, Hickok was more complex: when employed by Buffalo Bill to act in his show, Hickok proved a poor actor, frightened by having the lights on him, and had to be let go. In addition, despite his claims to have killed many armed men, it's likely that he only killed a few. However, he was certainly involved in shootouts, and thus he became remembered as a typical figure of the Wild West.

So by the end of the nineteenth century, theatrical shows and the press were depicting the West as a lawless place, where people settled arguments with violence. Other isolated events that had not received widespread attention at the time, became better known in the twentieth century, helping this depiction further. The gunfight at the OK Corral, for example, was just a single, thirty-second shootout that took place in Tombstone, Arizona, on October 26, 1881. It

"Buffalo Bill" helped mythologize the Wild West with his traveling shows in the 1880s.

## "These fictional exploits help create a folk hero—a shooter, gambler, spy, and a bandit"

was the culmination of a long-standing feud between a group of cowboys on one side, and law enforcers Wyatt Earp and his two brothers Virgil and Morgan, together with Doc Holliday, on the other. It might have been forgotten about but for a book—*Wyatt Earp: Frontier Marshal*—that was published about Wyatt Earp's life in 1931, two years after he had died, and later made into not just one, but two, films.

The creation of films from the OK Corral gunfight shows how the depiction of a lawless Wild West became well and truly entrenched. Once the movies arrived in the early twentieth century, cowboy movies would generally focus on violence for their narrative and pace. The 1960s were the peak era of the cowboy movie, or spaghetti western, and films such as The Magnificent Seven and The Good, The Bad and The Ugly date from this decade. The former helped depict the West as wild as it showed seven gunmen helping protect a village from "savage" thieves; in the latter, bounty hunting and gold help to depict the West as a place where the quest for money results in violence and lawlessness. The

barren landscapes and depictions of rugged masculinity—think of Clint Eastwood and the quiet menace of Lee Van Cleef—conjure up an image of brooding violence and a society where the usual rules and laws don't apply. The science fiction film *Westworld,* in 1973, played on people's fear of Wild West lawlessness by making it a place inhabited by robots who themselves "go rogue" and seek to shoot and kill the tourists who visit it, thus taking perceptions of violence and exaggerating them to their limit.

Given this long history of mythologizing, it is inevitable that today our perception of the Wild West is at best romanticized and at worst, false. Yet our fascination with it endures; and so the ghost towns of California will continue to play host to thousands of tourists from around the world, all wanting to see a shootout, or to hear a tinny piano being played in a Wild West bar. Perhaps our fascination with the Wild West—or the myth of it—lies in a subconscious desire to be free of society's constraints, conventions, and laws, and to live in an era that appeared to be less bound by rules.

## The Marlboro Man

**Macho, strong, and silent, the Marlboro Man epitomized the iconic American cowboy**

He was a fictional figure—in fact, the figurehead of an advertising campaign. Yet he became larger than life, depicting the rugged cowboy of American history, and even the fact that he was advertising something that could kill seemed appropriate.

The Marlboro Man was created by Leo Burnett in 1954, as a way to make filtered cigarettes popular with men—up to that point, they were seen as rather "feminine." The ads not only made cigarettes appeal to men; they also created an image of the strong, macho American man who was at home in the Wild West. They bypassed the already growing concerns about the health impact of smoking to suggest that cigarettes actually made a person more physically attractive. Although it was originally intended to portray a variety of working men—from builders to weightlifters— the cowboy quickly became so popular that Marlboro stuck with it as the iconic image in billboard and television advertising campaigns.

The best-known Marlboro Man was Darrell Winfield, who was not an actor or model, but a rancher. He fit the bill in terms of ruggedness and conspicuous masculinity so much that he was employed as the Marlboro Man for twenty years. Later, when several men involved in Marlboro ads died of smoking-related diseases, Marlboro cigarettes became known as "cowboy killers."

An iconic Marlboro billboard, featuring the Marlboro Man cowboy, above Sunset Boulevard in Los Angeles

# THE ORIGINAL WOLVES OF WALL STREET

## The USA has always held competitive capitalism in high regard, but at one time its entire economy was taken hostage by a few opportunistic men

Words by Alice Barnes-Brown

**W**alking around the USA's great cities, such as New York, you'll see their names everywhere—figures such as oil magnate John D. Rockefeller, Andrew Carnegie, and J.P. Morgan still loom large over American society. But these men rose to the top using a variety of questionable methods. Labeled as "robber barons" after the European aristocrats who once extorted money from anyone who happened to be on their land, these men disregarded the fundamental ideals America was built on to make themselves very wealthy indeed.

Though they became rich from a variety of different sources, anything from railways to fur, they all had one thing in common—they were opportunistic, and knew how to monetize practically everything. The conditions in 19th century America were perfect for them, creating a climate that allowed them to flourish.

Since Europeans first settled there, monopolies had always been able to thrive in America. Organizations such as the Virginia Company were given exclusive contracts by the colonial administration, enabling them to have complete control over an entire region. They were seen as a necessity, because in order to make the New World comfortable, it required large-scale public works and building projects, which could only be completed by big corporations.

Though American businesses grew in number after the Revolution, expansion into the west provided another golden opportunity for would-be monopolizers. When coupled with a rapidly industrializing society and the development of new technologies, the Frontier was the ideal place for these men to make their money. Rich in natural resources and almost completely untapped by White men, they moved fast in order to gain complete control over these riches.

In the case of oil, this was particularly prevalent. Factories, homes, and transportation across the US relied on fossil fuels like oil to run, so by knocking out the competition for the western oilfields in the early stages, it became possible to set the price of it, which is exactly what Rockefeller did. With no business regulation from the central government, the robber barons and their monopolies were essentially unstoppable.

In addition to the cheap and resource-rich land to the west, they were able to take advantage of swathes of cheap labor coming in from the east. With poor, hungry immigrants arriving from Europe and Asia in their thousands, venture capitalists were able to pay these desperate people pennies in exchange for backbreaking work, cutting costs while allowing their own profits to soar.

The abolition of slavery and the Civil War also benefitted them—many former slaves could now be employed on low wages, and the South's economy was ruined, meaning the robber barons could swoop in and turn a profit there, too. Attitudes to the South were telling—Thaddeus Stevens, a Northern member of the House of Representatives, once said; "we have the right to treat them as we would any other province that we might conquer."

To get rid of competition, men such as John Jacob Astor (a fur magnate who cheated Native Americans out of quality fur pelts, and sold them at much higher prices) and Rockefeller would arrange hostile takeovers, or conspire with other businessmen to drive their rivals out of business. Smaller businesses sometimes tried to complain to the authorities, but found their case fell on deaf ears. Moreover, in Astor's

Andrew Carnegie was one of the most divisive figures of the age

# Exposing Evil

**Were it not for these incredible journalists, the cruelty of robber barons may never have become known**

Though they were rarely held accountable by the government, robber barons were often heavily criticized by newspapers and magazines, who used top investigative journalists to find out what they were up to. Nellie Bly was one of these pioneering figures, working for the *New York World* in the 1880s. Thanks to her work, the paper was able to carve itself a reputation as a newspaper of the people, winning readers' trust by lambasting the rich.

Fellow journalist Ida M. Tarbell went even further. She was from a well-to-do family, but her father's oil business had—like so many others—been destroyed by Rockefeller. She wrote for *McClure's Magazine*, and became one of the robber barons' most influential enemies. Her 1904 exposé, "The History Of The Standard Oil Company," was read by millions, and it was one of the most thorough assessments of unethical business practices at the time.

These writers-turned-sleuths gave birth to a whole new style of journalism, known scornfully as "muckraking," a nickname given by Theodore Roosevelt himself. Their calling out of powerful, wealthy men may not have made these women popular with the authorities, but the wider public was all the better informed thanks to them.

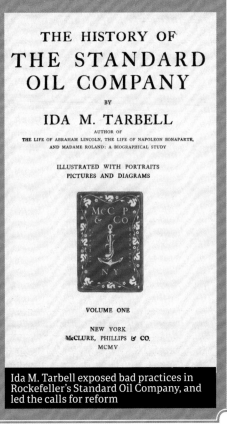

**THE HISTORY OF THE STANDARD OIL COMPANY**
BY
**IDA M. TARBELL**
AUTHOR OF
THE LIFE OF ABRAHAM LINCOLN, THE LIFE OF NAPOLEON BONAPARTE, AND MADAME ROLAND: A BIOGRAPHICAL STUDY

ILLUSTRATED WITH PORTRAITS PICTURES AND DIAGRAMS

VOLUME ONE

NEW YORK
McCLURE, PHILLIPS & CO.
MCMV

Ida M. Tarbell exposed bad practices in Rockefeller's Standard Oil Company, and led the calls for reform

case, he was not above using violence to silence his competitors, and his agents were swiftly dispatched to anyone who challenged him.

To add insult to injury, since these men controlled a vast amount of wealth, they had a huge influence over the government—so much so that in 1895, J.P. Morgan bailed out the entire US government with a $60 million loan. If it looked like policymakers were about to do something that affected their interests, these industrialists would pour money into lobbying and bribery to secure the outcome they wanted.

If that didn't work, they'd threaten government officials. This was particularly true of the railway magnates, who frequently had to interact with government to grow their operations. Leland Stanford—who was both the governor of California as well as the leader of the Pacific Association—bribed his colleagues so that his association could get nine million acres and a $24 million loan to build the Central Pacific railroad. When local authorities objected, he intimidated them and threatened to have the railway bypass their towns altogether. This was a vital lifeline for many remote communities, so they were hardly in a position to say no.

The robber barons were also known to meddle in the world of finance so that it paid them handsome dividends. James Fisk was especially guilty of this. He had made money with fraudulent stock market practices. During the Civil War, he had invested in Confederate war bonds. After the defeat, he quickly sold them to European investors, who had not realized the South had lost the war yet due to slow transatlantic communications. He also artificially inflated the price of gold by bribing public officials to keep government gold off the market, creating a higher demand—but it also created a panic on September 24, 1869, an event which later became known as Black Friday.

Despite these tactics, to some the robber barons were making America a great place to be. They were hailed as "self-made men" who proved that with hard graft, any man could make himself rich. For instance, Cornelius Vanderbilt bought his first boat at age sixteen with a $100 loan, but turned it into a vast shipping empire. They were transforming America into a steam-fueled superpower, bringing a form of order to the chaotic process of industrialization—or at least that's what they thought.

## "Industrialists would pour money into bribery to secure the outcome they wanted. If that didn't work, they'd threaten officials"

Rockefeller's Standard Oil pushed its competitors out of business by charging above and beyond for oil transportation

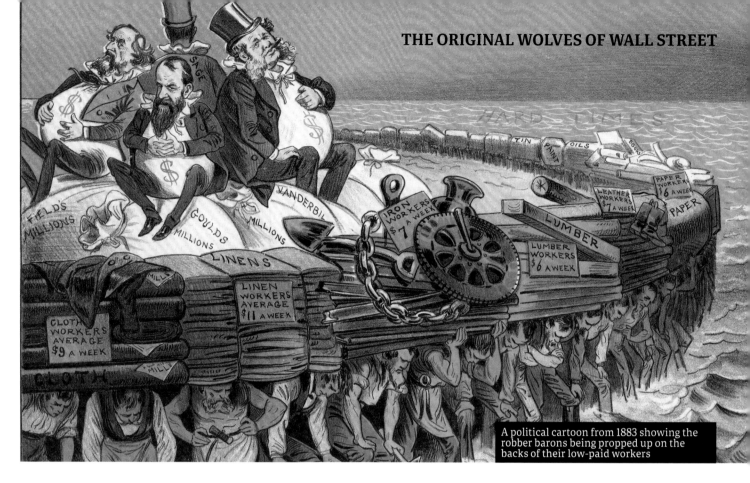

A political cartoon from 1883 showing the robber barons being propped up on the backs of their low-paid workers

To help their poor public image, many of these cutthroat capitalists turned to philanthropy in later life. Some, such as Leland Stanford, founded first-rate universities. Others built hospitals, schools, and museums, but none undertook more philanthropic work than Andrew Carnegie. Born to a poor weaver's family in Scotland, Carnegie was something of an outsider to his peers, and claimed to be worried about "mutual distrust" between the rich and poor. To alleviate this, he invested in 2,500 public libraries around the world, which he hoped would encourage the working classes to educate themselves. He believed his wealth could be used to enrich the public, so he also gave money to build Carnegie Hall, which remains one of the USA's top concert venues.

Regardless of their public-spirited and charitable work, the robber barons' workers held a different view of the rich industrialists. Tired of being exploited and abused by their employers, some had started to unionize in an attempt to secure better treatment for themselves, although not all workers were equal—African-Americans and women were often prevented from joining these organizations. The unions organized strikes, an unprecedented move which changed the face of American labor history forever.

The 1892 Homestead Strike was a protest against Carnegie's attempt to introduce lower wages and break the Amalgamated Association of Iron and Steel Workers. When a gun went off as the workers stormed a plant, a firefight broke out, leaving a few workers dead. While the workers succeeded in taking the plant, their victory did not last, and ultimately many workers had to accept pay cuts in exchange for getting their jobs back. Carnegie's ruthlessness had won out again.

However, the strikes had shown that resentment towards the robber barons was brewing, and the tide of public opinion was changing. Smaller businesses were starting to speak up, feeling cheated out of decades' worth of profit. The government had also changed somewhat in character, and got more involved in commerce. The public clamored for regulation of big business, and this time the government was willing to listen. The revelation that Rockefeller controlled ninety percent of American oil by 1890 was a key catalyst for change.

A campaign led by Senator Sherman of Ohio was one of the first steps on the road to regulating big businesses. The resulting Sherman Antitrust Act of 1890 prohibited trusts, such as Rockefeller's Standard Oil Company, which operated as a monopoly by having its board of trustees manage most of the nation's oil companies. The Act was ultimately used to dissolve Rockefeller's trust in 1911, forcing it to split up into thirty-four smaller companies.

Fuel to the fire was introduced when President Theodore Roosevelt took office in 1901. Known as the "Trust Buster," he took an active role in dismantling trusts, and began a campaign in 1907 that ultimately destroyed the American Tobacco Company's monopoly in 1911. However, he was keen to distinguish between the "bad" trusts that hindered trade and exploited their power, and the "good trusts," which did control entire industries—but so long as they did not adversely affect the consumers, could be left alone.

The reintroduction of competition to the American economy was a landmark point in its history. While it may not have taken down all of the US' monopolies and their robber baron owners, the Antitrust Act showed that the government was no longer willing to give big business free rein. As for the barons themselves, their names have lived on in history—partly because they were so notorious, partly because their charity and public works programs are still active in America today. Whatever you might think of their unethical practices, the robber barons made an undeniable mark on American society.

# THE MAN WHO SHAPED THE FRONTIER

Frederick Jackson Turner argued that the frontier was to thank for forming the character of America and its people

Words by Nell Darby

He was a product of the country he cared so much about—born during the American Civil War, in the young city of Portage, Wisconsin. Frederick Jackson Turner would grow up to become a historian for whom the American frontier represented something more than just a geographic entity—it reflected the soul of America itself.

Turner was born on November 14, 1861, the son of Andrew Jackson Turner and his wife Mary Olivia Hanford, who were both originally from New York state. They were an educated, literate family seeking to improve the lives of those in Wisconsin, a small state sandwiched between Minnesota to the west, and Michigan to the east. The Turners were very interested in the world around them and wanted to make a difference, whether that happened to be politically or intellectually.

Turner took after his parents, and after leaving school, attended the University of Wisconsin at Madison, where he would later settle down with his own family. After completing his degree, he started postgraduate work in Baltimore, Maryland, at Johns Hopkins University, under the guidance of Herbert Baxter Adams. Adams was himself an innovative historian and enthusiastic tutor, introducing postgraduate seminars, and co-founding the American Historical Association, which still exists today. His student, Turner, gained his PhD in 1890, by which time he was also teaching students back in Wisconsin. He had also married prior to receiving his PhD: on November 27, 1889, in Chicago, he wed Caroline Mae Sherwood, and the couple went on to have three children.

Unlike Adams, who had gained his doctorate in Heidelberg, Turner had been educated solely in the US, which was unusual for the time. It gave him a uniquely American outlook on history, one which he described as being shaped by a contemporary program. This outlook was presented to his own students as he started a long career as an educator himself. Turner's lasting legacy was what became known as his "Frontier Thesis," which synthesized his theories. This was a hypothesis he put forward in 1893 that the moving frontier line in American history had a long-lasting impact on pioneers and their lives—one that created a distinct nation. He argued that this moving frontier line resulted in the formation of American democracy, as well as in other distinctly American ways of life—egalitarianism, violence, and a lack of interest in high culture. These gave the pioneers a life that was distinct from their old ones in Europe, creating new customs to replace their old ones. There was less hierarchy than the old European classes of the aristocracy, the landed gentry, and the serfs below them: under the American frontier, all classes were equal, and all could acquire their own land.

Turner had first put forward these ideas in a paper delivered to the American Historical Association in Chicago. "The Significance Of The Frontier In American History" was applauded by academics and intellectuals, and became the first of several lectures and essays written or given by Turner over the next couple of decades. Unlike Adams, who had theorized that American institutions had much to thank German and English institutions for, Turner instead argued that it was the frontier history of America itself that had transformed its people and its institutions. He looked at the lives of explorers, trappers, and traders and how they eventually created a more urban life—one that reflected the frontier settlers' traits of self-reliance, individualism, and optimism. His was a thesis about social evolution, but one that was particular to his own country and its unique, albeit relatively recent, history. As one British newspaper phrased it, Turner saw the frontier as the means whereby "Americans adjusted to their environment and developed their sense of nationalism and democracy."

His work led to the establishment of university courses in frontier history, using Turner's work as a starting point. Although Turner wrote relatively little about history, his fame was assured. As one journalist noted in 1970, Turner has been described as "the man who wrote less and influenced his own generation more" than any other historian. Yet he lived long enough to become cynical about some of the descendants of the Pioneers. In the 1910s, he criticized those who destroyed natural resources out of greed or the desire to improve their own lives at the expense of others, and how these resources needed to be better protected.

By this time, Turner had finally moved on from the University of Wisconsin. In 1910, he moved to take a position he had been offered at Harvard University, becoming this institution's chair of history. He stayed there for fourteen years before retiring and moving to California. There, as far west as he could possibly go, he became a senior research associate for the Huntington Library in San Marino. He died in that city on March 14, 1932.

# His Father's Son

### Turner's father was, like his son, strongly interested in history

It was, perhaps, inevitable that Frederick Jackson Turner would grow up to be so fascinated by American history, and how people's experiences of the frontier would shape their identities. He was the child of a man who had moved west himself—Andrew Jackson Turner had been born in September 1832 on the east coast, in the town of Schuyler Falls, located on the edge of the Salmon River in New York state. The elder Turner had relocated to the frontier state of Wisconsin at the age of twenty-three, settling in Portage. There, he worked as a journalist and co-editor on the *Portage City Record*, before moving into Republican politics, taking on a number of positions including mayor of Portage, chief clerk of the Wisconsin State Senate, and Wisconsin railroad commissioner. Before his death in 1905, he had also written various pamphlets about local history—a subject he was passionate about.

# "OTHER WESTS THAN OURS"

## The Wild West is more than an American phenomenon: from Russia to Canada, vast landscapes and human greed have shaped national identities

Words by Nell Darby

Everyone has heard of the American Wild West. Thanks to movies and books, it will remain part of not only the American consciousness, but that of other nations too: yet it is not the only Wild West that exists. Across the world, from Canada to Russia to Australia, vast expanses of land have been settled over time, and the impact of this settlement and movement on the consciousness and sense of identity of nations has been debated and written about by historians and journalists. Therefore, the frontier in such countries is both literal and metaphorical: it is the borderline between different people—those not only from different countries, but different people within a country. Often, in history, this has come to mean those migrating to a country or an area and their push to settle there—and the impact of that on those peoples who were there first. Or it might mean the desire to civilize the land itself—to create structures, employment, and lives from what first appears to be desolate landscapes. The "wild" in Wild West can therefore mean a wildness in terms of landscape, but also a wildness among the people who have sought to live in such areas.

Frontiers are necessarily about control and ownership. The 49th Parallel, dissecting Canada ("British North America") from the United States of America, was chosen by Britain and America back in 1818, to establish the border from the Strait of Georgia to the Lake of the Woods. Soon 2.6-yard-high posts ran along this new border, to denote ownership, a border, and a boundary—keeping people in, or out, depending on how you looked at it. The idea of the "west," whether Canadian or American,

became tied to the concept of national identity, with settlers' and invaders' self-perceived superiority over displaced Native communities helping to create that national identity, one that saw this conquering and settling of land as both civilizing, and uncivilized, as the term "wild" also suggests.

In Canada, as in America, its concept of the Wild West owes much to money. In America, the Gold Rush of 1849 caused potential prospectors to head west in search of their fortunes, creating mining camps and towns in previously isolated spots that became known for alleged violence and lawlessness. Further north, and half a century later, Canada witnessed a similar rush. Gold was discovered in the Klondike region of the country in 1896, and as word spread about this news, a flood of individuals took the often dangerous path on foot and by river up the Yukon to the Klondike. Some 100,000 people are said to have headed for what has been described as one of the world's last untamed frontiers, to dig for gold in creek beds and in mines.

As was the case with the Californian Gold Rush, mining camps grew up like weeds, together with new frontier towns such as Dawson City, which soon gained a reputation for gambling and drinking. Native people were supplanted, evicted from their lands, and moved into reservations so that the miners could live, work, and drink; and although some prospectors only spent a time there before leaving, others migrated permanently to the area, not just to mine, but to service the miners by setting up shops, saloons, and other businesses. Prior to the Gold Rush here, the Yukon was seen by the wider

Concepts of Australian identity have centered around the bush, or Outback

world—and even by some in other parts of Canada—as a barren expanse of land away from civilization. But with the discovery of gold, and alleged "civilization" arriving to found Dawson City, it became talked about, written about, and romanticized about.

Just as America's Wild West was popularized and mythologized in the late 19th century with the likes of Buffalo Bill bringing his Wild West show to audiences outside of America, there were also attempts to romanticize the Canadian frontier. In the early 20th century, when the British press was writing about a fascination with the Canadian Wild West, themed shows were being performed in Britain—one being Barrett's Great Canadian Circus and Wild West Arena show.

This was the Canadian frontier and, as in America, a thesis was developed by academic historians to explore issues around what the frontier meant and what it represented. The key difference to America lay in when the frontiers had developed. In Canada, the settlement of the Canadian Prairies by incomers had started in 1896, later than in America. But like their southern neighbor, the Canadian Prairie provinces had helped support various democratic movements once this process of settlement had started. Canadian historian Harold Adams Innis, in *The Fur Trade In Canada*, published in 1930, saw "place" as being vital to the development of the Canadian West, and that cities and other settlements were key to the creation of markets, together with the input of indigenous peoples. Another historian, J.M.S. Careless, saw fur trapping, lumbering, and mining as commercial activities that had a key part to play in understanding Canadian identity.

If the American national character and consciousness was influenced by the nature of life on the frontier, and Canadian character by the experiences of those who trekked and rafted up the Yukon, what was life elsewhere influenced by? Several tried to establish what their national character was, and the frontier—wherever that was, whenever it had been established—was a key factor. As with Canada, South Africa had a shifting frontier, one that was affected by the discovery of gold in the 1880s. The Witwatersrand Gold Rush caused prospectors from around the world—including Australia and the US—to move in, first creating a mining camp, and subsequently large-scale development,

Is the South African national identity shaped by memories of its conflicts, such as the first and second Boer Wars?

## "In Australia, the rejection of 'Britishness' and the creation of a distinctly Australian character was seen as vital"

which led to the founding of Johannesburg. As with Canada and the US, economics were key. The desire for economic security led to the land clearances and the development of farms and of technology, but also the pushing of frontiers and the dislocation of Native communities. In South Africa's case, the Gold Rush led to increased political tensions that in turn led to the Second Boer War at the end of the 19th century.

In America, Canada, and South Africa, then, gold rushes had been key to both shifting frontiers and perceptions of communities and nations within those countries, and outside. Meanwhile, in Australia, the 20th century saw attempts to understand history's impact on how Australians saw themselves. In the 1950s, historian Russel Ward published *The Australian Legend*, which set out to map and explain the national character Down Under. When discussing Australian stereotypes about themselves, Ward decided that the Australian frontier (the bush) was similarly responsible for how its people were—they

were strong believers in equality, they were practical, and put a strong emphasis on friendship. Whereas the British stood for imperialism and patriotism, the Australians rejected intellectual and spiritual pursuits. This was a nation deeply affected by its history of convict voyages and settlements.

The British Empire played a key role in the development of the Australian and South African character; but in Australia, the rejection of "Britishness" and the creation of a distinctly Australian character was seen as vital. Britain had sought to control Australia, to own it and to house it with its own rejected individuals—over 160,000 convicts shipped to Australia over the course of eighty years. Convict colonies were established and expanded across the east of the country—Sydney, Hobart, Brisbane, and Melbourne. In 1822, the Bigge Report had recommended greater self-sufficiency on the part of settlers, but it resulted in land grabs bringing conflict with Australia's Native population. Conflict between convicts or former convicts, and Aboriginal Australians led to frontier

In Russia, as with other countries, vast landscapes and invasions or conflicts have helped create a national consciousness

How have relationships between Australia's Aboriginal population and its European settlers affected its identity?

*Zusammentreffen mit den Wilden.*

violence, as land was grabbed and cleared, both of trees and people. Yet it also led to a feeling of freedom among the settlers, who perhaps had greater opportunities than they would have had in Britain, in a far larger land. What is indisputable, though, is that both history and geography impacted on how Australians saw themselves.

Russel Ward argued that it was the history of British infiltration and control that had given birth to a national consciousness, but this had then been further developed by the lives of bushworkers and sheep shearers, who had worked in the vast, undeveloped plains of Australia. By the late 19th century, the stereotype of the Australian bushworker had been formed or, in Ward's words, it had been romanticized and popularized by the proliferation of bush poems and ballads being written and published in the 1880s and 1890s. This romanticizing of Australian life, however, owed something to the economic conditions of that period in its history: there was economic depression, conflict between different workers—such as sheep shearers and graziers—and growing city slums, as there were across the world in Britain.

The unpleasant realities of modern life for some led to a desire for a more romanticized version of reality, to be expressed in art and literature. The likes of Australian bush poet Henry Lawson (himself the son of an immigrant gold miner) therefore became part of the nation's culture, helping to cultivate stereotypes about Australian drovers, for example, while also drawing attention to contemporary problems, such as the impact of drought on people's fortunes, as can be seen in his poem, "Andy's Gone With Cattle." Lawson's popularity also lay in his nationalism, a rejection of British values that led to the creation of a distinctly Australian form of socialism, and an involvement by its working-class in politics. As in other nations, economic fortune or misfortune throughout different periods in its history had a hand to play in the development of a frontier-based national identity.

Ward's grappling with the concept of Australian national character, and how it had been formed, was influenced by American historian Frederick Jackson Turner's American Frontier theory; Ward argued that in Australian history, the indigenous Australian's conflict with settlers at the Australian frontier represented their equivalent of European transplantations at the American frontier. However, his work in *The Australian Legend* was not without controversy, and its thesis was particularly challenged by socialist historian Humphrey McQueen, who argued that Ward equated "class" with "convicts," making former convicts to Australia the focus of a class struggle, and ignoring other social classes and divisions. McQueen argued that, in fact, Australia did not have a class structure such as Ward had defined it, but only a "deformed" version of British structures. He therefore raised questions about whether the Australian national identity was based on democratic or egalitarian traditions that did not, in reality, exist.

There may have been arguments and debate about aspects of these theses and theories, but one aspect of these countries is undeniable, and unarguable. Australia, Canada, and America all share one thing: a sense of space. They have a national identity and consciousness that depends, at least partly, on the romanticizing of their huge landscapes—a wildness and emptiness that smaller nations, such as Britain, largely lack. If their identities are based on these landscapes, and those intrepid individuals who have traversed those spaces, where else might share these bases for identity?

## The Settlers in Canada

### A nineteenth-century children's novel explored issues around immigrant settlers

In 1844 Captain Frederick Marryat, a Royal Navy officer from London, published a children's novel entitled *The Settlers In Canada*. This was three years before his most famous book, *The Children Of The New Forest*, set during the English Civil War, was published. Like that book, *The Settlers In Canada* was a historical novel, but this one was situated in the 1790s. It was centered around the Campbell family in England, who lose their family estate and are forced to emigrated to Canada.

Marryat had been to Canada, and was the owner of land on the Canadian side of the Great Lakes. He used his knowledge of this area to form the setting of his book, showing how the Campbell family settle near Lake Ontario and work together to make their new farm successful. Along the way, they have to deal with weather, Native residents, bears, and forest fires. The book raises issues surrounding the relationship between settlers and Native Canadians; at one point, an indigenous woman is taken from her family by a party of settlers out hunting; Mr Campbell later explains "how the hunting party had brought home the woman, whom he pointed to in the corner where she had remained unnoticed by the visitors."

The Settlers In Canada told children what life might be like for 19th-century settlers in the Great Lakes region of Canada

# "Australia, Canada, and America have a national identity that depends, partly, on the romanticizing of their huge landscape"

Russia is certainly one possibility. It has the landscapes—the steppes of Russia, the Siberian wilderness—and a sense of isolation, located partly in Europe and partly in Asia, its population taking on aspects of both cultures. In Siberia, the Ural Mountains, the West Siberia Plain, and the Central Siberian Plateau are distinct geographic regions, but the wider area is still perceived as a cold, forbidding place whose residents are hardy and insular, and yet who live in an area rich in gold, diamonds, and coal. Russia's national identity has been influenced by several factors—its politics, people, and wars; its class system, monarchy, and, of course, the revolution of 1917 that eventually saw its Imperial Family executed—but its character is also influenced by its strong sense of "separateness" from other countries.

Even within the vast landscape of Russia, there is a history of invasion and settling. Hunters and traders from elsewhere in Russia traveled north to explore Siberia, overpowering the Native population. Siberia's eastern capital, Irkutsk, was on a key route from Mongolia and China westward to Europe, and so it was a strategic location. Add to this the gold, fur (especially sable), and sealskins that were found here, and it is inevitable that explorers and merchants would want to exploit its resources. In the late 16th century, seeking to expand Russian territory east, Yermak Timofeyevich conquered Siberia, and subsequently many Cossacks—men of middling status— settled there. This history of economic resources being exploited, and of invasion, led to the region becoming known as the "Wild Wild East" of Russia. Not only was it geographically isolated, thanks to its rivers and frozen lands, but there was little systematic governance, and it was both isolated from Moscow and little loved by it. The Cossacks who had settled in the region continued to take part in battles on behalf of the tsars of Russia, with garrisons and frontier posts being established. Siberian Cossacks wore traditional dress until they were replaced by uniforms in the early 19th century, but they remained iconic figures: mounted, bearded, armed with lances, and wearing high fleece hats.

In 1946, as the west sought to rebuild itself in the aftermath of World War II, economic historian Herbert Heaton published a journal article entitled "Other Wests Than Ours." Heaton, a Yorkshireman, had studied 18th century industrial life in his home county for his MA thesis, and similarly studied Yorkshire industry for his PhD. His own territory grew when he was invited to teach at the University of Tasmania—he left for Australia in 1914, and stayed until 1925, when he was offered a post in Ontario, Canada, leaving two years later, when he moved again, this time to the University of Minnesota, staying there until he retired in 1958. He therefore had experience living in three of these "frontier" countries–America, Canada, and Australia. With his journal article, he argued that there was "academic isolationism" in terms of how US history was taught, and that American history could only be studied in relation to the other countries that Europeans had migrated to from the sixteenth century to the twentieth. He saw similarities between all these countries with their own "Wild Wests." What had happened in America, he implied, was not unique: the American Wild West was little different to the Australian Outback. Both were wild landscapes that man had sought to control over the centuries; just as the countries they were part of had been "settled" by invaders from other nations. All these countries, or areas, had a history and a sense of nationhood or identity that was based on those experiences and histories of settlement.

Today, the study of "other wests than ours" continues, as academics reassess previous theories to look at the after effects of "settler colonialism," in terms of how Native communities were invaded or interacted with and also how national control has since been exerted over once individual territories and societies. Many now consider that hypotheses about frontiers can't completely explain how nations have been formed and developed; however, the frontier remains something of a romantic ideal, a narrative that helps us to understand our history, even if it does not offer an accurate understanding of our countries, our nations, and our societies, and how they have been constructed.

Canadian cowboys and cowgirls drive horses across the Saskatchewan prairie in a scene similar to ones further south in America

Historian Russel Ward argued that the Australian character stemmed from the arrival of convicts to the land in the 18th century

## The Australian Legend

### Russel Ward's groundbreaking book focused on who Australians really were

First published in 1958, when he was in his forties, Russel Ward's book looked at how Australians saw themselves, in terms of their ideals, traits, and personalities. He showed how Australian frontier life—involving farm workers moving around the outback in search of work, having a nomadic lifestyle—had come to influence the national identity, being focused on the country's literature. The bushworker had therefore had a key influence on how Australians saw themselves. Ward looked at all types of literature, including folk songs and ballads, to show how this literature reflected how the stereotype of the Australian bushworker and his life on this different frontier had, from the 1890s onwards, come to represent Australian life itself.

Ward went on to write several more histories of his country after *The Australian Legend*, which was itself originally his PhD thesis. These histories saw the middle class—the class he had come from himself—as imperialists, whereas the working class were more nationalist. It was his theory that the concept of the "noble bushman" had captured the imagination of the Australian nation that he is best remembered for, even though his arguments have since been critiqued by others.

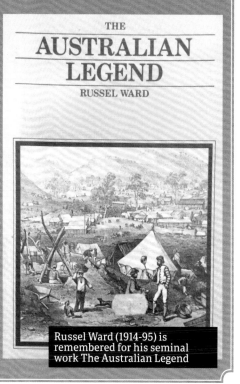

# THE AUSTRALIAN LEGEND

## RUSSEL WARD

Russel Ward (1914-95) is remembered for his seminal work The Australian Legend